Androgynous Democracy

Androgynous Democracy

Modern American
Literature and
the Dual-Sexed
Body Politic

AARON SHAHEEN

The University of Tennessee Press
Knoxville

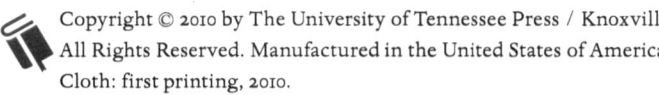 Copyright © 2010 by The University of Tennessee Press / Knoxville.
All Rights Reserved. Manufactured in the United States of America.
Cloth: first printing, 2010.
Paper: first printing, 2018.

An earlier version of the first part of chapter 1 was originally published as "'The Social Dusk of That Mysterious Democracy': Race, Sexology, and the New Woman in Henry James's *The Bostonians*" in *ATQ* 19, no. 4 (December 2005). Reprinted by permission of the University of Rhode Island.

Library of Congress Cataloging-in-Publication Data

Shaheen, Aaron.
Androgynous democracy: modern American literature and the dual-sexed body politic / Aaron Shaheen. — 1st ed.
     p. cm.
Includes bibliographical references and index.

ISBN-13: 978-1-62190-427-4

 1. American literature—20th century—History and criticism.
 2. Sex in literature.
 3. American literature—19th century—History and criticism.
 4. Politics and literature—United States—History—20th century.
 5. Politics and literature—United States—History—19th century.
 6. Modernism (Literature)—United States. I. Title.

PS228.S42S53 2010
810.9'3538—dc22   2009022561

DEDICATED TO THE MEMORY OF DALE SHAHEEN (1940–2004)

Failing to fetch me at first keep encouraged,
Missing me one place search another,
I stop some where waiting for you

CONTENTS

Acknowledgments ix

Introduction
    "Who Need Be Afraid of the Merge?" 1

Chapter 1.
    "The Social Dusk of That Mysterious Democracy": Race, Sexology, and the Modern Woman in Henry James's Postbellum America 17

Chapter 2.
    Commercial Androgyny: Reformulating the Modern Liberal Subject in Frank Norris and Charlotte Perkins Gilman 47

Chapter 3.
    Reactionary and Radical Androgyny: Two Southerners Assess the Depression-Era Body Politic 79

Chapter 4.
    Race, Gender, and Democratic Space in W. E. B. Du Bois and Marita Bonner 111

Epilogue
    Androgyny, Fascism, and Beyond 137

Notes 145

Bibliography 163

Index 175

ACKNOWLEDGMENTS

The task of thanking everyone who contributed to this book is indeed daunting. The fear of unintentionally leaving someone out makes me reluctant to name anyone at all. Despite such perils, I want to begin by expressing my deepest gratitude to those closest to me. My wife Amanda has been a part of this project from the beginning; she is my best editor, my closest confidante, and my most trusted advisor. My mother Julie has shown me through personal example that strength favors no one sex or gender. I also want to thank my sisters Lisa and Kelly for never letting me take myself too seriously.

This book has its genesis in 2002, when I first thought about writing a dissertation on the varied uses of androgyny in American literature. The idea received tremendous encouragement from not only my director David Leverenz, but also the members of the "coterie," my dear friends Jessica Livingston and Andrew Reynolds. David taught me that good scholarship is a lifelong labor of love; I hope my own fascination for literature stays as fresh and passionate throughout my career as David's has been. Jess and Andy, who entered the University of Florida's English graduate program the same year I did, showed me love, optimism, and the value of shoptalk over cheap beer. I am honored that they count me as their friend. As the dissertation developed, it benefited from the additional guidance of the other members of my committee, Susan Hegeman, Kenneth Kidd, and Louise Newman. Their commentary was tough, their expectations high, and their encouragement unwavering.

In 2005 I had the good fortune of landing a job in the English department at the University of Tennessee at Chattanooga. My colleagues at UTC have given me more affirmation and support than I probably deserve. I would like to thank my department head Verbie Prevost, whose heart is as big as her spine is stiff. Chris Stuart deserves equal praise. He not only introduced me to the right people at the University of Tennessee Press, but he has also proven to be a dear friend of incredible patience, goodwill, and resilience. I am equally thankful to my UTC colleagues Joe Wilferth, Marcia Noe, Bryan Hampton, Matthew Guy, Joyce Smith, Thomas Ware, Richard Jackson, Rebecca Cook, and Sybil Baker for their friendship, and to graduate assistants Deborah Jones, Katie McClelland, and Ashley Hopkins for their proofreading.

After the manuscript initially fell into the capable hands of Scot Danforth at the University of Tennessee Press, it received very thorough external evaluations from Dr. Leslie Petty of Rhodes College and a second (anonymous) reader. These rigorous but fair critiques helped me to understand once and for all the difference between a revised dissertation and a full-fledged book. From there, UT Press's Stan Ivester, Thomas Wells, and freelancer Monica Phillips were instrumental in moving the manuscript through the copyediting and proofing stages. I am deeply grateful that the manuscript has passed through so many capable hands on its way to final printing.

INTRODUCTION

"Who Need Be Afraid of the Merge?"

The Romantic Roots of Androgyny in America

Alexis de Tocqueville's *Democracy in America,* one of the first great works to detail the culture and government of the young republic, suggests how the specter of androgyny has long resonated at the level of national representation. Though remaining optimistic about the nation's general prospects, the book reveals a certain anxiety about the relations between American men and women. In his chapter "How the American Understands the Equality of the Sexes," Tocqueville writes: "I believe that the social changes that bring nearer to the same level the father and son, the master and servant, and, in general superiors and inferiors will raise woman and make her more the equal of man."[1] Tocqueville justifies his anxiety by explaining what democracy appeared to have done in Europe, especially in postrevolutionary France:

> There are people in Europe who, confounding together the different characteristics of the sexes, would make man and woman into beings not only equal but alike. They would give to both the same functions, impose on both the same duties, and grant to both the same rights; they would mix them in all things—their occupations, their pleasures, their business. It may readily be conceived that by thus attempting to make one sex equal to the other, both are degraded, and from so preposterous a medley of the works of nature nothing could ever result but weak men and disorderly women.[2]

The Frenchman's remarks suggest just how close democracy could come to unleashing widespread social and gender panic. Indeed, this new governmental form had set the United States and France out into uncharted waters, and the citizens of both countries quickly sensed the economic, social, and political confusion involved in severing ties to aristocratic regimes that maintained clearly prescribed roles for the relations among men and women. More specifically, Tocqueville's comments reflect the fear generated by French counterrevolutionaries, who suspected that equality and democracy would embolden women beyond conventional limits. Abhorred by the bloodiness of the Reign of Terror, these reactionaries depicted revolutionary women as maenads or mannish furies intent on stripping men of their civic privileges and rendering them politically, if not physically, impotent.[3] Should America try to make men and women the same in all civic and cultural functions, the Frenchman wonders, what would become of its fledgling democracy?

Yet by the time Tocqueville published his famous book in 1840, neither memories of the bloody excesses of the French Revolution nor the fear of unnaturally masculine women quelled interest in androgyny. In fact, on both sides of the Atlantic, interest in the concept only grew. Back on the continent, for example, the French mystic Pierre-Simon Ballanche conceived of the mysterious male-female figure as an embodiment of emerging democracy and social equality. He regarded the prelapsarian Adam and Eve, ignorant of their nakedness and of their different sexual anatomy, as two parts making up a spiritually androgynous Humankind. In his *Vision d'Hébal* (1831), Ballanche argued that the Fall resulted not only in acknowledgment of sexual division, but also in subsequent breakdowns into social and racial classes. After being exiled from the ahistorical, nonpolitical world of Eden, Adam and Eve were left to wander through historical time and space to find a way to return to their androgynous unity.[4] Like his contemporary Ballanche, the German romantic theologian Johann Gottfried von Herder espoused a universal history (*Universalgeschichte*) that described human development as a movement away from a primitive androgynous harmony into a present world of division and sexual inequality.[5] Arguing for a type of organic nationalism, Herder further pictured the universe as an organism that consisted of smaller, interrelated organisms such as ethnic units; as a part of this organic chain, individuals were intimately linked to their surroundings and to each other. "The most natural state . . . is *one* nation, with one national character," Herder claimed. "[A] nation is as much a natural plant as a family, with only more branches."[6] The cultures that therefore emerged from various communities' unique experiences with their local surroundings became hardened and perpetuated in language, and hence this linguistic solidarity served as the basis for Herder's concept of the *Volk*. In this sense, though humans had lost their primitive androgynous harmony, they still maintained a certain organic and spiritual immanence with each other and their specific natural surroundings.

In the antebellum United States, transcendentalists used variations of French mysticism and Herderian nationalism as a means of promoting their own androgynous visions for American democracy. The emphasis on the fluidity of consciousness among God, humans, and nature that served as the backbone of transcendental philosophy had its roots, just like Herderian thought, in a rejection of John Locke's experiential-based materialism. Unlike Locke, who regarded human identity as the result of the outside world's active inscription upon the passive, unformed mind, Herder believed that existence presupposes activity, and therefore the human mind actually does not merely receive impressions from the outside world, but instead creates impressions based on those experiences. In this sense humans and nature, subject and object, even man and woman, are symbiotically linked within their *Volk* communities.[7] This postulation was akin to Kant's notion of intuitive-based "Reason," which Ralph Waldo Emerson saw in "The Transcendentalist" (1842) as the groundwork for transcendental fluidity. Emerson's insistence in *Nature* (1836) that "[w]ords are signs of natural facts," and that "[p]articular natural facts are symbols of particular spiritual facts" is clear evidence of Herder's organic influence.[8]

Emerson further reworked Herder's notion of symbiosis to help create an American ethos based on the spiritual and psychic unity of all men and women. Many of his opinions on the matter were supplemented by his understanding of Emanuel Swedenborg, the Swedish mystic who wrote extensively on the androgyny of souls and angels. Especially under this second influence, Emerson saw true men and women of genius as those who sought out and internalized these angelic traits. "The finest people marry the two sexes in their own person," he wrote in an 1843 journal entry. "Hermaphroditus is then the finished soul."[9]

The Sage of Concord was also fascinated by Plato's thoughts on both androgyny and the creation of the Ideal State. According to Plato's *Symposium,* man and woman were initially combined into one globular form. Fearing that their kind might one day rule Olympus, Zeus rent these androgynes in two with his thunderbolts, and subsequently men and women have desperately sought out ways to regain their original wholeness. In reading *The Republic,* Emerson regarded the ideal city-state's elite stratum, known as the guardians, as mentally androgynous beings, uniting feminine compassion and gentleness with masculine endurance and courage. The notion of personal and political cohesion found in these two works no doubt prompted Emerson in 1843 to write in his journal, "I notice that an Emperor in his robes is dressed almost in feminine attire, because the supreme power represents woman as well as man, the moral principle as well as the intellectual principle."[10] While Emerson's thoughts on the matter no doubt challenged prevailing mid-nineteenth-century notions that men and women belonged to different biological, psychological, and cultural "spheres," his conception of androgyny remained male-centered. His version of the ideal leader, after all, is a man clothed in womanly attire, not a woman clothed in manly attire.[11]

The Swedenborgian notions that proved instrumental in Emerson's androgynous ideals were equally influential for Julia Ward Howe. Best known for her "Battle Hymn of the Republic" (1862) and her commitment to abolition, Howe also wrote a novel manuscript posthumously entitled *The Hermaphrodite*. Today the 1847 manuscript exists only in published fragments, but from them we are able to understand the main character's hermaphroditism not only in physiological terms, but also as a sign of the spiritual perfection and wholeness so often attributed to androgyny in both the Platonic and romantic traditions.[12] Despised by many of those who learn his secret, the protagonist Laurence finds himself at death's door at the end of the manuscript. In one particular scene a doctor who has come to examine him reveals the secret of his anatomy to Briseida, the sister of Laurence's Italian friend Berto. "'Ah!' said Briseida, who had read something of Swedenborg, 'a heavenly superhuman mystery, one undivided, integral soul, needing not to seek on earth its other moiety, needing only to adore the God above it, and to labour for its brethren around it.'"[13] Though the scorn and ridicule that Laurence suffers throughout the story anticipate the pathologizing of androgyny in the postbellum era, his persona of Christlike tenderness suggests that he is more spiritually and physiologically evolved than single-sexed humans. As Briseida sees it, Laurence reaches the cosmological telos that Herder, Ballanche, and others envisioned in their writings.

Although Howe's incomplete manuscript has nothing overtly or covertly to do with American nationalist sentiment (Laurence hails from some European locale, and the story itself takes place mainly in Germany and Italy among members of the nobility), it is of additional relevance because it speaks with all sincerity about the "verifiable" existence of hermaphroditism among human beings. This perception, as we shall see, began to change in the next few decades of the nineteenth century. But in 1847 medical science still entertained the notion held since ancient times that genital sexual difference developed from one innately hermaphroditic corporeal frame. In such a view, a penis was simply a uterus that developed externally and vice-versa. *The Compleat Master-piece,* a widely read tract on human sexuality written under the pseudonym of Aristotle, delineates this "one-sex" model. After explaining the details of female genitalia in prose to a presumptive male reader, the *Master-piece* resorts to rhyming couplets, explaining:

> Thus the Womens Secrets I have survey'd
> And let them see how curiously they're made:
> And that, tho' they of different Sexes be,
> Yet in the whole they are the same as we:
> For those that have the strictest Searchers been,
> Find Women are but Men turned Out side in:
> And Men, if they but cast their Eyes about,
> May find they're Women, with their Inside out.[14]

The Compleat Master-piece had gone through many editions since its original publication in 1684, and it provided eighteenth- and early-nineteenth-century Americans—common folk as well as physicians and the educated elite—with a relatively comprehensive view of human sexuality. Given the widespread belief that any given human body contained the bedrock for both male and female genitalia, Julia Ward Howe could construct a plausible rendering of a character whose dual-sexed wholeness was therefore tantamount to his apparent spiritual wholeness.

Another of Swedenborg's American devotees, Margaret Fuller, espoused an affirmative version of androgyny in her 1845 *Woman in the Nineteenth Century*. Based on an earlier article entitled "The Great Lawsuit: Man versus Men, Woman versus Women," published in a July 1843 issue of *The Dial*, the treatise leveled a heavy indictment upon American democracy for leaving its women citizens politically disenfranchised and socially isolated: "It is inevitable that an external freedom, an independence of the encroachments of other men, such as has been achieved for the nation, should be so also for every member of it." Democracy, she asserts, should not only lead to women's political enfranchisement but also promote a national ethos of female self-development: "What woman needs is not as a woman to act or rule, but as a nature to grow, as an intellect to discern, as a soul to live freely and unimpeded, to unfold such powers as were given her when we left our common home."[15] For Fuller, the country's democratic potential could only come to fruition when society encouraged women to cultivate their own inner masculinity and men to cultivate their own inner femininity: "Male and female represent the two sides of the great radical dualism. But, in fact, they are perpetually passing into one another. Fluid hardens to solid, solid rushes to fluid. There is no wholly masculine man, no purely feminine woman." The ideal republic is made up of men and women who resemble the archetypes Apollo and Minerva, for in the sensitive and intuitive man and in the strong and bold woman, Fuller asserts, is the true power of democracy and the full embodiment of the nation-state.[16]

Perhaps America's greatest expression of the androgynous-democratic ideal came from Walt Whitman, who, like Emerson, was deeply influenced by Herder. Herder's emphasis on near-primitive *Volk* communities provided Whitman with the impetus to write about a young, virile, and energetic America.[17] Beginning with *Leaves of Grass* in 1855, Whitman formulated a new kind of national narrative for his country, one James E. Miller, Jr. calls a "lyric-epic."[18] As traditional genre theory holds, the lyric and epic exist on opposite ends of the poetic spectrum. Whereas the lyric is an extremely personal, introspective, and short poetic expression, the epic is expansive, active, and community-based. As a lyric-epic poet, then, Whitman endeavors to reconcile the tension contained within the concept of the "united states." Thus he speaks as a singular self, but also as other people of the growing republic, both male and female. This particular dynamic most clearly links androgyny and nationalism in Whitman's poetics. In biographer Justin Kaplan's opinion, androgyny "seemed only natural and right" to one wishing to represent the dual-sexed body politic.[19] "One's-Self I Sing," for example, not only begins in traditional epic fashion with an invocation to the muse, but it also recognizes America as an androgynous body politic:

> One's-Self I sing, a simple separate person,
> Yet utter the word Democratic, the word En-Masse.
>
> Of physiology from top to toe I sing,
> Not physiognomy alone nor brain alone is worthy for the Muse,
> I say the Form complete is worthier far.
> The Female equally with the Male I sing.
>
> Of Life immense in passion, pulse, and power,
> Cheerful, for freest form'd under the laws divine,
> The Modern Man I sing.[20]

Though written just after the Civil War (1867) and not included as the opening poem of *Leaves of Grass* until the 1871 edition, "One's-Self I Sing" harks back to the antebellum optimism that democracy brings the sexes together—if not physically to inhabit one body, at least spiritually and metaphorically to inhabit one body politic. Moreover, the temporal projection of Whitman's poem, as well as his heralding of "Modern Man," harks back to Ballanche's theory that with the progression of time and the perfection of democracy, prelapsarian androgyny is recoverable.

Whitman's expansive, transgendered voice provides a sense of democratic egalitarianism not previously seen in American poetry. Early on in the 1855 edition of *Leaves of Grass*, the poet proclaims, "Every kind for itself and its own . . . for me mine male and female." Thus admitting no shame in combining female and male traits in his own poetic character, he then challenges the reader with the direct question, "Who need be afraid of the merge?"[21] Obviously the poet is not afraid of merging, for as the embodiment of democracy, he is "the poet of the woman the same as the man, / And I say it is as great to be a woman as to be a man." At a later moment in the poem, the merge is portrayed as both a marriage between a man and a woman as well as a type of psychic transference: "I turn the bridegroom out of the bed and stay with the bride myself, / And tighten her all night to my thighs and lips." After a line break the poet then proclaims: "My voice is the wife's voice, the screech by the rail of the stairs, / They fetch my man's body up dripping and drowned."[22] Whitman suggests a temporal progression of the marriage, which ends with the husband's untimely death and the poet's transference of consciousness to the grief-stricken wife.

In his poem "The Sleepers," also contained in the 1855 edition of *Leaves of Grass*, Whitman's expansive I/eye once again gives him the protean power to be both men and women. Over the course of a night, the national poetic persona peers into houses across the American landscape to become the different people he sees: "I am the actor, the actress, the voter, the politician, / [. . . .] I am she who adorn'd herself and folded her hair expectantly, / My truant lover has come, and it is dark."²³ The poem provides a clear example of what Benedict Anderson has famously called an "imagined community." Anderson claims that with the postmedieval increase in public literacy, people used various forms of print media to imagine themselves as working in unison with other constituents of their nation-state:

> The idea of a sociological organism moving calendrically through homogenous, empty time is a precise analogue of the idea of the nation, which also is conceived as a solid community moving steadily down (or up) history. An American will never meet, or even know the names of more than a handful of his 240,000-odd [sic] fellow-Americans. He has no idea what they are up to at any one time. But he has complete confidence in their steady, anonymous, simultaneous activity.²⁴

By the time *Leaves of Grass* was first published, the United States had already reached the Pacific Ocean (California was admitted to the Union in 1850), and in a poem such as "The Sleepers," readers are able to imagine and vicariously experience the vastness of the country and the male and female citizens who constitute it. In a move that goes beyond the typical instance of "imagining" that Anderson describes, the speaker *becomes* the many different-sexed Americans he sees, showing once again that the lyric-epic form is successful only if it is a poetic androgyne who gives it voice.

The Postbellum Turn

As America entered the postbellum era, new questions about the role and legitimacy of democracy invariably challenged previous conceptions of androgyny. David Leverenz refers to this particular time in American history as a type of Contact Period, a term usually reserved for initial encounters between early European explorers and native inhabitants of the New World. In this second age of contact, "many African Americans, immigrants, and women dreamed of rising to respectability, and some achieved it."²⁵ Leverenz's term is apt for two reasons. First, it bespeaks a time when America had to rethink its past reliance on race—and later sex—as a means of bestowing full citizenship. Second, just as early explorers used Old World tropes and symbols to demarcate, legitimate, or explain unfamiliar or surprising New World phenomena, Americans after the Civil War relied on familiar male-female models (and variations of those models) to explain other types of diversity for which there was no name or for which there was barely even an ideological concept. Indeed, only by the mid-nineteenth century did binaries such as blackness/whiteness, heterosexuality/homosexuality, and bourgeois/proletarian achieve codified articulation and relative mass comprehension. Ethnology, the forerunner of modern-day anthropology, was only beginning to codify human phenotypical differences into a consistent, albeit Eurocentric, pattern of race and ethnicity. Sexology, which attempted to classify various kinds of sexual expressions, conditions, and maladies, came onto the scene as late as the 1850s and 1860s. And only by the middle of the nineteenth century did new types of class codifications begin to solidify as the result of industrial capitalism's gaining strength and of workers' abandonment of the countryside in search of urban wage labor. In light of these vast and frightening changes, Americans often relied on gender differences they understood (or at least thought they did) to represent other types of difference, diversity, or ambiguity within the American polis that were new and that barely made sense.

Consequently, what we now recognize as diversity in terms of race, class, sexuality, regional identity, or even political affiliation was often articulated by a language of sexual distinction that inevitably evoked androgyny, especially when certain identities showed little evidence of "purity" or polar absoluteness. In the years following the Civil War, for example, the reunification of the country was often symbolized in fiction and the press as a marriage between a northern groom and a southern bride.[26] In keeping with Plato's myth of the androgynes, the reunification of the male North and the female South provided a metaphorical sense of wholeness to a body politic violently severed by four years of war. In other instances, the close of the Civil War evoked a humorous blurring of genders. The capture of Jefferson Davis suggested, if not androgyny, at least transvestism as northern presses fueled speculation that the hapless Confederate president tried to escape Union troops in the Georgia wilderness disguised in a bonnet and hoopskirt.[27] And in a later instance, the presidential election of 1884 witnessed the short-lived rise of the "mugwumps," those Republicans who crossed party lines to vote for Democrat Grover Cleveland. Attempting to keep other Republicans from leaving the fold, party loyalists often relied on the language of sexual indeterminacy to castigate these mugwumps, calling them, among other things, "eunuchs," members of a "third sex," and "political hermaphrodites."[28]

Similar to political identity, biracial identity was often infused with the language and imagery of the androgyne. Despite the widespread postbellum perception that black men were oversexed beasts, blackness itself was regarded as a less advanced form of humanity akin to (white) women's intellectual and moral inferiority.[29] These and related sentiments prompted some very curious remarks from famed Harvard professor Louis Agassiz. In a letter dating from the 1860s to abolitionist Samuel Gridley Howe, he warned that government policies implicitly promoting race mixing would transfigure the United States from a "manly population descended from cognate nations" into "the effeminate progeny of mixed races . . . half negro, sprinkled with white blood."[30] According to Agassiz, then, should sexual contact between the "masculine" white race and the "feminine" black race result in offspring, such a child would be not only a half-breed, but also a type of racial hermaphrodite.

Also, by the advent of the Civil War, America had entered into the era of "modern" sexuality. In this new era, sex and sexuality were recognized as key components of a person's core identity. As such, sexual activity became more than simply a reproductive function done under strict religious guidelines; it was now an instrument of personal fulfillment—within and even outside of marriage.³¹ The advent of modern sexuality left an indelible mark on androgyny that has lasted to this day. Whereas to varying degrees antebellum thinkers such as Emerson, Fuller, Howe, and Whitman felt that androgyny was a transcendental, physiological, or spiritual quality meant to usher in a new era of democratic equality, the advent of modern sexuality either dismissed androgyny/hermaphroditism as nonexistent or it lifted it from its genital-based context and pathologized it. As Michel Foucault explains, the decade of the 1860s marked a crucial moment in the history of sexuality as it witnessed the first attempts by doctors to codify sexual perversions and conditions and to make hermaphrodites fit into one of two sexes. Foucault's famous case study of Herculine Barbin is a real-life example of how French authorities imposed a juridically undisputable sex on one who had previously lived, at least in Foucault's opinion, in a "happy limbo of a non-identity."³²

The medical and juridical consolidation of anatomy into a clearly bifurcated system of male and female genitalia reached America at roughly the same time it did in Barbin's native France. This apparent need for such consolidation came at a time when feminism and homosexuality challenged assumptions about sexual boundaries. In fact, medical historian Alice Domurat Dreger calls the period directly following the much publicized 1868 death of Herculine Barbin the "Age of Gonads":

> [S]cientific and medical men, faced with and frustrated by case after case of "doubtful sex," came to an agreement that every body's "true" sex was marked by one thing and one thing only: the anatomical nature of the gonadal tissue as either ovarian or testicular. Not coincidentally, such a definition virtually eliminated "true" hermaphroditism in theory and practice, even if—probably because—people with challenging bodies kept popping up. Without the material and consequent social problems presented by the hermaphroditic body, this particular construction of "true sex"—namely, that sex is ultimately determined by the gonad—might never have occurred.³³

Two medical cases in America—one dating from 1629 and the other from the Civil War—support Dreger's general paradigm. The first recorded case of hermaphroditism in the American colonies dates back almost four hundred years to one Thomas/Thomasine Hall, an indentured servant from Virginia whose indeterminate genitalia convinced him/her to live as both man and woman depending on the circumstances that arose. Eventually learning of Hall's genital uncertainty, local magistrates forced him/her to wear garments of both sexes. While certainly the magistrates imposed the outlandish punishment to prevent Hall or anyone else of ambiguous genitalia from additional attempts at deception, it is also true that the punishment is in keeping with a pre-nineteenth-century pattern of recognizing the possibility of the existence of physiological hermaphroditism.³⁴ Since Hall was a person who possessed genitalia of both sexes, it was only suitable that s/he wear clothing that denoted as much.

In keeping more in line with gonadal imperatives, however, later cases in America would require individuals with indeterminate genitalia to conform to a doctor's ruling of what sex they best approximated. Take, for example, the case of M. B. H., a Union soldier who, when being examined for a Civil War battle injury, was found to possess questionable genitalia. As Dr. B. Cloak examined the patient further, he learned that M. B. H., while living as a man, had experienced monthly bloody discharges and only once or twice in his life did he ever have an erection. Ultimately, the doctor deemed M. B. H. a female on account of these discharges and certain psychological factors, such as a reported indifference to sexual activity. As female, M. B. H. had made a mistake, in Dr. Cloak's opinion, in enlisting in the Civil War.³⁵ This case shows not only the increasing perception that hermaphroditism was impossible, but that nations, especially during times of tremendous military struggle, required distinct lines of demarcation among its male and female citizens. Moreover, in cases where it proved impossible to determine a clear presence of single-sexed gonads, doctors felt compelled to find—or invent—such evidence, even if it meant taking nonanatomical factors such as sex drive into account.

"The Rough Going of Historical Process": The Critical Intervention

Androgyny did not disappear after the Civil War; rather, it simply wedded itself to other late-nineteenth-century intellectual discourses, including (but certainly not limited to) medical and evolutionary science, racial uplift, socialism, feminism, and psychology. *Androgynous Democracy* is particularly concerned with how the concept of androgyny, once detached from either genital-based corporeality or antebellum romantic notions, was appropriated by these and other intellectual discourses, and how in turn a number of authors from that same time borrowed from those discourses to formulate their own paradigms of democratic national cohesion.

In operating from these assumptions, *Androgynous Democracy* is clearly grounded in Foucauldian historicism, but it is equally indebted to the work of Thomas Laqueur and Judith Butler, who have both challenged the conventional distinctions previous scholarship has made between gender and sex. Laqueur, for instance, famously reversed Freud's postulation that "anatomy is destiny" by arguing that abstract perceptions of gender have historically controlled our understanding of sexual anatomy. "Historically," he explains, "differentiations of gender preceded differentiations of sex. . . . Anatomy in the context of sexual difference was a representational strategy that illuminated a more stable extracorporeal reality."³⁶ Judith Butler has made a similar claim about "extracorporeal reality," or the persistence of gendered conceptions of the body in western thought. She arrives at her conclusions by critiquing a whole range of thinkers, from Sigmund Freud to Julia Kristeva, exposing the essentialism implicit in their theories. Such essentialism shows that gender "ought not to be conceived merely as the cultural inscription of meaning on a pregiven sex (a juridical conception); gender must also designate the very apparatus of production whereby the sexes themselves are established."[37]

Readers may be surprised that physiological instances of hermaphroditism comprise only a small part of my study. But as I have already mentioned, physicians at the turn of the century were largely dismissive of physiological hermaphroditism, insisting that even the most questionable medical subjects really belonged to one sex or the other. Still, even as doctors rejected hermaphroditism as an anatomical category, androgyny persisted in a number of other intellectual discourses as a legitimate topic of inquiry, and therefore if Laqueur's and Butler's assumptions about the pervasiveness and durability of gender are correct, androgyny is and always has been a concept that reaches far beyond the genitalia. It is for this reason that I rely overwhelmingly on the term "androgyny" instead of "hermaphroditism" in this study, for androgyny typically bespeaks a sense of masculine-feminine duality beyond mere anatomy.

This study focuses specifically on Henry James, Frank Norris, Charlotte Perkins Gilman, John Crowe Ransom, Grace Lumpkin, W. E. B. Du Bois, and Marita Bonner. Certainly many other writers at this time were interested in gender fluidity in general and androgyny in particular; authors ranging from Robert Herrick to H. D. to Ernest Hemingway were fascinated by the concept, yet they typically did not tie androgyny to larger issues of national destiny.[38] The seven figures featured in the following chapters, however, expressed an abiding interest in androgyny, and their interest had a direct bearing on their thoughts about some of the most prominent issues America confronted before and after the turn of the twentieth century. Among those issues were postbellum reconciliation and the struggle for universal suffrage (James); America's remarkable economic ascendancy in the first decades of the twentieth century, which led to the development of a consumer culture (Norris and Gilman); the threat of socialism after the Great Depression had weakened the country's faith in both capitalism and religious fundamentalism (Ransom and Lumpkin); and the flight of blacks from the southern countryside to northern cities in search of economic and social advancement (Du Bois and Bonner).

Indeed, androgyny proved a malleable concept that provided a way to negotiate and identify these authors' limits (or sometimes their lack thereof) of democratic inclusion. At times it served as an "abject" figuration against whom, in Judith Butler's observation, nation-states "circumscribe[d] the domain of the [enfranchised] subject."[39] Yet, at other times, writers tried to revive antebellum notions of androgyny only to find that their world had changed far too dramatically to reconcile those notions to modern circumstances. These views, as contradictory as they may be, nonetheless signal a larger modern consistency of the desire for communal wholeness and order, even if dual-gendered "wholeness" turns out to be simply another form of male prerogative. Such a desire for unity no doubt came as a response to the many challenges America faced. From the time of the peace treaty at Appomattox in 1865 to the end of the Second World War in 1945, the United States experienced a number of rifts and conflicts, including violent labor struggles, the contentious enfranchisement of African Americans, the first wave of feminism, the Spanish-American and Great Wars, the genocidal violence leading to the "closing" of the frontier in 1890, the emergence of mass culture, the shrinking of the rural populations as urban wage labor became more prominent, and the advancement of science and technology that in one way or another contributed to these other events.

Yet if the androgyne's apparent timelessness may have intrigued some modern American writers in search of wholeness, it also contributed in a more recent time to androgyny's critical repudiation, especially among many second-wave feminists. The repudiation began with the publication of Carolyn Heilbrun's 1973 *Toward a Recognition of Androgyny*. At the center of the book is an impulse to seek out what Heilbrun calls "a hidden river of androgyny," which she claims has been integral to humans' notions of inner wholeness for centuries.[40] Heilbrun's book proved so controversial that it generated a special session at the 1973 Modern Language Association annual conference. The then-fledgling journal *Women's Studies* devoted a full issue to the papers that came from the session. In the opening essay of the issue, Heilbrun defends her postulation against accusations of essentialism. She attributes previous misunderstandings and attacks to "simply a debate over terminology." Though she had used the terms "masculine" and "feminine" to denote aggression and gentleness respectively, she "would agree wholeheartedly" with any other terms that suggested the same conventional, culturally inscribed types.[41] An additional essay by Nancy Topping Bazin and Alma Freeman came to Heilbrun's defense, emphasizing, though in a more essentialist vein, that "[t]he eternal human quest . . . is to discover and identify with the true self, to embrace the polar opposites and find again the primal wholeness which has been lost."[42]

For Cynthia Secor, however, androgyny's mythological grounding evades historical scrutiny. "My fundamental objection to the concept of androgyny," she states, "is that it is rooted in a static image of perfection, in eternity, an image which cannot take into account the rough going of historical process." As a result, Secor could not accept the term "androgyny": "[I]n perpetuating the categories of masculine and feminine, it necessarily continues conceptually to define women in relation to men. The term as historically used, and as it tends to be used in the present, maintains the polarity represented by genders, thus undercutting the very sense of independence and selfhood it would seem to encourage."[43]

With the advent of postmodern feminism in the 1980s, *Toward a Recognition of Androgyny* got a second look, this time from Toril Moi, who understood Heilbrun's concept of androgyny as inherently deconstructive, as a "recognition of [gender's] falsifying metaphysical nature."[44] Moi's alternative perspective helps us to recognize both the falsities and the persistence of the masculine-feminine binary on which androgyny is inextricably based. Judith Halberstam generally agrees with Moi, showing that even when one attempts to deconstruct the binary to show its inherent signifying instability, we must also recognize that no deconstruction can exist without the enduring presence of the two oppositional terms that constitute the binary.[45] And since androgyny has been largely an extragenital, extracorporeal concern throughout the last 150 years of American history, its implications reach into the gendered concepts that have historically sexed the body and set up social hierarchies. As a concept of debate and politics, androgyny will only disappear when gender disappears, but such a disappearance seems hardly imminent.

Despite the deconstructive tendencies of our current postmodern age, it is still necessary to recognize American nationalism's historical complicity in holding tight to the masculine-feminine binary. In approaching this subject matter, I therefore come neither to praise androgyny (as Heilbrun did) nor to bury it (as many second-wave feminists did), but to historicize it. Since the roles of men and women have obviously changed much over the years, I am careful not to attempt to provide any overarching narrative of gender. Doing so would only reinscribe an ahistorical fixity that I try to avoid at all costs. I wish to let the authors and their specific historical and social contexts define what constitutes male and female as well as masculine and feminine.

Each chapter depicts two different "voices" in conversation with one another. In most instances, the exchange takes place between two different figures, though chapter 1 showcases only one author, Henry James, whose writings from different stages of his career create their own revealing dialogue. Despite the number of interlocutors involved in any given conversation, the first voice in each chapter proposes a way in which androgyny could be used, for better or for worse, to delineate the outermost boundary of democratic enfranchisement. The second voice in the chapter then responds to those proposals, usually revealing (in James's case unwittingly) their continuing reliance on male privilege. It is certainly no coincidence that the second voice in every chapter but the first belongs to a woman; for much of the period I examine, women were legally denied many of the rights given to men, and even after landmark events such as the passage of the Nineteenth Amendment in 1920, they still fought patriarchal assumptions embedded in the culture at large.

This book's specific trajectory traces the development of modern American nationalism from its origins in the post–Civil War era to its moment of crisis in the 1930s, a decade that witnessed both the devastation of the Great Depression at home and the rise of fascism abroad. Chapter 1 begins in the 1880s as Henry James comes to the realization that notions of androgynous wholeness voiced by romantic writers featured in this introduction no longer held any sway. At issue for James in his 1886 *The Bostonians* is how to reinvent the modern American citizen in an age marked by the political enfranchisement of blacks, women's suffrage, and the emergence of sexological and evolutionary discourses that tie androgyny to homosexual pathology and racial degeneration. As protagonists Olive Chancellor and Basil Ransom attempt to uncover Verena Tarrant's potential homosexuality—that is, her psychical androgyny—they muse upon her racial origin and what that origin means for a nation reuniting after four years of civil war. By late career, James's opinions had begun to change. Looking at "The Manner of Our Speech," "The Speech of American Women," "The Manners of American Women," and *The American Scene*, four pieces the writer composed during and after his last visit to America in 1904, I argue that James cautiously envisioned greater public affirmation of androgyny through the construction of a disembodied national voice, a *vox Americana* that consisted of distinct "masculine" and "feminine" elements. Ironically, though James held transcendentalism at arm's length throughout his professional life, his writings from this later period largely endorse the romantic notion of androgyny once propounded by Emerson, Fuller, and Whitman.

If in chapter 1 I explain how sexology and evolution led James to conclude that the only way to accommodate white women and African Americans into the new paradigm of citizenship was to transcend the body in favor of an androgynous *vox Americana*, then the first part of chapter 2 explains how sexology's and evolution's co-optation of androgyny could explain, of all things, the development of America's consumer culture in the first decades of the twentieth century. The second chapter therefore addresses the rise of what I call "commercial androgyny." The country's economic ascension in the first two decades of the twentieth century helped create a new paradigm of economic liberalism, one that combined in individual citizens of both sexes the production and consumption impulses. This new notion of the liberal subject was in some senses a sharp departure from the assumptions of the "separate spheres" paradigm of the nineteenth century, in which men were perceived as biologically predisposed to production while women were equally predisposed to consumption. In his 1901 novel *The Octopus*, Frank Norris ties the new parameters of the liberal subject to evolutionary discourses of atavistic androgyny, thus creating a narrative that "naturalizes" capitalism through Anglo-Saxon men and women whose primitive impulses to both produce and consume are linked directly to national destiny.

In the second part of chapter 2, I discuss Charlotte Perkins Gilman, who, while also affirming the legitimacy of evolutionary science, rejected the new configuration of the androgynous liberal subject found in Norris's writings. In *Women and Economics* (1898) and her utopian novel *Herland* (1915), Gilman critiques the discursive historical processes that have gendered economic spheres. Relying on evolutionary science that clearly revealed an Anglo-Saxon bias, Gilman's writings search instead for universal "human" qualities and propose reforming relations between American men and women through a different and nongendered understanding of production and consumption. Particularly in the feminist-utopian *Herland*, Gilman explores how the entire discourse of androgyny is part of a masculine signifying order that helps prop up America's economy and self-conception.

Despite Gilman's personal efforts, the notion of commercial androgyny persisted throughout the first decades of the twentieth century, making southern poet and critic John Crowe Ransom, the central figure in the first part of chapter 3, deeply suspicious about the overall stability of the American economy. Ransom's fears were realized with the eventual crash of the stock market in 1929. As a response to both the market crash and the nation's potential susceptibility to radical takeover, Ransom set upon a defense of southern nationalism in his contributions to the Agrarian symposium *I'll Take My Stand* and in his book on theology *God Without Thunder* (both published in 1930). Ransom's project in both works is not to dismiss androgyny, but rather to strip it of its capitalist parameters and reformulate it as the central tenet of religious fundamentalism. For Ransom, belief in an androgynous Christian godhead (consisting exclusively of God the Father and a feminine Holy Ghost) would serve as the best defense against a welfare state that, in its misguided effort to provide economic stability for American citizens, would create social, racial, and sexual disarray.

The chapter's second half then allows the southern proletarian author Grace Lumpkin to respond to the masculine impulses embedded in the Agrarian vision of androgyny voiced by Ransom. Lumpkin addresses these issues in *To Make My Bread*, her 1932 novel based on the violent textile mill strike in Gastonia, North Carolina, in 1929. Initially resisting Ransom's volkish sensibilities, the novel explores to what extent striking southern workers can safely and successfully dissolve gender boundaries under the aegis of class. Ostensibly, the novel's "protagonist" is the dual-sexed proletarian social body, though in the striking workers' creation of a union, women laborers in particular question what it means to join a radical movement that regards them as little more than pseudo-men. These troublesome issues, still looming large at the end of the novel, indicate not only the American Communist Party's difficulty in adopting a clear and consistent stance on "the woman question" during the tumultuous 1930s, but they also anticipate Lumpkin's eventual turn toward conservative southern nationalism later in her career.

In its discussion of black leader W. E. B. Du Bois and Harlem Renaissance author Marita Bonner, the fourth and final chapter brings together the various evolutionary, sexological, racial, and Agrarian themes that have run throughout the rest of the book. The volkish sense of national belonging that punctuates Ransom's (and later Lumpkin's) love of the agrarian South was not the exclusive ideological territory of whites. The Herderian notions of organic nationalism that I have described earlier in this introduction resonated just as deeply with Du Bois and Bonner. I contextualize both authors' works within the discourse of the *Volk* movement, which had been developing in Europe and America throughout the nineteenth century. In resisting the evolutionary and racial uplift discourses that had linked blackness to androgyny throughout much of the nineteenth century, Du Bois reformulated his "black folk" to position manhood, not racial purity, as its prime component. Yet in setting up the money obsessed inner-city black man as the unmanly foil to his black folk, he often relied on the various nineteenth-century discourses of androgyny that denigrated or mocked black manhood.

In her writings from the 1920s and 1930s, Marita Bonner, the featured figure in the second half of chapter 4, exposes the fallacies in Du Bois's volkish scheme and suggests that the heterogeneous American inner-city neighborhood provides the most hospitable site for the transgression or blurring of racial and gender boundaries. As fascism was on the rise in Europe during the 1930s, Bonner implicitly probed how the United States' notions of order and civility were simply a mask for the violent suppression of racial and gender fluidity.

If chapter 4 ends with the looming question of fascism and the attendant issues of racial purity and rigidly defined gender roles, the epilogue investigates androgyny's own potential link to the hyper-nationalism on which fascism was historically based. The epilogue begins with an assessment of the sixth chapter of *A Room of One's Own*, in which Virginia Woolf critiques Mussolini's wish to commission fascist literature. In Woolf's eyes, Mussolini's project is destined to fail because it will be written from a hypermasculine point of view rather than from an androgynous perspective. Thus, while Woolf clearly sees androgyny as the antidote to fascism, a review of the authors I have investigated in this study shows that fascism, for all its masculine bravado, nonetheless accommodates androgynous paradigms of national cohesion.

Androgyny has indeed been a key concern in the history of America's ideological formation. In the modern rage for order it appeared as both monstrosity and sublime ideal, as both perdition and salvation. As we shall see in the first chapter, questions of nationalism and post–Civil War reunification concerned not only democracy, but also the ambiguously gendered and racialized citizens who would embody that democracy.

CHAPTER 1

"The Social Dusk of That Mysterious Democracy": Race, Sexology, and the Modern Woman in Henry James's Postbellum America

The American transcendentalists who rose to prominence in the antebellum period regarded androgyny as the spiritual result of a nation dedicated to egalitarian democratic principles. These notions were short-lived, however, as the Civil War and the disastrous Reconstruction that followed made any true national union seem like a distant, if not impossible, reality. The disillusionment with the romantic period in general, and with transcendental notions of androgynous harmony in particular, were no more apparent than in Henry James. No doubt fueling this pessimism was the failure of his transcendentalist father, Henry Sr., to achieve the philosophical or literary fame to which he aspired. In fact, the poor critical reception of *The Bostonians*, when it initially appeared in serial form in both Britain and America, caused James to muse upon his father's professional failures in an 1885 letter to his brother William:

> I fear *The Bostonians* will be, as a finished work, a fiasco, as not a word, echo or comment on the serial (save your remarks) have come to me (since the row about the first two numbers) from any quarter whatever. This deathly silence seems to indicate that it has fallen flat. I hoped much of it, and shall be disappointed—having got no money for it I hoped for a little glory. . . . But how can one murmur

at one's success not being what one would like when one thinks of the pathetic, tragic ineffectualness of poor Father's lifelong effort, and the silence and oblivion that seems to have swallowed it up?[1]

There is a sad irony in how James's letter compares the failure of his novel, which lampoons a group of transcendentalist-influenced radicals, to his father's earnest efforts to become one of the philosophy's leading spokesmen. And just as Henry Jr. did not altogether purge transcendentalism from his novels, a point *The Bostonians* makes clear, neither did he completely ignore the transcendentalists' vision of androgyny; he did, however, arrive at very different conclusions on the subject.

By evoking androgyny in his writings, James also signals a larger shift taking place in American and European medical discourses. With the rise of sexology around the middle of the nineteenth century, the terms "androgyny" and "hermaphroditism" came to describe pathologically degenerative same-sex attraction. As Michel Foucault explains, "Homosexuality appeared as one of the forms of sexuality when it was transposed from the practice of sodomy onto a kind of interior androgyny, a hermaphrodism of the soul."[2] The conflation of androgyny with same-sex attraction dates at least as far back as the 1860s with the writings of sexologist Karl Ulrichs, himself a homosexual. The idea was soon appropriated by other notable sexologists, such as Edward Carpenter and Havelock Ellis in Britain and the Viennese sexologist Richard von Krafft-Ebing. Krafft-Ebing's monumental *Psychopathia Sexualis*, originally published in German in 1886 and republished in other languages in subsequent decades, provided the most detailed explanation to date; homosexual men were "females in feeling; in women, males." Krafft-Ebing spoke of psychical androgyny as a type of psychological sickness rooted in stunted evolutionary development; for him, homosexuals "approached the opposite sex anthropologically," meaning that homosexuality was an atavistic trait that had its roots in a primitive physiological hermaphroditism.[3]

No doubt having a famous physician for a brother helped James keep current on the many theories circulating in these medical communities. Wendy Graham explains:

> James's incorporation of a feminine identity was a socially mediated act; that is, it was influenced by James's desire to avoid unwelcome duties (military service and supporting a family) and his upbringing. It is also true that James's self-portraits (fictional, epistolary, and autobiographical) are consistent with sexologists' constructions of homosexuality during his lifetime. [Forensic scientist J. L.] Casper published in the 1850s and 1860s. [Karl] Ulrichs and Carl Westphal published in the 1860s. By the 1880s a mass of information about homosexuality had accumulated, and much of it was remarkably uniform in outlook,

in that it labeled homosexuality as simple gender inversion. By the 1880s inversion had become a mainstream concept.[4]

It is no surprise, then, that the many effeminate men and masculine women so common in James's fiction would resemble the medical portraits drawn up by many of these prominent physicians and scientists. Thus, even outside of a specific homosexual context, androgyny was a consistent theme for James. Carolyn Heilbrun, for example, has credited *The Portrait of a Lady* with helping to usher in a new phase of "androgynous" literary creativity. As opposed to strictly "feminist" novels, androgynous novels such as *Portrait* ask the reader to identify "with the male and female characters equally," just as its author has done. Kelly Cannon has claimed that James and many of his male protagonists subscribed to "a nonaggressive [gender] model that draws upon the androgynous quality at the core of [societal] marginality."[5]

Yet the emerging science of sexology did more than co-opt androgyny for its new classifications of homosexual identity. Bound up in this new codification was the question of race. As sexologists Havelock Ellis and John Addington Symonds (himself a personal acquaintance of James's) wrote in the 1890s, "And now that the problem of religion has practically been settled, and that the problem of labour has at least been placed on a practical foundation, the question of sex—with the racial questions that rest on it—stands before the coming generations as the chief problem for solution."[6] Thanks in large part to Siobhan B. Somerville's scholarship, we are beginning to understand the larger implications of Ellis and Symonds's remarks. Attempting to give coherence to these vague suggestions, she argues that "the formation of notions of heterosexuality and homosexuality emerged in the United States through (and not merely parallel to) a discourse saturated with assumptions about the racialization of bodies."[7] Somerville sees the discourse of race and sexuality intersecting at three basic points. First, just as race and evolutionary theorists of the time attempted to classify individuals along a "continuum" of absolute whiteness and blackness (with the mulatto holding a place in the middle), sexologists attempted to classify homosexuals along similar lines. Somewhere between the axes of heterosexual men and women existed what sexologist Edward Carpenter termed the "intermediate sex"—that is, persons with same-sex desire. Secondly, sexology and evolutionary discourse theorized that both same-sex and interracial desire were either steps backward along the evolutionary path or else they were "unnatural" psychological perversions.[8]

Third—and perhaps most important for this chapter—sexologists attempted to prove through comparative anatomy that (white) homosexuals had bodily features similar to blacks. These comparisons, explains Somerville, had special implications for black and white women in particular: "In characterizing either lesbians' or African American women's bodies as less sexually differentiated than the norm (always posited as white heterosexual women's bodies), anatomists and sexologists drew on notions of natural selection to dismiss these bodies as anomalous 'throwbacks' within a scheme of cultural and anatomical progress."⁹ For example, sexology made much of black women's reportedly larger-than-average clitorises—a feature that seemed to resemble a primitive or atrophied penis. An 1892 study tellingly entitled "Is Evolution Trying to Do Away with the Clitoris?" observes a direct contrast between the anatomical "imprisonment" of the clitoris of the "Aryan American Woman" and the "free" clitoris of "negresses."¹⁰ But the clitorises of lesbians—and especially white lesbians—posed a different scenario. As one medical journal from 1921 makes clear, "[A] physical examination of [lesbians] will in practically every instance disclose an abnormally prominent clitoris." The author then continues, "This is particularly so in colored women."¹¹

This chapter therefore gauges American democracy's ability to come to terms with androgyny—in both its homosexual and racial dimensions—by way of certain writings in the James canon spanning from *The Bostonians* to a number of essays and addresses the author composed between 1905 and 1907. After fearing in *The Bostonians* that homosexual desire was destructive because of its presumed scientific link to racial degeneration, James began to see new hope for androgyny by means of a dual-gendered, yet disembodied, *vox Americana*, which he believed marginalized or mitigated the problematic sexualized and racialized bodies that would give it voice. This reversal is no small move in James's late career, for by revitalizing his hope in androgyny via a disembodied voice, James shows that he was never able to divorce himself completely from the romantic notions of national unity that occupied the discourses of androgyny in the antebellum period.

When Henry James started compiling notes for *The Bostonians* in 1883, he summarized his intentions for the new project: "I wished to write a very *American* tale," he claimed, "a tale very characteristic of our social condition, and I asked myself what was the most salient and peculiar point in our social life. The answer was: the situation of woman, the decline of the sentiment of sex, the agitation on their behalf."¹² In the author's attempt to capture the entire postbellum age within the confines of women's liberation, one cannot help but wonder if something else is left out. Given the immense upheaval the United States had experienced since 1861, writing an "American" tale in the early 1880s would be a project of almost epic proportion. The Thirteenth, Fourteenth, and Fifteenth Amendments had finally given African American men legal citizenship and voting rights, yet American women—black and white alike—were denied the vote. Though women would not be given the vote until well into the twentieth century with the ratification of the Nineteenth Amendment, they were making their voices known at the time James was formulating ideas for his novel. It is evident from the novel's subject matter—with its themes of women's suffrage, the "Boston marriage," and postbellum sectional discord—that James was attuned to the social and political controversies stirring in his native land. Still, it would have been unthinkable for the author, whose famous directive in "The Art of

Fiction" is to be a writer "on whom nothing is lost," to overlook the racial issues that were so much a part of Gilded Age America.[13]

To what extent James knew about the imbrication of racial and sexual discourses is not entirely clear. We do know, however, that James was at least vaguely aware of a metaphorical link between androgyny and Africa, if not between androgyny and blackness outright. Having written a review for Alvan S. Southworth's memoir *Four Thousand Miles of African Travel: A Personal Record of a Journey Up the Nile* in an 1875 issue of *The Nation*, James remarks: "Mr. Southworth's style is, it must be said, sometimes rather odd, as, to take another instance, when he speaks of Egypt as a 'hermaphrodite land, half savage, half civilized.'"[14] It is worth noting that James chose to linger on this particular line in a review of only a few pages in length. Though Southworth presumably speaks of hermaphroditism in terms of masculine civilization and feminine nature, it is impossible to know exactly what James himself thought of the analogy.

Regardless of what a hermaphroditic Egypt may have meant for James, the previously quoted notebook entry about his intentions for *The Bostonians* makes one thing certain: whatever link might exist between homosexuality/androgyny and blackness would ultimately come to bear on the American New Woman. Originating from a published debate in 1894 between British novelists Sarah Grand and Ouida, the term "New Woman" initially described an educated, white, middle- or upper-class woman who sought greater access to education, the marketplace, and politics. In America, as Carroll Smith-Rosenberg argues, the term could be applied retroactively to white women who made their first inroads into public discourse through abolition in the years leading up to the Civil War. These "first generation" New Women, cautious of public derision, insisted upon their femaleness, arguing that they could use their inherent femininity to purify a political system too often viewed as competitive, corrupt, and cutthroat.[15] Yet when the struggle for universal suffrage gained even greater force by the late nineteenth century, the sexological conceptualization of androgyny came to represent women's desire to make their mark in the public arena.[16] Smith-Rosenberg identifies Havelock Ellis as the one who was perhaps most responsible for conflating androgyny—in the form of homosexuality—with the emergence of the New Woman. "The modern movement of [women's] emancipation," he stated, "has involved an increase in feminine criminality and in feminine insanity. . . . In connection with these, we can scarcely be surprised to find an increase in homosexuality which has always been regarded as belonging to an allied group."[17]

The New Woman's public visibility precipitated larger questions about the predictability and psychic complexity of women in general. At times, these questions became caught up in larger issues of not only sexuality, but also race. Critic Lisa Duggan has engaged such issues in a fascinating assessment of the events surrounding the 1892 murder of Freda Ward by her lover Alice Mitchell in Memphis, Tennessee. Alongside this story Duggan posits the various lynching narratives made known by Ida B. Wells, who, in the same year and in the same city, edited the anti-lynching pamphlets *Southern Horrors*. In both cases, Duggan pays particular attention to the role of the "unstable" woman. In the lesbian murder case, this persona is exemplified in Freda Ward, the outwardly "feminine" love object of Alice Mitchell's ostensibly mannish desire. What makes Ward unstable in the public's opinion is that she could choose to involve herself in a lesbian relationship *or* she could choose to reject Alice's love altogether and marry a male suitor, thus living up to Victorian American ideals. Thus, Freda's bisexual "instability" manifested itself as a type of psychical androgyny.

Duggan also points out how the unstable white woman appears in Ida B. Wells's depiction of various southern lynching narratives. Challenging the conventional notion that white women were the passive, hapless victims of black men's sexual desire, Wells refigures this narrative to expose the white woman as actually having a choice to engage in sex with a black man.[18] As these events in Memphis unfolded, the country was vexed and alarmed: the modern woman, poised at the brink of the twentieth century, could exercise her own agency, choosing either heterosexuality or homosexuality; and she could even choose her own love object, black or white. While it would be hasty to classify Freda Ward and the women in Wells's pamphlets as unequivocal exemplars of the New Woman, the rising visibility of the New Woman throughout the late nineteenth century no doubt amplified concerns that all women—even those without formal educations, those of different races, or those not from middle-class backgrounds—possessed desires and agencies that challenged domestic paradigms of virtuous womanhood.

James himself was intrigued by various types of unstable women, writing stories that depicted their frequent opaqueness or capriciousness. In *Daisy Miller* (1878), for example, Winterbourne can never decide if Daisy is "exceedingly innocent" or an "unscrupulous" flirt.[19] Similar mysteries characterize the alluring Madame de Vionnet, Chad Newsome's possible lover in *The Ambassadors* (1903). But Verena Tarrant, the young, eloquent suffragist of *The Bostonians*, may elude the reader more than any other of James's female characters. The narrative notes quite early that Verena has a "singular hollowness of character." Because we rarely have access to her thoughts, we are unsure of her sexual inclinations—or perhaps even her own racial makeup.[20]

Likewise, more than any other novel in the James canon, *The Bostonians* reflects the overlapping postbellum discourses of feminism, race, and sexuality. Consistently throughout the novel, James endows his two protagonists Olive and Basil with the ability to perceive homosexual desire in racialized terms. Not surprisingly, their perceptions come to bear on Verena. In wishing to make Verena her intimate companion, Olive sees this young radical as a racialized, exotic Other whom she can guide and control. Insofar as Basil Ransom perceives Verena to be involved in a lesbian relationship, he, too, sees her in racialized terms. His perception is perhaps more complex than Olive's because he is both attracted *to* and repelled *by* Verena's perceived blackness and psychic androgyny. In short, she presents a challenge: having "surrendered the remnants of his patrimony" by failing to eke out a living on his Mississippi plantation, Ransom is looking for a way to reclaim his manhood (43). In his struggle to woo her—and thus domesticate her through marriage—he is not only rescuing the young suffragist from lurid lesbianism and blackness, but also reestablishing his own place in the gender hierarchy.

That Ransom ultimately wins out over his cousin Olive suggests that James may be making a larger statement about the role of race and androgyny in the postbellum imagination. Just as James sees the nation not yet willing to take on larger issues of sexual liberation at the end of the nineteenth century, he cannot conceive of a racially diverse America, an America that makes room for blacks within its citizenry or national iconography. Through its overlapping (homo)sexualized and racialized imagery, *The Bostonians* reflects a nation's deeper broodings about the social makeup of American modernity.

The reform-minded Olive Chancellor is, in James's artistic vision, the postbellum legatee of the transcendentalist movement. Her progressive stance on women's emancipation, her Boston lineage, her abolitionist sympathies, and her argumentative personality in many ways make her the fictional reincarnation of Margaret Fuller. Just as James was ambivalent about transcendentalism, so too was he about its leading female voice. This ambivalence was one he no doubt inherited from his father, who himself had mixed personal relations with Fuller. The commitment to social and political reform that Olive Chancellor has in common with Fuller is what separates her from the subtly rebellious "drawing room feminists," such as Isabel Archer, Milly Theale, and Maggie Verver, with whom James himself seemed to identify and sympathize.[21] While James the artist may have embraced Fuller's dictum that "there is no wholly masculine man, no wholly feminine woman," James the social critic probably did not. In other respects, however, James moved well beyond Margaret Fuller for his portrait of Olive, suggesting that her sexual desire for other women may be read as a type of psychical androgyny. The narrator tells us: "It was a curious incident of [Olive's] zeal for the regeneration of her sex that manly things were, perhaps on the whole, what she understood best" (137). The "manly things" the narrator mentions carry over into her de-sexed appearance. Her lack of ornamentation and "plain dark dress" emphasizes that "[s]he had absolutely no figure, and presented a certain appearance of feeling cold" (40, 48).

Within the larger context of the overlapping discourses of androgyny, evolution, and race, Olive represents what sexologist Karl Ulrichs termed an *Urninde*—a woman "with a masculine love-drive."[22] Olive's resemblance to this particular type of psychical androgyne, I contend, keeps James from racializing her as he will Verena in subsequent pages. According to Ulrichs's writings from the 1860s, *Urnings* and *Urnindes* were respective terms for homosexual men and women found in white, bourgeois populations. Though their same-sex desire was an anomaly, these individuals themselves were neither pathological nor dangerous to society.[23] In fact, the more civilized classes of *Urnings* and *Urnindes* might also possess "fine romantic feeling" similar to Olive's romanticizing of Verena.[24] For James, Olive's class status and her penchant for understanding "manly things" make all the difference; if nothing else, such similarities draw her closer to her creator. Casting a black racial hue on Olive might therefore appear too close to an indictment of James himself, seeing as they both have not only same-sex desire in common, but also a patrician Boston pedigree, a mutual aversion to marriage, and an impressionable imagination.[25]

From its outset the novel makes clear that Olive has a deep-seated hatred of anything conventional: "[S]he always felt more at her ease in the presence of anything strange. It was the usual things of life that filled her with silent rage; which was natural enough, inasmuch as, to her vision, almost everything that was usual was iniquitous" (42). As the novel will show soon enough, this disdain for the humdrum of Victorian American domestic life can be seen in both sexual and racial terms. It is "natural enough" to Olive that the quotidian and conventional are "iniquitous"—that heteronormativity and the bourgeois manifestations of whiteness it supports are as *unnatural* to her as women's suffrage is to her cousin Basil.

When Olive then shows up at Miss Birdseye's house with Ransom in tow, she meets Verena and finds in her a potential love object. Enthralled by the speech Verena gives later that evening, Olive invites the young suffragist to meet her the following day. Through subtle probing during this second meeting, Olive wonders if Verena might be a more outwardly feminine variant of her own psychically androgynous type. She then admits, "You seem to me very wonderful. I don't know what to make of you" (100). We do understand only a page later, however, that Olive's imaginative faculties have gotten the best of her. Regarding Verena, she thinks:

> It was just as she was that she liked her; she was so strange, so different from the girls one usually met, seemed to belong to some queer gipsy-land or transcendental Bohemia. With her bright, vulgar clothes, her salient appearance, she might have been a rope-dancer or a fortune teller; and this had immense merit, for Olive, that it appeared to make her belong to the "people," threw her into the social dusk of that mysterious democracy which Miss Chancellor held that the fortunate classes know so little about, and with which (in a future possibly very near) they will have to count. (101)

Given these racially coded images, Olive is less likely to see Verena's complexion as überwhite (Dr. Prance had noted the night before that Verena looked "certainly very pale" and must be "anaemic" [82]), but instead as a blank page upon which Olive can paint her own portrait of racial and sexual desire. Though this premise may appear contradictory, it is really no more than an interpretive reaffirmation of James's role as a proponent of psychological realism; for psychological realists contend that the psyche, often caught up in a solipsism of desire, superimposes its own sense of reality on the outside material world.

In Olive's mind, Verena runs the gamut from Bohemian to a circus rope-dancer. Considering the narrow definitions of whiteness extant in the nineteenth century, these exotic figures are very much racialized. The most tantalizing aspect to Verena's gypsylike appearance is that her racial origin is ambiguous. With the transient lifestyle attributed to Bohemians, the narrative implies, Verena might very well be the daughter of an exotic moor or a Middle Eastern sultan—or even, given her father's Hebrew first name, Selah, a wandering Jew. Yet given the passage's emphasis on both darkness (the "social dusk") and impending political enfranchisement, Verena more likely appears in Olive's mind as an adumbration of the American polis once the manacles of racial oppression and prejudice have been lifted from African Americans. Her clothing is not only "bright"—suggesting the garish hand-me-downs of black slaves—but also "vulgar," implying that Verena is common in the sense that she is now "of the people." She is the new "flower of the great Democracy" (128) for whom both abolition and universal suffrage have been fought in their respective eras. The novel recognizes early on, after all, that the suffragists of the postbellum era were the abolitionists of the 1830s, 1840s, and 1850s (56, 111). It is worth noting here the importance of the novel's title, for Boston was not only the center of women's suffrage in the nineteenth century; it was also the center of abolitionist activity in the years leading up to the Civil War, providing a headquarters for William Lloyd Garrison and his American Anti-Slavery Society, as well as the ardent reformers Lydia Maria Child and Maria W. Stewart.

In James's novel, Miss Birdseye most clearly embodies this double legacy of reform. "She was in love, even in those days, only with causes, and she languished only for emancipations. But they had been the happiest days, for when causes were embodied in foreigners (what else were the Africans?), they were certainly more appealing" (56). Though too young to have participated in abolitionism, Olive seems especially sensitive to the American lower classes, of which newly freed slaves were most certainly a part. We cannot help but wonder if Olive, like Miss Birdseye, "did not sometimes wish the blacks back in bondage" so as to be able to free them all over again (56).

It is no surprise, then, that Olive conflates racial and sexual liberation: "She liked to think that Verena, in her childhood, had known almost the extremity of poverty, and there was a kind of ferocity in the joy with which she reflected that there had been moments when this delicate creature came near (if the pinch had only lasted a little longer) to literally going without food. These things added to her value for Olive" (128). As James intimates, the sober-minded suffragist may be casting herself as William Lloyd Garrison opposite Verena's Frederick Douglass. In such a case, the escaped slave narrative of mid-nineteenth-century America seems to work its way subtly into the text. As literary historians tell us, the popularity of antebellum slave narratives was attributed in large part to northern women who, like Olive, had the education and the leisure time to invest in reading. Given an Urninde's purported sensitivity to art and sentiment, it seems that "the romance of the people" (62) Olive conjures in her mind guides her feelings for Verena.

Yet Verena's "value" for Olive goes well beyond romantic sentiment. Despite the embarrassment of being from the Boston gentry, she cannot help but think in pecuniary metaphors. The more Verena resembles an escaped slave, the more Olive's fantasies circulate in the realm of commerce: "[T]he prospect of suffering was always, spiritually speaking, so much cash in [Olive's] pocket" (129). The narrative pronounces this race-cash nexus most prominently when Olive takes the necessary steps literally to buy Verena's freedom from her mesmerist father. Olive suspects that Selah loves his daughter only because she can make him rich through her work in the women's liberation movement. The meeting between Olive and the mesmeric healer had "the stamp of business," the novel states. "It assumed that complexion very definitely when she crossed over to her desk and wrote Mr. Tarrant a cheque for a very considerable amount." Without hesitation Olive then commands, "Leave us alone—entirely alone—for a year, and then I will write you another" (176).

Once Verena is safely purchased, Olive begins educating her about the history of women's oppression. Olive takes great pride in effecting a racial and sexual "uplift" of sorts, taking Verena away from her father—itself a move unmistakably linked to slavery—and turning her into a more visible spokeswoman for sexual liberation. Under Olive's guidance/ownership, Verena will fulfill all the duties expected of her: she will stay true to the cause of women's liberation and she will *not* marry any prospective suitor, especially Basil Ransom. In Olive's opinion, she is not possessing Verena, but merely saving her. Olive claims, "You must be safe, Verena—you must be saved; but your safety must not come from your having tied your hands" (152). In one instance Olive echoes the paternalistic rhetoric of southern masters, who argued that slavery was in the best interest of slaves because they lacked the intellectual and mental wherewithal to live in a free world. Nevertheless, her bondage metaphor is racially suggestive: the enamored Olive cannot bear to let Verena loose, especially to the conservative former slave owner Ransom; if so, the loss would be tantamount to Verena being thrown back into slavery, almost as if that is literally where she had come from. The point becomes even clearer when Olive bluntly states that Ransom has "the delicacy of one of his own slave-drivers" (363), and therefore Verena must steer clear of him at all costs.

Clearly Olive's broodings about Verena's loss of agency at the hands of her southern cousin is indeed curious considering this desire for mastery. Not long after purchasing Verena's "freedom" from her parents, she takes her on a long tour of Europe in hopes of removing her as far as possible from all those in Boston who would control her. The decision to flee in the face of oppression is evocative of Frederick Douglass, who in 1845 went to Europe with the help of the predominantly white American Anti-Slavery Society. While Douglass's official purpose was to give lectures throughout England and Ireland, he stayed there for two years in order to give his white benefactors time to purchase him from his former Maryland master.[26] The rather striking resemblance between Olive and Verena's relationship on the one hand and Douglass's relationship with his white abolitionist patrons on the other reveals the extent to which Olive is unwilling to acknowledge Verena's own female subjectivity, be it ultimately black or white. Verena may be, at least in Olive's mind, the reincarnation of Frederick Douglass, and thus her possible blackness seems to make the condition of her female individuality less consequential, except that it may stir Olive's erotic impulses. By the time the novel takes place in the 1870s, several women's slave narratives had hit the reading public, including those by Harriet Jacobs and Sojourner Truth. The fact that *The Bostonians* and Olive herself both seem to rely on Douglass's narrative instead of those by former women slaves suggests the limited extent to which white women involved in nineteenth-century racial uplift could truly empathize with black women.

Indeed, Olive's greatest flaw in the novel is that her interest in Verena is ultimately self-serving insofar as Verena provides Olive a blank canvas on which to let both her libido and her abstract reformist ideals run free. For Olive, Verena's potential blackness is therefore perhaps most valuable not because of how it can give voice to the concerns of black women in a time of social upheaval, but because it allows Olive the chance to position herself retroactively within the tradition of the antebellum-abolitionist-turned-postbellum-suffragist. As Nina Auerbach rightly puts it, "the main drawback [of Olive's feminism] is the intrusion of other women."[27] Significantly, in coming to grips with Verena's attraction to Basil Ransom, Olive eventually recognizes Verena's individual female (heterosexual) agency. Perhaps as a direct result of this epiphany, the narrative no longer couches Olive's lesbian desire for the young suffragist in the suggestive racialized terms that often pervade the earlier parts of the novel.

Yet if Olive is able ultimately to make this progression, her cousin Basil is not. Piqued by Verena's sexual allure and possible lesbianism, Basil, like his cousin earlier in the novel, gives Verena form by racializing her. In the process of wooing Verena, Ransom will have to work through his own libidinal desire, ultimately to claim her through marriage as a model of virtuous southern womanhood. Moreover, I read Ransom as anxious about Verena's sexual "instability" because failing to domesticate her would further cripple his sense of masculinity, a concern that critic Nina Silber has shown was widespread among southern men in the years following the emasculation of surrender at Appomattox.[28] He understands from the outset that visiting the "city of reform" will be a test of his manhood. As Olive's sister Mrs. Luna tells him in the novel's opening pages, Olive "would reform the solar system if she could get hold of it. She'll reform you, if you don't look out" (38). As a former slaveholder and a staunch believer in the patriarchal order, Basil feels doubly besieged by these remarks. The thought of Olive transforming him harks back to the female abolitionists of the 1830s, those such as the African American Maria W. Stewart, who publicly castigated black and white men alike for not opposing slavery more virulently.[29]

To succumb to Olive's radical program would compromise Basil's manhood in other ways as well. Abolitionist men had often sought a model of masculinity quite different from the one of acquisitive aggression that was becoming so prominent in the business communities of the mid-nineteenth-century North. Modeled chiefly on the meek and somewhat androgynous Christ, Cynthia Griffin Wolff explains, this new sense of manhood "encouraged expressions of lavish affection between (heterosexual) men. Male friends routinely exchanged kisses when greeting one another and passionate letters when separated."[30] A southern aristocrat, Ransom does not feel at home in the industrial-capitalist North, and for him to accept this sentimental version of manhood would further alienate him from familiar gender norms.

James further enhances Basil's emasculation by reversing the conventional plot structure of a national reconciliation subgenre that grew in popularity during the last decades of the 1800s. In these works, typified by John De Forest's 1867 novel *Miss Ravenal's Conversion from Secession to Loyalty* and William Gillette's 1886 play *Held by the Enemy*, sectional reunion was depicted as the marriage between a northern man and a southern woman.[31] Thus, by putting Basil in the subject position typically reserved for southern maidens, James is able to amplify the southerner's sense of alienation among northern radicals and the general futility of reinstituting a premodern patriarchy in an America that had decided to commit itself—North and South—to industrialization.

When he meets Verena at Miss Birdseye's, an androgynous-looking cast of characters in attendance immediately unsettles him. Aside from Olive—whom the narrator has already pinned as being "unmarried by every implication of her being" (47)—there is also Dr. Prance, who "looked like a boy, and not even like a good boy" (67). Noticing how all the women at the meeting flock to Verena once she enters the room, Ransom considers the young suffragist's potential lesbianism. Verena is beautiful, but she is "*disturbingly* beautiful"—that is, her physical appeal has a caveat that might make a southern gentleman pause (239, italics mine). As the narrative hints, her character might be marred not only by psychic androgyny, but also by a certain racial ambiguity: "The girl was very pretty, though she had red hair" (60). The seeming trepidation with which the narrative admits this detail is well worth pondering. Red hair often comes across now, as well as it did over a hundred years ago, as a sure signifier of Irish blood. Irish Americans, despite their obvious phenotype, had an immensely difficult time verifying or claiming their whiteness in the nineteenth century. In the eyes of Anglo-Protestant America during the mid-1800s, Noel Ignatiev explains in *How the Irish Became White*, the Irish not only brought with them to the New World a distasteful Catholicism, but also a "lower class" status similar to that of blacks. In some instances, Irish immigrants and blacks even married, further exacerbating anxieties among many Anglo-Americans in northeastern cities.[32]

If red hair signifies a type of "blackness" for Basil, it also gives that blackness an erotic charge. He feels a furtive thrill in fantasizing about Verena's potential psychic androgyny and racial otherness when he first meets her. She was "such an odd mixture of elements; she had the sweetest, most unworldly face, and yet, with it, an air of being on exhibition, of belonging to a troupe, of living in the gaslight, which pervaded even the details of her dress, fashioned evidently with an attempt at the histrionic" (82). Several aspects of this short description are highly suggestive. Being "on exhibition," Verena can have particular resonance in the southern male imagination as being a black slave who is put up for sale. Indeed, the auction block and the theater shared many performative similarities. Just as a theater presentation puts actors and actresses before a crowd of paying customers, the slave auction required its human commodities to speak, flash their teeth, flex their muscles, and show off their agility as a means of making them suitable for commerce. Therefore, when Olive tells Verena that Basil is "becom[ing] one of his own slave-drivers," we may very well see Ransom in exactly that role when viewing Verena for the first time.

With her "unworldly" face and her "bright, vulgar clothes," the suffragist also resembles a type of minstrel character (82, 101). Ever since Thomas Dartmouth Rice first "jumped" Jim Crow at New York's Bowery Theater in 1832, blackface minstrelsy had become the most popular and pervasive form of entertainment in nineteenth-century America. Certainly James would have been familiar with the tradition's various characters and motifs, given its mass appeal. Although women very rarely performed in blackface, the whole minstrel tradition was heavily involved in spoofing and questioning racial purity, class propriety, and even heteronormativity.[33] With men dressing up as women and whites dressing up as blacks, minstrelsy left no part of genteel Victorian American society untouched or undefiled. Basil's perception of Verena as a performer implies that she swims in this sexual and racial uncertainty that the world of blackface embodies.

Yet James's narrative provides a significant twist to Verena's "blackface" appearance, for if she really is not "white" under the narrow definition to which Basil subscribes, the "very pale" Verena might be performing a type of whiteface (82). In this case, the beauty of Verena's "unworldly face" is qualified by an air of falseness that obfuscates her worldly origin. Much of antebellum minstrelsy's popularity stemmed from its ability to allay white working class fears about blacks. With the black population constantly on the increase in northern industrial cities, whites felt their jobs were in danger.[34] If depicting "black" buffoonery tries to cover up a deep-felt anxiety, whiteface works in the opposite direction, showing just how easy it is to mask or obscure one's racial pedigree. As W. T. Lhamon, Jr. explains, "blackface made whiteness a sign, too"—which is to say that the codes and signification of whiteness are just as arbitrarily marked and understood as those of blackness.³⁵ Ironically, Basil himself is complicit in these arbitrary markings as—within the terms I read him—he thinks he can "purify" Verena racially and sexually.

Basil's exoticizing and eroticizing of Verena suggests a larger historical trend among the slaveholding class. As historians of antebellum southern culture have noted, a strong sexual tie often linked masters and women slaves. Bertram Wyatt-Brown, for example, claims that while wholesale application of Freudian paradigms is "always risky," he does understand how the Madonna/Whore Complex often worked its way into a white southern man's perception of a female slave. It is no secret that the white plantation matron held particular significance in antebellum southern culture as the emblem of virtue and domesticity. But southern men felt themselves unable to sexualize this woman who purportedly symbolized the best of southern morals. The young southern man also found that he could not compete for the affection of his own virtuous mother in an Oedipal triangle that would involve his father. Wyatt-Brown therefore argues that "[i]n repressing his fantasies, he splits the sexual and affectional impulses in his relations with women. Sex becomes associated with an inferior, an expendable woman whom, outside of wedlock, he both enjoys and socially despises."³⁶ With regard to Verena, Ransom finds himself caught in a similar Madonna/Whore bind.

Insofar as the southerner perceives the beautiful Verena to be the object of lesbian desire, she corresponds to the stereotypical black seductress so commonly found in minstrel or fictional representations of the time. True, Basil wants to "convert" Verena to both heteronormativity and whiteness, yet he revels in the momentary possibility of lesbian desire and the supposed blackness it evokes. More simply put, the challenge excites him in much the same way current-day pornography depicting lesbian sex might be said to tantalize a heterosexual male viewer: if the male viewer could somehow enter into that scene, perhaps his own masculine attractiveness would redirect the women's libidinal desire onto himself instead of just each other.

Verena's psychic androgyny and racial exoticism must eventually give way to whiteness and heteronormativity in Basil's mind. The challenge before him is worth the struggle only if in the end he can claim his prize, which in this case is a heterosexual and white bride who willingly succumbs to his plan of southern domesticity. Sometime after the novel's midpoint, he tells Verena of his wish to marry her. While trying to win her favor, he reassures her that he wants to preserve her coveted voice:

> Believe me, Miss Tarrant, these things will take care of themselves. You won't sing in the Music Hall, but you will sing to me; you will sing to every one who knows you and approaches you. Your gift is indestructible; don't talk as if I either wanted to wipe it out or should be able to make it a particle less divine. I want to give it another direction, certainly; but I don't want to stop your activity. Your gift is the

gift of expression, and there is nothing I can do for you that will make you less expressive. It won't gush out at a fixed hour and on a fixed day, but it will irrigate, it will fertilize, it will brilliantly adorn your conversation. Think how delightful it will be when your influence becomes really social. Your facility, as you call it, will simply make you, in conversation, the most charming woman in America. (379–80)

Since it was Verena's eloquence that erotically bound Olive to her, Basil suggests that giving her voice "another direction" is to redirect her libidinal impulses toward men instead of women. Under his guidance and "cultivation," that voice will speak instead for the world of the domestic sphere, thus removing her from the public debate concerning women's full citizenship in America. Basil's reliance on organic metaphors is representative of contemporaneous linguists' contention that women were inherently ill-equipped for public speech. For example, in her own analysis of *The Bostonians,* Caroline Field Levander has shown how linguists such as the famed Otto Jespersen explained that women's brains, unlike men's, were simply incapable of prioritizing information in terms of importance.[37] In this view, Verena's insistence on equality is therefore traceable to her inability to recognize natural hierarchies delineated along sexual boundaries.

Yet Basil's celebration of domesticity also seems to question the naturalness of both interracial and androgynous desire. The sexological discourse of the day argued that both interracial desire and homosexuality were "a type of congenital abnormal sexual object choice."[38] Thus in marrying Verena and "making" her both heterosexual and white according to Victorian American norms, he is somehow restoring a biological balance in Verena's genetic makeup. Basil can enact his own type of "irrigation" and "fertilization," using the wedding bed to cultivate her into a stable woman.

Verena, too, speaks of pastoral settings when articulating her own nationalist vision, although hers harks back to a prelapsarian existence. When giving a speech at Mrs. Burrage's home midway through the novel, Verena implores the men in her audience to envision a new egalitarian America: "You would like so much better to walk there, and you would find grass and trees and flowers that would make you think you were in Eden. That is what I should like to press home to each of you, personally, individually—to give him the vision of the world as it hangs perpetually before me, redeemed, transfigured, by a new moral tone" (268). Like Pierre-Simon Ballanche in the earlier part of the nineteenth century, Verena believes that sexual equality through democratic entitlement provides a path back to a prelapsarian Eden. Yet at times such as these when Verena speaks before a crowd of like-minded men and women, Basil Ransom, as Levander has observed, "constructs Verena's desirability as a product of the tone of her voice and simultaneously as the rationale for not hearing its content."[39] Her voice transports him to locales where Verena is a nymph "sinking on a leopard skin . . . with the native sweetness of her voice forcing him to listen till she spoke again" (229). James's use of "native" and "leopard" here suggests that as long as Verena speaks of women's liberation, she is neither American nor white, but rather a magical inhabitant of some exotic African land whose sole purpose is to seductively await domestication by a white man. The African exoticism of Basil's fantasy is especially resonant, for when Mrs. Luna had joked earlier that Verena might one day "run off with some lion-tamer," she did not know at the time how close she was to the truth (213).

Within the sexualized and racialized terms of my reading, the narrative ultimately gives Ransom the final (albeit qualified) victory over Olive, providing him an assuredly white and heterosexual bride. In the novel's last scene, he whisks Verena away just as she is about to give her suffrage speech before a riotous Boston crowd. The plot's reliance on a conventional ending suggests that the author as well as his Victorian American readership quake at the thought of endorsing more transgressive possibilities of sexual and racial liberation. Neither sexually liberated (hetero- or homosexual) women nor newly freed African Americans can achieve a place in what Shane Phelan calls the "national imaginary." In racializing lesbian desire only to have it succumb to heteronormative whiteness, the novel suggests that neither population has found placement among the "persistent images and rhetoric that, however inadequately and imperfectly, signal to a population who and what it is."[40]

Dissatisfied by earlier critics' "incuriosity" about James's own sexuality, Eve Kosofsky Sedgwick's *Epistemology of the Closet* treated James's "The Beast in the Jungle" to its first queer reading.[41] What has emerged since then is a complex portrait of a man who understood himself to be psychically androgynous in the late-nineteenth-century sense of the term, but who also managed to "privatize" his sexual impulses in order to maintain a Victorian sense of propriety. There is still considerable debate about the extent of homosexual intimacy James allowed himself—whether he was content with simply writing suggestive letters to younger men or whether he was in fact sexually active.[42] Although James seems never to have felt apologetic or ashamed of his same-sex attraction (at least as far as critics can tell), he understandably saw no reason for his sexual inclinations to be mentioned or known in the public sphere. To make one's homosexuality visible, as the Oscar Wilde trials of 1895 proved, would certainly have devastating personal and professional repercussions. And, indeed, having held a professional rivalry with Wilde for the better part of two decades, James kept close tabs on the trial, calling it in a letter to a friend "hideously, atrociously dramatic." But the real threat, one can easily imagine, is that the "squalid gratuitousness" of the public hearings threatened to call more attention to other unmarried male writers, especially those whose fictional characters frequently experience disastrous heterosexual relationships.[43]

This privatizing impulse is at work in *The Bostonians*. Although James may allude to such lesbian goings-on between Olive and Verena, and though much of the novel is filtered through Olive's consciousness, the reader will never encounter any *explicit* scenes of lesbian desire. As Terry Castle states, "though we can't see what exactly is 'going on' between Olive and Verena, 'it' nonetheless seems to stare us brazenly in the face."[44] James cuts the reader off from viewing anything that might be too revealing. While at home studying women's history, for example, Olive and Verena "watched the stellar points come out at last in a colder heaven, and then, shuddering a little, arm in arm, they turned away, with a sense that the winter night was even more cruel than the tyranny of men—turned back to drawn curtains and a brighter fire and a glittering tea-tray and more and more talk about the long martyrdom of women" (185). We must therefore stand on the sidewalk of Olive's Charles Street home wondering about things we cannot see for ourselves. What goes on behind drawn curtains, be it idle conversation or even lesbian sex, is sanctioned in the private sphere, a place where not even the reader is allowed.

From this safe narrative distance, there is even a hint of tenderness to the scene, suggesting that James does not necessarily condemn lesbian desire. David Van Leer insists that "[t]he negative implications of the process by which readers identify Olive's lesbianism do not mark James's personal discomfort with homosexual passion.... James's problem with homosexuality concerns not its moral dimension, but the ways in which it can be represented in literature."[45] Yet to Van Leer's assertion I might add the issue of homosexuality's representation in the larger realm of American national expression. James's deeper reservation lies not in Olive's homosexuality, but in her insistence on making Verena's sexuality a public issue. Verena would then become just as much a "slave" to Olive's public ambition as she does to Basil's domestic one. In fact, Olive loses Verena for good when the young woman is about to make her Boston public debut. In absconding with Ransom, Verena escapes from the many devious characters—Matthias Pardon and Selah Tarrant, most notably—who want selfishly to capitalize on her public name.

Also, through racializing Verena and placing her within a white patron/escaped slave narrative, Olive doubly devalues James's coveted realm of privacy. Thus his thoughts on homosexual (in)visibility roughly parallel his attitudes concerning racial (in)visibility. *The American Scene,* James's account of his 1904–5 visit to the United States, shows the particular difficulty the author had in conceiving of blacks as having a place in the postbellum national imaginary. In this book James can only imagine blacks to be "alien," never a part of America's larger depiction of itself.[46] For example, when watching several African Americans loitering about the streets of Richmond, Virginia, James registers shock at the scene: the free black, "all portentous and 'in possession of his rights as a man,'" is the same "Southern black as [America] knew him not."[47]

A later chapter in *The American Scene* recounts James leaving Charleston, South Carolina, for St. Augustine, Florida. Boarding the train, he finds that a black porter had indifferently dropped his luggage in the mud. While James may regard the porter as embodying a certain postbellum upward mobility, albeit modest, his presence also no doubt evoked considerable anxieties about the limits (if any) of democratic enfranchisement and economic agency.[48] Thus the only way that James can imagine race infused within the national imaginary is in a decidedly preindustrial, antebellum southern context. Immediately after he sees the porter drop the baggage into the mud, he meditates on how "[o]ne had remembered the old Southern tradition, the house alive with . . . darkies for the honour of fetching and carrying" (*AS* 312). The porter's apparent insolence triggers James to imagine a time when slaves had no legally recognized subjectivity, a time when any effrontery would almost surely invite a trip to the whipping post. Since emancipation, the role of American blacks had changed dramatically, but neither James nor the country for whom he purports to speak can conceive of blacks as a part of mainstream postbellum life.

This sentiment sheds light on *The Bostonians*. In one particular scene, Verena and Basil visit Harvard's Memorial Hall, a building erected to commemorate "the sons of the university who fell in the long Civil War" (246). Realizing that the Mississippian might not feel comfortable visiting a memorial for Union soldiers, Verena tells Ransom that perhaps they are better off not to enter. Overtaken by curiosity, Basil remains unfazed:

> [T]hey lingered longest in the presence of the white, ranged tablets, each of which, in its proud, sad clearness, is inscribed with the name of a student-soldier. The effect of the place is singularly noble and solemn, and it is impossible to feel it without a lifting of the heart. It stands there for duty and honour, it speaks of sacrifice and example, seems a kind of temple to youth, manhood, generosity. Most of them were young, all were in their prime, and all of them had fallen; this simple idea hovers before the visitor and makes him read with tenderness each name and place—names often without other history, and forgotten Southern battles. (246)

James uses Memorial Hall as an indication of what symbols, attitudes, and sentiments clearly have been admitted into the postbellum national imaginary. As David Blight has observed, "the forces of reconciliation overwhelmed the emancipationist vision in the national culture," and at the forefront of these reconciliation forces were the many monuments that sprang up in the North and the South in the decades after the war, which commemorated a nonpartisan commitment to white manhood, honor, and bravery.[49] Worth considering, then, is what the narrative leaves out of this description. While the Civil War was fought in large part to liberate and patriate almost four million slaves, there is no such mention of race in the passage. Enshrined upon Memorial Hall's "*white* ranged tablets" are what the narrative implicitly sees as Anglo-American virtues of "duty and honour," "sacrifice," "youth, manhood, [and] generosity" (italics mine). When we speak of America, the narrative implies, *these* are the qualities that we dare mention—even though (as the novel indeed fails to mention) one of the men enshrined on those tablets is Colonel Robert Gould Shaw, the white leader of the ill-fated Fifty-fourth Massachusetts Colored Regiment. Gesturing toward white solidarity, Memorial Hall even goes so far as to commemorate southern battles (and presumably the white southerners who fought in them), but once again, the narrative stops short of making room in the national imaginary for blackness.

Similarly, Memorial Hall implicitly ennobles heteronormative virtues of manhood and womanhood. The stone tablets suggest that student-soldiers, guided by inner principles of duty and courage, claimed their rightful place as men within a traditionally gendered framework. Had these men survived the war, they surely would have been expected to return to Harvard, graduate, enter the marketplace or the professions, and then get married. The "singularly noble and solemn" atmosphere also holds sway over Verena, impressing upon her the "true" virtue of heteronormativity—of men who live up to their full potential as men. As Blight further explains, "romance triumphed over reality, sentimental remembrance won over ideological memory."[50] Obviously in awe of Ransom's own sense of manhood, she loses sight of her own feminist ideology and stabilizes herself literally and metaphorically by silently "[sitting] down on a low stone ledge, as if to enjoy the influence of the scene" (246). Her attitude shown here anticipates her repudiation of psychic androgyny by the end of the novel. She is impressed by the virtues that the hall represents, and she accepts her "low," fixed position on the stone ledge. After reading this scene one need not be too surprised to find the southerner winning her over by the novel's end.

True enough, *The Bostonians*'s denouement reinscribes a patriarchy that can imagine neither blackness nor androgyny in the national imaginary. Yet in the novel's closing passages, James seems to second guess his own ending, as the final sentences read: "But though [Verena] was glad [to leave the company of the suffragists], [Ransom] presently discovered that, beneath her hood, she was in tears. It is to be feared that with the union, so far from brilliant, into which she was about to enter, these were not the last she was destined to shed" (433). So where has James left us by the novel's last sentence? His calculated yet frustrating choice to make Verena a relatively empty vessel only adds to our demand for definite answers. The novel's ambivalent and inconclusive ending is perhaps the best one imaginable, reflecting as it does the Gilded Age's deep anxiety about an unknown future. These issues continued to preoccupy James even into the next century.

Romanticism Redux: The Androgynous Vox Americana

Trying to locate the Jamesian spokesman in *The Bostonians* is nearly impossible. While the narrative certainly seems to sympathize at certain times with all the main characters involved in the drama, it does not seem to endorse any one of them unilaterally. This complexity is nowhere more evident than when Basil rants to Verena about the diminishment of the masculine voice in America. He wants to save his country from

> the most damnable feminization! I am so far from thinking, as you set forth the other night, that there is not enough woman in our general life, that it has long been pressed home to me that there is a great deal too much. The whole generation is womanized; the masculine tone is passing out of the world; it's a feminine, a nervous, hysterical, chattering, canting age, an age of hollow phrases and false delicacy and exaggerated solicitudes and coddled sensibilities, which, if we don't soon look out, will usher in the reign of mediocrity, of the feeblest and flattest and the most pretentious that has ever been. The masculine character, the ability to dare and endure, to know and yet not fear reality, to look the world in the face and take it for what it is—a very queer and partly very base mixture—that is what I want to preserve, or rather, as I may say, to recover; and I must tell you that I don't in the least care what becomes of you ladies while I make the attempt! (327)

The irony of this passage is comic: in this tirade Basil embodies not only the masculine critique of the Boston suffragists, but also the feminine emotionality he fears and despises. By the end of the novel, then, he seems hardly any more heroic than his doppelgänger Olive. Olive, at least, attains some personal growth in the novel, even if that growth is measured by the sad recognition of Verena's inconstancy and her own authoritative impulse to control Verena's future.

In light of Basil's ironic tirade, it may very well be that in James's reckoning, neither the isolated masculine nor feminine voice could carry out America's social and political discourse. In subsequent years James invested a significant amount of mental and creative energy working out the various conundrums that the New Woman brought with her as she publicly questioned the ideology of separate spheres. As I have argued in the first part of this chapter, James's earlier reluctance to embrace the visibility of the New Woman was in large part due to the ways in which sexology linked psychical androgyny to racial degeneracy. But as Basil's invective also signals, the New Woman was not going away. In fact, it was the Basil Ransoms of America—grounded in their chivalry, agrarianism, and gentility—who were on their way out, to be replaced in due time with a man deeply ensconced in materialism and commercial competitiveness. Coming to terms with the New Woman would therefore mean finding a more "artful" form of androgyny for her to embody as she made her way in the public realm.

By looking at *The American Scene,* "The Question of Our Speech," "The Speech of American Women," and "The Manners of American Women," which were all published between the years 1905 and 1907, I argue that James's notion of androgyny was in transformation. His solution to the gender and racial disarray he found in modern America was to form a new and cohesive embodiment of American identity. Ironically, however, this new embodiment was not based in corporeality at all, since *The Bostonians* had shown just how problematic racialized and sexualized American bodies could be. Instead, the author sought out a "voice" for his native country, one that would actually reside most comfortably in the New Woman. In James's opinion, it is relatively inconsequential that it takes a living body to produce a voice; speech not only defines the citizen—it becomes the citizen.

My reading of these four later works attempts to situate James's thoughts on modern American womanhood between Caroline Field Levander, who sees in these nonfiction works little or no development in James's thinking on the issue, and Jessica Berman, who sees perhaps too much development. According to Levander, James limits his thinking on matters of women's speech to tonality rather than content, a contention that puts James rather awkwardly in the same camp as his creation of decades past, Basil Ransom. In her assessment of "The Speech of American Women," for example, she claims, James disagreeably "links women's focus on the content rather than the sound of their voices with their burgeoning interest in the public sphere."[51] Levander proposes here and elsewhere an awkward either/or proposition: For James, women must either speak eloquently within the confines of the domestic sphere, or they speak outside that sphere with a terrible and repelling dissonance.

Unlike Levander, Berman sees in these later writings James's receptivity to the New Woman's public speech—as long as the speech's content is accompanied by eloquence. In this respect, I think Berman is correct, though I partially disagree with her later contention that "in order to achieve and perpetuate itself as a nation, America must follow the lead of its women, adopt this new tone, and itself become ideally feminized."[52] Berman, I suspect, overstates the case when claiming that James envisions an America that is "ideally femininized" as a result of a feminine and female-generated voice. For James, the ideal *vox Americana* is instead comprised of both masculine and feminine elements, and the culture he sees resulting from this new voice will reflect this gendered mix. The nascent androgynized *vox* therefore became the author's greatest attempt to settle the gender chaos in a country he abandoned but could never forget.

The four works under examination are all related in some way to the trip James took to America in 1904 after a twenty-year absence. While in Massachusetts in June 1905, he delivered the commencement address entitled "The Question of Our Speech" to the graduating class of the all-female Bryn Mawr College. The next year he published a series of installments in *Harper's Bazaar* entitled "The Speech of American Women." Later in 1907 he wrote a follow-up piece, "The Manners of American Women," in the same magazine. And finally, also in 1907, James published *The American Scene*, which recounts the author's travels in the North, Midwest, and South two years earlier.

As these works bear out either directly or indirectly, James had a strong interest in American women in general and the New Woman in particular. The one thing James makes perfectly clear in all of these writings is the singularity of the American woman's position in the world. In "The Speech of American Women," James says it most clearly: "The conditions of American life in general, and our great scheme of social equality in particular, have done many things for her, and left many others undone; but they have above all secured her this primary benefit that she is the woman in the world who is least 'afraid.'"[53] Here James seems more at ease mentioning "social equality" than he did in the 1880s. What makes the New Woman masculine is not necessarily her sexual desire for other women, as *The Bostonians* would have had us believe, but rather her bold willingness to be seen in various public spheres, be they institutions of social reform, commerce, education, or social intercourse.

Yet this bravery can be a positive attribute only if it is used properly, which includes developing a civic voice that bespeaks national civility, charm, and unity. Much of James's interest in American women's voices no doubt stemmed from his disillusionment with American men, who, he felt, were too involved in commercial affairs to be of any long-lasting significance to American culture. As he claims in "The Speech of American Women," "the American male, in *his* conditions, is incapable of caring for a moment what sounds his women emit. . . . Of what sounds other than the yell of the stock-exchange or the football field does he himself, we on these lines hear it asked, give the cheering example?" (39).

Here James has put his finger on a common phenomenon among industrializing western countries of the late nineteenth and early twentieth centuries. According to theorist Ernest Gellner, nationalist unity fully matured when states became industrialized. Before that time, states were usually characterized by the "low" cultures of their various fragmented peasantries. As industrialism set in, many of these low cultures disappeared, to be replaced with a "high" culture, which achieved national unity primarily through standardized education, mass literacy, and consequent professional classes. Given the presence of a high culture, "a situation arises in which well-defined educationally sanctioned and unified cultures constitute very nearly the only kind of unit with which men willingly and often ardently identify."[54] Obviously, then, capitalism was key to the development of the nation-state because it gave citizens—and men especially—a common lexicon of technology, competition, and commercialism that made them relatively interchangeable and expendable in modern industrial society.

Yet for Henry James, national unity based on a commercial lexicon and vocational interchangeability was still too vulgar, crass, and soulless. "The Question of Our Speech" draws out the general parameters of a linguistic homogenization to better suit modern America. Being nascent New Women, the graduates of Bryn Mawr College could benefit from the men's disappearance into the recesses of commercial life and fill the vacuum by developing a public voice based on James's idea of civility. But there was more than personal decorum at stake. James points out to his female audience that "there is no such thing as a voice pure and simple: there is only, for any business of appreciation, the voice *plus* the way it is employed.... [W]hen such influences [of beauty and refinement], in general, have acted for a long time we think of them as having made not only the history of the voice, but positively the history of the national character, almost the history of the people."[55] This, for James, is the *vox Americana* to which he exhorts the American New Woman to cultivate in her fellow citizens.

As the commencement address also makes clear, nations arise and perpetuate themselves through narratives that themselves constitute the historical pedagogy of the people as well as provide the basis for their current-day speech. No doubt this address would have particular resonance for the graduates of Bryn Mawr, many of whom surely would have entered the working world as teachers or school administrators, both acceptable professions for unmarried women of the middle class. This dual-pronged function of narrative is evidence for critic Jessica Berman that James was coming to terms with modern American womanhood, which "mov[ed] beyond the parameters of the nineteenth-century domestic model and into the conflicted discourse of the progressive woman."[56] For Berman, as I have mentioned earlier, James's *vox Americana* is an attempt to feminize the nation. In her reading, James is claiming that very little about American men is redeemable, and so the whole onus of national character rests firmly on the backs of those such as the Bryn Mawr graduates, left as they are, in James's words, "on every inch of the social arena that the stock-exchange and the football field leave free" ("SAW" 39). But by occupying this liminal space between the world of domesticity and the world of greater political enfranchisement, these New Women of modern America are not feminizing the nation in James's vision so much as they are androgynizing it. Anne McClintock has suggested that the modern nation-state is a type of Janus figure whose faces are male and female. While the male face represents the "progressive agent of national modernity," the female face embodies "nationalism's conservative principle of continuity."[57] In James's own configuration, the American man's mind-numbing preoccupation with competitive business pursuits leaves the New Woman to represent both masculine progressiveness and feminine continuity.

Moreover, one must take into account how James's notion of ideal masculinity subtly pervades these later writings, showing that the *vox Americana* is a composite of the best of masculine and feminine virtues. To understand James's breakdown of male and female attributes, it is useful to look at Walter Pater's aesthetics, which influenced James significantly. Pater's 1893 *Plato and Platonism* contends:

> Manliness in art, what can it be, as distinct from that which in opposition to it must be called feminine quality there,—what but a full consciousness of what one does, of art itself in the work of art,

> tenacity of intuition and of consequent purpose, the spirit of construction as opposed to what is literally incoherent or ready to fall to pieces, and, in opposition to what is hysteric or works at random, the maintenance of a standard.[58]

In other words, the difference Pater makes between masculine and feminine art is the difference between control and chaos, integrity and fragmentation. Though James ultimately sides with no one particular character in *The Bostonians*, Basil Ransom's tirade on the disappearance of the masculine voice closely follows Pater's dichotomy. Basil's idea of masculine character, based on "the ability to dare and endure, to know and yet not to fear reality, to look the world in the face and take it for what it is," roughly echoes the sense of control and mastery found in Pater's concept of masculine art.

This breakdown James makes in *The Bostonians* by no means suggests that women cannot express themselves artistically. As *The American Scene* implicitly argues, essential feminine artistic qualities do exist. Early in the book James recalls visiting Chocorua Mountain in New Hampshire. The landscape evokes "tenderness" with its "postures and surfaces . . . slimness and thinness and elegance" (19). James asks his reader: "What was that but the feminine attitude?—not the actual, current, impeachable, but the old ideal and classic" (19). True enough, there is a suggestion of weakness to these classic features, but only if men allow their penchant for control to turn into a passion for conquest. The landscape wished "to be liked, to be loved, to be stayed with, lived with, handled with some kindness, shown even some courtesy of admiration" (19). This allure of the feminine landscape has all too often summoned avaricious men to her hills to possess and destroy it. But lest we see the feminine landscape as destructively codependent, James imagines the landscape as wishing for a mutually beneficial relationship:

> [T]he "Do something kind for me," is not so much a "Live upon me and thrive by me" as a "Live *with* me, somehow, and let us make out together what we may do for each other—something that is not merely estimable in more or less greasy greenbacks. See how 'sympathetic' I am," the still voice seemed everywhere to proceed, "and how I am therefore better than my fate; see how I lend myself to poetry and sociability—positively to aesthetic use: give me that consolation." (19–20)

To remedy the gender polarization in modern America, citizens must strive for a way to make masculine and feminine impulses cohabitate in mutually productive, nondestructive ways. As this passage and the quotation from Pater show, James's notion of the classic masculine and feminine is reciprocal. Whereas the masculine artistic faculties of control and endurance can decay into conquest and destruction, feminine art can decline from tenderness and sociability into ranting and raving. There are, in other words, good traits and bad traits in both masculinity and femininity, and the trick for the New Women of America is to find the best of both and champion a national ethos based on an androgynous national voice.

In fact, the masculine-feminine reciprocity was something James had written about as early as 1878 when describing the writer Charles Sainte-Beuve:

> [T]here is something feminine in his tact, his penetration, his subtlety and pliability, his rapidity of transition, his magical divinations, his sympathies and antipathies, his marvelous art of insinuation, of expressing himself by fine touches and of adding touch to touch. But all this side of the feminine genius was in Sainte-Beuve reinforced by faculties of quite another order—faculties of the masculine stamp—the completeness, the solid sense, the constant reason, the moderation, the copious knowledge, the passion for exactitude and for general considerations. In attempting to appreciate him, it is impossible to keep these things apart; they melt into each other like the elements of the atmosphere.[59]

Though such sentiments are latent throughout the four works I examine, James has the most to say about the melding of masculine "exactitude" and feminine "fine touches" in "The Manners of American Women." Because the New Women are still novitiates in the art of cultivated speech, they should look to a gentlemanly form of conduct even if there are no gentlemen to be found. Once again emphasizing reciprocity, the author explains that charm, amiability, and tenderness are enhanced by "manly competence and control."[60] In earlier times aristocratic gentlemen used to take responsibility for the conduct of women—be they wives, daughters, or sisters. Traditionally, "[i]t is from his maintenance . . . that the woman, as a social creature, gets her cue and best sanction for her maintenance." But having "abdicated" his role as teacher, the American man leaves women to internalize the masculine sense of "discipline" for her own self-maintenance (78). The real test comes for women when they must give up their "queenship"—that is, their arrogant sense of self-entitlement—to enhance the American voice (78).

This voice is, in many respects, akin to art, a subject James knew very well. First of all, the voice is something that must be practiced if it is to be perfected. Repetition and imitation provide a "stage of development" for those seeking competent articulation. And to this end, James sets himself up as a possible mentor—the androgynous novelist teaching androgynous elocution. Secondly, as James reminds the graduates of Bryn Mawr in "The Question of Our Speech," "there is only, for any business of appreciation, the voice *plus* the way it is employed" (26). In other words, the *vox Americana* is not just substance, but also form. The form is itself a delicate mediation between feminine charm and masculine control; the masculine keeps the feminine from becoming too hysterical and the feminine keeps the masculine from becoming too brutish and aggressive. Yet ultimately, speech-as-form comes back to a question of function: "[S]peaking badly is speaking with that want of attention to . . . any other controllable motion, or voluntary act, of our lives" ("QS" 23). In other words, if Americans are sloppy in their verbal articulation, they are no doubt remiss in other areas. The lesson of clearly formulated speech comes back to the idea found in "The Art of Fiction": "Try to be one of the people on whom nothing is lost." Patriotism is wasted on those whose mouths are full of nothing worth saying.

It seems almost too perfect that the one city in America where this cohabitation of masculine and feminine is most apparent for James is the District of Columbia—not only the nation's capital, but also the midpoint between the North and the South. Washington's geographic location mediates between these two regions' gendered identities. James believes that any culture completely dominated by either masculine or feminine impulses is bound for disaster. Whereas he finds the North to be overrun with masculine business interests (the phallic skyscrapers of Manhattan say it all), he sees the South as entirely too feminine. While vacationing in Charleston, South Carolina, the author realizes that the Civil War has made the South shift from one extreme to another: "The feminization is there just to promote for us some eloquent antithesis; just to make us say that whereas the ancient order was masculine, fierce and moustachioed, the present is at the most a sort of sick lioness who has so visibly parted with her teeth and claws that we may patronizingly walk all round her" (*AS* 307).

Yet in Washington, James finds that American men are not unduly given over to commercial endeavors, an observation that gives the author greater encouragement that they, too, can be purveyors of the androgynous *vox Americana*. Unlike Mark Twain and Charles Dudley Warner, who satirized politicians' greed in *The Gilded Age* (1873), James shows a sincere affinity for the culture of Washington. Among its citizens, "smiles and inflections" make up the "medium of exchange," not stocks, bonds, and shares. James continues: "I have described this anomaly, at Washington, as that of Man's socially 'existing'; since we have seen that his fidelity to his compact throughout the country in general has involved his not doing so" (*AS* 247, 257). In the broader view, Washington presents itself as an androgynous metropolis whose male and female components are so much in accordance with one another that they prompt James to call the capital the "City of Conversation" (*AS* 252). Even more important, James's trip to the city on the Potomac proves that men can and must eventually find a way to cultivate their speech. National cohesion simply will not endure if it only exists for half of America's population.

But what of race in James's configuration of the androgynous *vox Americana*? His dislike for sexual polarity, so evident in his remarks on the masculine North and the feminine South, also resists a larger movement in America to codify races along gender lines. James visited America and published his writings on that trip—all within a three-year time span, from 1904 to 1907. During these years, Theodore

Roosevelt occupied the White House, and in his own way he was also deeply concerned about the gendering of the nation. Having risen to prominence for his famous (albeit overblown) charge up San Juan Hill in 1898, Roosevelt became vice president under William McKinley and then ascended to the presidency after McKinley was assassinated in 1901. Advocating a tough-minded "Big Stick" policy that ushered in the beginning of American imperialism, Roosevelt did more than perhaps any other individual of the time to "masculinize" the nation by insisting on a virile, hardy, and civilized American "race." Born a New York patrician, Roosevelt prided himself on being a rugged frontiersman—though he lived only a little over two years on a ranch in South Dakota, and much of that time he spent back in New York. Drawing on his time out West, Roosevelt claimed that the frontier experience is what made the American race unique from other "white" races, and, as Gail Bederman rightly argues, "the hero of Roosevelt's story was a *race* whose gender was implicitly male."[61]

Not surprisingly, Roosevelt was not quite sure what to make of African Americans, but given his gendering of whiteness as masculine, blackness was either feminine or childlike. In either capacity, if civilized whiteness proved to be the apex of human evolution, black men fell well short of the mark. African Americans might be more advanced than blacks of other nations and continents because of their frequent contact with whites, according to Roosevelt, but nevertheless it would take "many thousand years" before black Americans could develop to be "as intellectual as the [ancient] Athenian."[62] Yet underneath his condescension lay the somewhat counterintuitive fear that blacks threatened white supremacy, since their biological inferiority might sap white manhood of its virility. To assuage the anxiety that white America was committing so-called race suicide, Roosevelt went to great lengths to parade his masculine whiteness all around the nation—whether in speeches, in photographs, in heavily publicized trips to the wilderness, or in autobiographical writings.

Yet just as troubling for someone such as James was Roosevelt's evolutionary scheme, which insisted that the refinement and civilization the white American race had gained over the years was predicated on virile masculinity. Nothing seemed to threaten Roosevelt more than the insidious encroachment of effeminacy among fellow white men because it suggested devolution. He feared "a certain softness of fibre in civilized nations, which, if it were to prove progressive might mean the development of a cultured and refined people quite unable to hold its own in those conflicts through which alone any great race can ultimately march to victory."[63] For this reason Roosevelt thought it necessary to keep white men competitive, virile, and athletic, for a healthy American culture must be "fostered by vigorous, manly out-of-door sports, such as mountaineering, big-game hunting, riding, shooting, rowing, football and kindred games."[64] James would no doubt appreciate his fellow Harvard alumnus's desire for cultural refinement among American men. At the same time, however, he would presumably detest the means by which the refinement is attained, given the author's fear that manhood had appeared to relegate itself either to the football field or the stock exchange. By providing a link between homosexuality and racial degeneration on the one hand and a link between American civilization and virile masculinity on the other, evolutionary science had provided a physiological rationale that could prevent James himself from claiming an American identity.

Given these difficulties, how could James insist on cultural cohesion if it meant acknowledging the polarity of the sexed and racialized bodies that always seemed to be threatening the polis? He had dealt with these issues before when writing *The Bostonians,* only to conclude that postbellum America was as fragmented as it had been at the height of the Civil War. Subsuming racialized and sexualized bodies under the larger aegis of a unified disembodied voice was his only way out of the bind. By the time James returned to America the immigrant bodies within the American body politic had grown well beyond what he had known as a boy living in New York. In the first decade of the twentieth century, for example, six million immigrants came through New York Harbor, most of them either Jewish or Italian. In these early years 12.2 percent of the entire American population said it could not speak or write English. That number had risen to 22.8 percent by 1910.[65] In "The Question of Our Speech," James is very mindful of the changes this "vast contingent of aliens" could have on the American character. Indeed, it frightens him to think that "from the moment of their arrival, they have just as much property in our speech as we have, and just as good a right to do with it as they choose" (29). Moreover, the English language might be used by these other races and ethnicities as one might use a "freely figured oilcloth" that lays on the kitchen floor or staircase. And to finish his tirade about the potentially negligent immigrants, James claims that the broken English they produce will become a vulgar commodity: "durable, tough, cheap" (29). The point to glean from the material image of the oilcloth is this: if the "aliens" use English improperly, they will turn James's coveted disembodied *vox Americana* into something akin to a disposable material product. A voice can be most beneficial because it has the power to transcend materiality and thus steer clear of the marketplace—a place that he feels polarizes citizens more and more by sex, class, and race.

In fact, James feels that African Americans, newly arrived immigrants, or other marginalized persons might actually benefit economically and socially by embracing the androgynous, transcendent *vox.* Thus while the author certainly seemed to have feared the masses—as my own reading of *The Bostonians* bears out—he was at the same time an advocate of a "social utopianism," as John Carlos Rowe puts it, that not only contradicted his nativistic impulses but also put him in the strange company with transcendental thinkers of an earlier generation.[66] Ultimately, language, not bodies, is at the core of James's utopian vision. A later passage from the Bryn Mawr address details this utopian vision with its heavy insistence on linguistic assimilation:

> It is prosperity, of a sort, that a hundred million people, a few years hence, will be unanimously, loudly—above all loudly, I think!—

speaking it, and that, moreover, many of these millions will have been artfully wooed and weaned from the Dutch, from the Spanish, from the German, from the Italian, from the Norse, from the Finnish, from the Yiddish even, strange to say, and (stranger still to say) even from the English, for the sweet sake or the sublime consciousness, as we may perhaps put it, of speaking, of talking, for the first time in their lives, *really* at their ease. . . . [T]he thing they may best do is play, to their heart's content, with the English language, or, in other words, dump their mountain of promiscuous material into the foundations of the American. ("QS" 28)

The language James uses in this passage is striking for a number of reasons. Speaking easily and "artfully" ultimately allows these individuals to make a living and join the larger American community. And while it is true that as late as 1905 he still had a difficult time conceiving of blacks in particular within the national imaginary, these assertions in "The Question of Our Speech" suggest that it is not impossible for them to gain such ascendancy.

At first glance, James appears to follow Roosevelt's scheme of gendering race, putting the non-Anglo others in the same position as the New Woman; even those who already speak some form of English—presumably African Americans and lower class whites—are aligned with the Bryn Mawr graduates. Yet while James *seems* to feminize these various populations, he actually androgynizes them by giving them the right kind of voice, which for him mitigates the significance of their culturally marked bodies. The language James uses in the passage above bears out such a move. Given the way I read *The Bostonians* in terms of blackness and same-sex eroticism, the words "promiscuous material" have broader resonance: the idea behind the American linguistic melting pot—or the *pot au feu*, as James so eloquently calls it in *The American Scene* (50)—is the purifying or effacing effects it has on diverse corporeality (insofar as "material" denotes physical matter), be it black or white bodies, homosexual or heterosexual bodies. This is no small point, for it allowed someone such as James—whose sexuality and gender identity he felt to be in flux throughout his life—to stake a claim in American national character, though he himself had not lived in the United States since the 1870s. One must remember, after all, that the title of his commencement address is "The Question of Our Speech," not "The Question of Your Speech."

Though James treats the issue of race and assimilation with trepidation, his remarks suggest that he acknowledges the United States' democratic potential. Given that James died in 1916, he did not live to see American women's full political enfranchisement, which came in 1920. But certainly he had come a long way since 1886, when issues of race and sexuality had apparently muddled his idea of American civic participation. Though we may legitimately criticize James's *vox Americana* for simplifying or mitigating the deep racial and sexual rifts in the country, we can nevertheless credit him for having the courage to question the nativist impulses so common in those of his own race and caste.

While most critics regard the trip to America as a reaffirmation of James's choice to expatriate, they must also be willing to concede that his native land still remained his greatest source of artistic inspiration. This claim is no doubt ironic, given the fact that one of the main reasons he left the country was because he found it lacking the cultural refinement of Europe. Throughout James's long career, America was a portrait always in the process of becoming. In an 1885 letter to his brother William, James confessed to the shortcomings of *The Bostonians:* "The whole thing is too long and dawdling. This came from the fact (partly) that I had the sense of knowing terribly little about the kind of life I had attempted to describe—and felt the constant pressure to make the picture substantial by thinking it out—pencilling and 'shading.'"[67] One can easily see that he was never satisfied with his portrait of America as he created it in the mid-1880s. In later years, however, the author seemed less disappointed and more fascinated by his inability to "flesh in" the country and its inhabitants. In the chapter entitled "Richmond" in *The American Scene,* James attempts to come to terms with the changing visage of America after having first reflected on the relations between blacks and whites in Virginia. "What is the picture, collectively seen," he asks the reader, "but the portrait, more or less elaborated, of a multitudinous People, of a social and political order?—so that the effect is, for all the world, as if, with the body and the limbs, the hands and feet and coat and trousers, all the accessories of the figure showily painted, the neat white oval of the face itself were innocent of the brush" (280). What better image might the author of *The Portrait of a Lady* provide than a portrait of America? While the sketched features of the "People" suggest it is male (note the trousers) and perhaps white, we can never say for sure as long as the face is still missing. His reliance on visual representations of the American polis once again leads him to more unease. One might wonder, for example, if the portrait is in the process of being filled in or of being erased and remade.

Therefore, while such emphasis on the *vox Americana* provided a way to circumvent troublesome issues of corporeality, even James could not completely seem to convince himself that the voice exists without the body. Ultimately we are never sure if the voice is an attempt at democratic inclusion so much as it is a means of deferring problems of race and androgyny for another generation. As the next chapter explains, however, the body could not be overlooked for long, especially when its sexual makeup and evolutionary history could explain the United States' economic ascendancy in the opening decades of the twentieth century.

CHAPTER 2

Commercial Androgyny: Reformulating the Modern Liberal Subject in Frank Norris and Charlotte Perkins Gilman

Though by the first decade of the twentieth century Henry James found his own way to reconcile romantic notions of androgyny with postbellum demands for a new model of national cohesion, his proposal for a transcendental *vox Americana* did little if nothing to address the material reality of the citizens—the New Woman or anyone else—who would literally embody that voice. Evolutionary and sexological science, with their suggestions of racial degeneracy and homosexuality, had come to remind James again and again that the body, in fact, was the national voice's greatest nemesis. As this chapter explains in greater detail, making androgyny acceptable and respectable in materialist-economic realms was no easy task. In many cases, it involved rechanneling evolutionary discourse toward a larger theoretical project: reformulating the ideological and gendered parameters of the modern liberal subject. Attuned to this project, both Frank Norris and Charlotte Perkins Gilman offered a profound meditation on how prevailing concepts of androgyny were used to create a new form of civic participation for a nation positioned to be the new century's foremost economic superpower.

Debates about the imputed human characteristics of the theoretical liberal subject are traceable to the classical political philosophy of the seventeenth and eighteenth centuries. The liberal subject's gender neutrality has its ontological grounding in John Locke's famous *Essay Concerning Human Understanding*, which asserts that the human mind at birth is a "white paper, void of all characters, without any *ideas*," and waiting to be inscribed upon by experiences in the external material world.[1] As Thomas Laqueur suggests, the liberal subject that evolved out of John Locke, Jean-Jacques Rousseau, and Adam Smith was neuter in order to represent the universality of God-given natural rights: "Social-contract theory at its most abstract postulated a body that, if not sexless, is nevertheless undifferentiated in its desires, interests, or capacity to reason. In striking contrast to the old teleology of the body as male, liberal theory begins with a neuter individual body: sexed but without gender, in principle of no consequence to culture, merely the location of the rational subject that constitutes the person."[2]

Yet by the nineteenth century, the Lockean liberal subject's tabula rasa became less a marker of gender neutrality and more a canvas on which the ideology of the separate spheres could inscribe its own discursive meanings. As Linda K. Kerber has remarked, "Separate spheres were neither due to cultural accident nor to biological determinism. They were social constructions, camouflaging social and economic service, a service whose benefits were unequally shared."[3] Thus the construct of the separate spheres took hold of American culture in the first part of the nineteenth century by assuring citizens that neither industry nor democracy presaged the end of male control of the family or of economic production. In fact, when Alexis de Tocqueville expressed his fears in *Democracy in America* that democracy might androgynize American citizens, he assuaged those fears by reminding himself, "The Americans have applied to the sexes the great principle of political economy which governs the manufacturers of our age, by carefully dividing the duties of man from those of woman in order that the great work of society may be better carried on."[4]

More and more, the economic centrality of the agrarian homestead gave way to the new ideological paradigm that situated economic production squarely in the hands of men, whether that form of production was material/industrial, intellectual, governmental, or artistic in nature. Certainly women participated in production; in fact, America's first textile factories located in Lowell, Massachusetts, were largely staffed by unmarried women. But as critics and historians have explained, the ideological parameters of gender and social propriety were such that working-class women were, by their very need to labor in industry, precluded from inclusion as "women" in the strictest bourgeois sense of the word.[5]

In the thirty years leading up to the Civil War, American industry prompted unprecedented consumer activity. More and more, producers and merchants geared stores and commodities toward women with enough disposable income (or really their husbands' income) and free time to make shopping a regular part of their lifestyle.[6] By the middle of the nineteenth century, medical, religious, philosophical, and legal communities found their own ways to prove that women were innately suited for consumption.⁷ Thus both men and women came to embody certain aspects of the Lockean liberal subject, though those aspects were very different economically speaking. Obviously men—as producers of commodities, law, or high culture—were the most visible embodiments, but as the nation's chief consumers, women were afforded a certain social identification and civic participation in their own right. Such an identity, however, carried with it the assumption that consumption would mark the outermost limit of social enfranchisement.⁸

But by the dawn of the twentieth century, the parameters of the liberal subject began to shift yet again. The new century, as Christophe Den Tandt explains, was dominated by a new figure, one he calls the "corporate androgyne." Like the nineteenth-century model of liberal subjecthood, this new model citizen was still male, but he differed from earlier models in that he achieved his heightened form of masculinity "from an ability to bracket off [his] sense of individuation and to merge with entities modeled as feminine bodies—the urban market, the corporation."⁹ Yet men achieved manhood not only through metaphorically merging with feminine corporate entities, as Den Tandt claims; they also did so, I argue, by merging with another realm largely considered feminine: consumption. In fact, as Thorstein Veblen's 1899 *Theory of the Leisure Class* attests, men had already begun advancing so far into the female realm of consumption that consumption, especially when carried out on an opulent scale, became a veritable mark of manhood. "Conspicuous consumption of valuable goods is a means of reputability to the gentleman of leisure," he claims, and "the failure to consume in due quantity and quality becomes a mark of inferiority and demerit."¹⁰

Hailed by these shifts, American authors including Frank Norris and Charlotte Perkins Gilman confronted the ways in which consumption and production brought their gendered histories with them into the twentieth century. In his "epic of the wheat," *The Octopus* (1901), Norris is particularly concerned with negotiating a space for androgyny in the national construction of the liberal subject. The novel illustrates how, in accordance with the Platonic myth, men and women come together through marriage to form an androgynous whole. The force drawing them together, I argue, is guided by "androgynous atavism," a term denoting a character's instinctual drive for heterosexual union as a means of self-completion. This drive is in keeping with Norris's understanding of evolutionary theory, which postulated that the lowest forms of life on the evolutionary scale were themselves hermaphroditic. The androgynous configuration that so preoccupies Norris is (hetero)sexist and racist at its core, for it occurs mainly among Anglo-Saxons and favors the male component of that composite by allowing him to consume right alongside his wife without impingement on his masculinity. The female component, however, must content herself with production in a form all too familiar: biological reproduction.

Gilman, on the other hand, rejected androgyny, considering it to be largely based on culturally inscribed characteristics that ideologically pigeonholed women as weak, dependent, and incompetent. For Gilman, history had done great injustice to the liberal subject, for even when it was coded as androgynous in an attempt to achieve human totality or commercial legitimacy, it still bespoke masculine privilege, as Norris's novel surely attests. By dismantling the gendered assumptions that structured her society's notions of production and consumption, Gilman shows that the liberal subject is most representative of humanity while still a tabula rasa. For her, the greatest challenge came in articulating this nongendered vision using a linguistic signifying system steeped in gender hierarchy. Yet despite these differences, her theories share with Norris a racial essentialism that precludes non–Anglo-Saxons from full national enfranchisement. In the end, the tabula rasa upon which Gilman inscribes her image of the modern American liberal subject is not so much blank as it is, racially speaking, white.

Androgynous Atavism: Norris's Octopus

Frank Norris's writings show a consistent interest in androgynes and Amazons. In a 1901 essay entitled "Novelists of the Future: The Training They Need," he even goes so far as to proclaim that the masculine woman is his muse: "The muse of American fiction is no chaste, delicate, super-refined mademoiselle of delicate poses and 'elegant' attitudinizing, but a robust, red-armed *bonne femme*, who rough-shoulders her way among men and among affairs, who finds a healthy pleasure in the jostlings of the mob and a hearty delight in the honest, rough-and-tumble, Anglo-Saxon give-and-take knockabout that for us means life." It would seem that Norris's painting apprenticeship in Paris during 1887–89 brought him in contact with androgynous embodiments of democracy such as Eugène Delacroix's famous depiction of Marianne in his painting *La Liberté guidant le peuple,* for not only is his muse a "hearty, vigorous girl with an arm as strong as a man's," but she is also a "Child of the People."[11] Norris's interest in muscle-bound women goes beyond a mere repudiation of Victorian delicacy, for androgyny (or any variation thereof) is key to understanding Norris's creative process and his evolutionary vision.[12] The manly Anglo-Saxon female muse helps Norris, whose fiction invariably possesses national and epic themes, to position himself within the Whitmanian tradition as a writer who is both a singular male subject and an androgynous, transcendental embodiment of The People.

When writing *The Octopus,* Norris certainly had populism on his mind. The novel is a fictionalized account of the 1880 Mussel Slough shootout, which was the outcome of a land dispute in California's San Joaquin Valley between U.S. marshals acting on behalf of the Southern Pacific Railroad on the one side and the railroad's embittered rancher-tenants on the other. Going back on a previous gentleman's agreement, the railroad hyperinflated the price of the ranchers' leased land before agreeing to sell it to them. Faced with eviction, bankruptcy, and public humiliation, the ranchers defended their homesteads with arms. All in all, eight men were killed in the incident, and though the surviving ranchers were convicted for their instigation of the violence, their sentences were astonishingly lenient. In the eyes of most Californians, they were epic heroes who protected their homes from a huge and uncaring industrial monopoly.[13]

The fictional account of these events focuses mainly on two wheat ranch owners, Buck Annixter and Magnus Derrick, and the many friends and relatives who work on or near their land. The main conflict develops as the Pacific and Southwestern Railroad (the fictional analogue of the real Southern Pacific Railroad), led by the Jewish Mr. Shelgrim and his toady S. Behrman, inflate the price of the rancher-tenants' land. The ranchers, fearing mass eviction, then create the League of Defence [sic]. Meanwhile Annixter falls in love with Hilma Tree and Derrick becomes corrupted as he tries to manipulate the railroad commission to do the league's bidding. The story reaches its climax when the league members meet their demise against armed representatives from the railroad. All of these proceedings are observed by the poet Presley and his friend Vanamee, who both try to make sense of the bloodshed.

In his rendering of these events, Norris makes androgyny the theme that ties his populist, economic, and evolutionary visions together. The reclusive Vanamee sets up the proper paradigm that others in the novel should follow if they are to find peace and economic prosperity in modern industrial America. Vanamee's progression in the novel involves coming into contact with primordial hermaphroditic impulses that guide him toward finding his other half, Angéle Varian. Only by gaining the spiritual wholeness provided by Angéle is he able to move into the marketplace as a consumer.

Before the action of the novel begins, Vanamee had fallen in love with Angéle Varian during a college vacation in Tulare County. But their love affair was cut short when Angéle was raped by someone known simply as the "Other." After nine months she gave birth to a daughter and immediately died. When the novel commences, Vanamee is still unable to come to terms with his grief, and he walks aimlessly about the American West, only stopping in his native California for short stints before moving on again. Vanamee's love for Angéle hearkens back to the Platonic myth of the androgynes, those dual-sexed beings whose separated halves clung to one another in search of their previous wholeness: "It was small wonder that Vanamee had loved her, and less wonder, still, that his love had been so intense, so passionate, *so part of himself.* Angéle had loved him with a love no less than his own. It was one of those legendary passions that sometimes occur, idyllic, untouched by civilisation, spontaneous as the growth of trees, natural as dew-fall, strong as the firm-seated mountains."[14] Theirs was to be "the Perfect Life, the intended, ordained union of the soul of man with the soul of woman, indissoluble, harmonious as music" (134).

Despite his grief and wanderings, Vanamee is never too far removed from economic processes of production and consumption that keep money in his wallet, food in his stomach, and clothes on his back. When he acts in the service of the marketplace as a plowman on Annixter's wheat ranch, his atavistic longing for androgynous completeness becomes most apparent. For example, the description of the plowing is erotically charged, and it becomes clear that the action symbolically positions Vanamee as both male and female. On the one hand, the land is depicted as female, and the plowing done by the men, including Vanamee, is the agricultural equivalent of lusty heterosexual penetration: "It was the long stroking caress [of the plow], vigorous, male, powerful, for which the Earth seemed panting" (130). Yet Norris's description of the pseudo-sex act between the male plowers and the female land takes a curious turn: as Vanamee plows on, the phallic plow seems to take on a life of its own in his hands and *he* appears to be penetrated psychically as much as the soil is physically: "Underneath him was the jarring, jolting, trembling machine; not a clod was turned, not an obstacle encountered, that he did not receive the swift impression of it through all his body, the very friction of the damp soil, sliding incessantly from the shiny surface of the shears, seemed to reproduce itself in his finger-tips and along the back of his head" (129).

Vanamee's role as both penetrator and penetrated in this lusty primordial scene suggests an atavistic androgynous trait residing deep within him. Atavism, also known in evolutionary circles as "reversion," was described by Charles Darwin as the resurfacing of a trait that was "lost for many, perhaps for hundreds of generations."[15] In previous chapters I have suggested that sexologists were instrumental in pathologizing androgyny as homosexuality. At the same time, a number of prominent scientists regarded hermaphroditism as the very origin of normative evolutionary patterns. In *The Descent of Man* (1871), for example, Darwin suggests that "some remote progenitor of the whole vertebrae kingdom appears to have been hermaphrodite or androgynous."[16] By 1901, the year *The Octopus* was published, German sexologist Otto Weininger's *Sex and Character* took this idea of atavistic androgyny even further. By looking at a range of life forms along the evolutionary chain that included flowers, water fleas, beetles, and horses, Weininger concluded that "whether it refer to the brain or to any other part of the body[,] absolute sexual distinctions between all men on the one side and all women on the other do not exist. . . . It can be shown that however distinctly unisexual [that is, sexually polarized] an adult plant, animal, or human being may be, there is always a certain persistence of the bisexual character, never a complete disappearance of the characters of the undeveloped sex." Weininger believed that all human cells are made up of male arrhenoplasm and female thelyplasm, and therefore there was no such thing as "man" and "woman," but only male and female "conditions" encapsulated in a universal corporeal frame.[17] Should a man therefore contain certain womanly characteristics—be they hormonal or psychological—they can be attributable to a higher than normal distribution of thelyplasm in his body.

Norris himself no doubt learned of androgynous atavism through his undergraduate biology courses at the University of California at Berkeley with professor Joseph Le Conte. By the time Le Conte taught Norris in the 1890s he had established himself as one of the foremost Darwinians in America, and like Darwin, Le Conte believed that "the highest form [of living creatures], viz., unisexuality, was developed out of bisexuality or hermaphroditism."[18] Le Conte further espoused an evolutionary paradigm which suggested that the physiological development of an individual (ontogeny) roughly imitated an entire species's development from hermaphroditism to sexual differentiation. In human cases, the change was more subtle since it typically occurred while in utero, but in certain sea creatures such as jellyfish the development was more pronounced. Le Conte was clearly an influence in Norris's naturalistic rearing, and his musings on the hermaphroditism of sea creatures may have also influenced Norris's decision to cast the ambiguously sexed octopus as the chief corporate metaphor in a novel that jumbles nineteenth-century gender and economic categories.

My aim here is to use Vanamee as an example of this "normative" pattern of evolutionary development. If scientific naturalism is the chronicling of humans' evolutionary link to the world of instinctual drives and natural selection, literary naturalism is the fictional rendering of how certain primitive, animalistic traits can promote human survival and national perpetuation. The recluse's own male and female atavistic impulses, which come alive during the plowing scene, compel him to fulfill his lack through seeking out Angéle, his other half. In a later scene he sets out to visit Angéle's grave. After Vanamee begs Father Sarria to help him magically conjure Angéle, the priest lashes out, "I thought you were a man; this is the talk of a weak-minded girl" (148). What at first seems like an insult proves to be all too prescient, for if thinking and speaking like a little girl is what it takes to find his lost love, Vanamee "was ready to be deluded" (150). Vanamee's apparent regression toward girlhood is the ontogenic outcome of his step backward into primordial sexual undifferentiation in the earlier plowing scene. As a result he becomes both producer and reproducer. Later in the novel Angéle miraculously comes back to Vanamee in the form of her sixteen-year-old daughter, also named Angéle, who looks just like the original. This form of reification, as Mark Seltzer suggests, is evidence of Vanamee's masculine productive drive: "Vanamee's reincarnative power . . . amounts to a mechanical reproduction of persons" that allows Norris to exclude women from the procreative process.[19] Yet Vanamee's act of creation is as much organic as it is mechanical, for the text suggests that the young mystic's feminine parturient impulses are the result of his initial ability to harness the forces of the "elemental Male and Female" (131) while plowing—and being plowed—in the field.

By the novel's end, Vanamee has recovered not only his other-sexed half through finding Angéle's daughter, but also his place within the industrial economic system as a consumer-producer. In a final discussion with Presley, the narrative suggests that material reality is greater than romance alone: "Romance had vanished, but better than romance was here. Not a manifestation, not a dream, but her very self" (638). Having materially "produced" both the wheat and Angéle, Vanamee has the requisite finances and sense of self-completion to emerge from his romantic isolation and enter the marketplace as a consumer. Since it was Angéle's death that sent him in flight across the desert for sixteen years, it is safe to assume that in (re)materializing her he fits into a larger Darwinian evolutionary narrative that begins with nomadism and ends with rooted civilization. In other words, as long as he stays in the California marketplace as a shepherd or ranch hand, he has the monetary potential to consume at a rate in accordance with his class status. After all, despite such asceticism, the novel suggests that he is originally from the bourgeoisie—even "college bred," like his dandified friend Presley (36). Given his upbringing, one can logically assume that he can now settle back down and find additional material rewards. Angéle's greatest value is her ability to be replicated, not only like a trinket on a factory assembly line, as Seltzer has intimated, but also like the wheat itself. In this sense, Vanamee is the producer of the commodity he plans to consume on the wedding night. Presumably, the consummation of the wedding vows will ineluctably hasten more consumption of commodities needed to keep house and raise a family.

If romance has vanished in the recluse's reckoning, it is reconstituted as an epic narrative of material accumulation on the personal and national level. True, Vanamee's consumption impulse is hard to track, especially because the focus shifts so dramatically to Presley in the second half of the novel. Yet one thing we do know about him is the comfort he feels within a community of male consumers—particularly the men who eat a massive feast after a hard day's work plowing the wheat field. "It was a veritable barbecue, a crude and primitive feasting, barbaric, homeric," the narrative explains (132). With volkish enthusiasm, Vanamee "saw nothing repulsive ... [in] this feeding of the People, this gorging of the human animal, eager for its meat" (132). Still, given the fact that this feast takes place after a full day of wheat production on a large, proto-corporate ranch, it is hard to forget that these men, epic though they may be, are surely consuming mass-produced commodities. In fact, the soiree at Mrs. Gerard's home, which Presley attends as Mrs. Cedarquist's guest, exposes how the plowers in the field are integral in making millionaires out of the husbands whose wives attend these lavish dinners. At first glance, class difference makes these two groups seem worlds apart; but given the cosmic forces that tie everyone together in the capitalist economy (hence the metaphor of the octopus's tentacles), one wonders if these manly men who gorge themselves on meat are all that different from the refined women who pleasantly nibble their "raw Blue Point oysters" and sip their Haut Sauterne (602).

Buck Annixter and Hilma Tree offer a vision of what goes wrong if one does not find a proper balance between consumption and production. Like Vanamee and Angéle, they first appear as severed halves in search of androgynous wholeness. Though the narrator describes Annixter as determined, aggressive, and direct, he is also a brooding, choleric malcontent whose weak stomach and irrational hatred of "feemales" make him guilty of the same faults he finds in women. Resembling

Norris's muse figure, Hilma Tree is a young woman whose large frame, thick neck, strong arms, and slow gait give her a distinct Amazonian look. Her last name even attests to her androgyny, suggesting a phallic yet feminine nature. In short, Annixter is so masculine that he is almost feminine; Hilma is so feminine that she is almost masculine.

The dialectical reciprocity between Annixter the "man's man" and Hilma the "man's woman" is central to their self-completion.[20] After finally realizing that he cannot live without Hilma, Annixter comes into contact with his atavistic androgynous impulses, and as a result his gruff masculine exterior falls away. "In that rugged composition, confused, dark, harsh, a furrow had been driven deep, a little seed planted, a little seed at first weak, forgotten, lost in the lower places of his character" (366). Just as Vanamee and the soil are simultaneously penetrated by the phallic plow when planting the wheat seed, Annixter metaphorically becomes the feminine soil that contains the gestating seed of love for Hilma:

> By a supreme effort, not of will, but of the emotion, he fought his way across that vast gulf that for a time had gaped between Hilma and the idea of his marriage. Instantly, *like the swift blending of beautiful colors,* like the harmony of beautiful chords of music, the two ideas melted into one, and in that moment into his harsh, unlovely world a new idea was born. Annixter stood suddenly upright, a mighty tenderness, a gentleness of spirit, such as he had never *conceived* of, in his heart strained, swelled, and in a moment seemed to burst. Out of the dark furrows of his soul, up from the deep rugged recesses of his being, something arose, expanding.... The little seed, long since planted, gathering strength quietly, had at last germinated. (367–68; italics mine)

This passage is most poignant because it suggests that Annixter, like Vanamee, gives birth to himself through the acquisition or materialization of his other-sexed complementary half. As the various organic metaphors of seeds, germination, and soil also suggest, Annixter is as much mother to his new self-conception as he is its father, and the more penetrated and maternal he becomes in this description, the more "upright" and masculine it makes him.

If the narrative is fairly abstruse when detailing Vanamee's and Angéle's consumption in the marketplace, it more than makes up for these gaps when describing Hilma's betrothal to Annixter. Shortly after exchanging wedding vows, they commence upon a renovation of the ranch that quite literally takes on epic proportions. Curiously, the narrative couches their consumption excursion within a larger logic of labor and production. Before their shopping spree begins, "Hilma abruptly declared they had had enough of 'playing out,' and must be serious and get to work" (406). Understanding the shopping as "labor," Hilma seems as much involved in the production of the commodities she buys as Annixter does in the production of wheat. Annixter, too, is ecstatic over these new purchases, going about his "work" with the rigorous methodology of one rotating crops or mobilizing a harvesting crew. In a move that ultimately assuages guilt over consumer gluttony, Norris provides a tautological capitalist fantasy that makes consumption look like ample reward for the hard work of, well, previous consumption.

The week they spend in San Francisco buying all their new furniture is, according to the narrative, "delicious"—underscoring the sense of blissful work *qua* consumption that the marketplace sanctions under the aegis of androgynous wholeness (406). "Nearly an entire car load of carpets, curtains, kitchen furniture, pictures, fixtures, lamps, straw matting, chairs, and the like were sent down to the ranch" (406). The listing of the commodities, which runs for nearly two full pages of text, gains such poetic, rhythmic consistency that it echoes the various catalogs found throughout Whitman's longer poems. In the novel's reasoning, all this amounts to a reformulation of the epic form that rivals the lyric-epic *Leaves of Grass*. Now the new flow of commodities mediates the social exchange between members of the nation. Even the much maligned Pacific and Southwestern Railroad is involved in the exchange, as it is the means by which all the new commodities are brought back to the Annixter household.

While the shopping spree in San Francisco clearly shows how easily a man such as Annixter can feel primordial wholeness in a department store, Hilma's production impulse is certainly not as transgressive. If "get[ting] to work" (i.e., producing) simply means consuming commodities in a department store, her androgyny manifests itself tautologically. The immense irony of this situation is even more evident in Hilma's mannish, gargantuan size—her sturdy hips and broad shoulders—which makes her especially suitable for the traditional role of birth and motherhood, for being the "perfect woman" (504). But even in childbirth the phallocentric hypocrisy of Norris's androgyny is evident. When Hilma miscarries at roughly the same time Annixter is shot, it is clear that Annixter, his "feminine side" having previously been recovered, is as psychically or physically involved in birthing the stillborn child as Hilma.

The primal androgynous completeness that men and women find in one another is lost on the exclusively production-minded League of Defence, a collection of rugged ranchers united to save their means of production—the land—from the monopolistic Pacific and Southwestern Railroad. The masculine ethos of agrarian production that binds these ranchers together is made all the more striking in comparison to Annie Derrick, the wife of the league's leader, the manly rancher Magnus Derrick. A devotee of Paterian aesthetics, she winces at the "direct brutality of ten thousand acres of wheat" being produced outside her door (60).

Annixter's initial participation in the hypermasculine League of Defence keeps his atavistic androgynous impulses at bay. Of course his attitude changes when he gets married. Acting together as husband and wife, Hilma and Annixter are so enraptured with one another that they almost forget about the outside world in much the same way Vanamee and Angéle do once they (re)unite. It is no coincidence that once Annixter finds Hilma his commitment to the league and his hatred for the railroad wane. After the honeymooners finish their shopping spree in San Francisco, they even travel back home in a Pullman owned by the very railroad company the league has sworn to thwart. Eventually Annixter's past catches up to him, and he is called upon by the men of the league. Annixter reluctantly makes good on his commitment and pays the price. In a skirmish at the irrigation ditch, he is shot to death.

In Norris's cosmic logic, the ranchers are a part of the "elemental Male and Female" that guides production and consumption, though they have refused to see it. Instead they subscribe to an outdated notion of national cohesion that has no true efficacy in the modern American industrial economy. The ranchers' greatest flaw is that they speak in epic terms of "The People" when they never really have a secure notion of what it means. Their version of the *Volk* does not take into account a growing middle class made up in part of people who have moved from the farm to the city to engage more fully in mass production and consumption. Even though the farmers live outside the city, their livelihood is intimately caught up in the consumption of wheat in the urban areas. The league casts itself as the hypermasculine legatee of this Jeffersonian agrarianism instead of seeing itself for what it really is: the progenitor of agribusiness whose reliance on "feminine" consumption is just as necessary as the reliance on its own "masculine" production.

As the capitalist Cedarquist tells Presley, "Our century is about done. The great word of this nineteenth century has been Production. The great word of the twentieth century will be—listen to me, you youngsters—Markets" (305). There is some dramatic irony in this statement. Though the novel takes place in the late 1800s, the author, writing in the new century, knows what the members of the league cannot see. The rubric of the "Market" is general enough to engulf both production and consumption. Cedarquist's remark also has deeper racial ramifications for the novel. As Norris explains in his 1902 article "The Frontier Gone at Last," the triumph of Anglo-Saxon world hegemony was first as a violent conquest of the North American continent and later as an economic conquest of global markets: "But though we are the same race, with the same impulses, the same blood-instincts as the old Frisian marsh people, we are now come into a changed time and the great world of our century is no longer War but Trade."[21] Himself an exemplar of Anglo-Saxon manhood, Annixter comes to this realization too late and dies before producing any progeny. The League of Defence's privileging of "War" over "Trade," however, causes its own downfall. Within Norris's naturalist logic, even Anglo-Saxons such as Magnus Derrick who refuse to move beyond their masculine productive drive are left weakened and crippled. Knowing no other way to make a living, the former league leader becomes an assistant to the freight manager of the very railroad he once violently opposed. Now a "tamed lion" whose "old-time erectness was broken and bent" (624,

622), Derrick shows that resisting commercial androgyny paradoxically means losing one's masculinity and phallic prerogative.

Norris's epic of androgyny does not end there. The poet Presley proves in many respects to be the one who most clearly evades the commercial androgyny paradigm. While Norris's novel sees androgyny as an atavistic trait that, once it has resurfaced, can be used to further the prosperity of the marketplace and the state, the novel also seems attuned to androgyny's seamier side. As I have shown in the previous chapter on Henry James, sexology went to great lengths to pathologize men and women who did not fit into Victorian norms of gender and sexuality. For Basil Ransom in James's *Bostonians*, Verena's threat resides not just in her possible lesbianism, but also in the mixed racial makeup that could account for her lesbianism. Norris portrays Presley with much the same uncertainty; he is sickly, sexually ambiguous, and rather effeminate.[22] A brooding poet recovering from that most romantic of diseases, consumption, he has features that are "of a delicate and highly sensitive nature.... One guessed that [his] refinement had been gained only by a certain loss of strength" (8). Always on the periphery of all-male communities, he is neither an employee of the ranch nor a part of the League of Defence. While the ranchers are having their first league meeting, he stylishly "lounge[s] on the sofa, in corduroys and high laced boots, smoking cigarettes," playing with Annie Derrick's cat, Princess Nathalie (95). On the day of the shootout, his only participation is to stay back with the women and nurse all the wounded brought back to the homesteads.

Given his effete appearance and consumption habits (his clothes in particular), why does Presley threaten the commercial androgyny paradigm? Balance is the key: whereas Magnus Derrick's exclusive commitment to masculine production leads to ruin, Presley's effete consumption habits lead to alienation. Moreover, Presley cannot produce anything that buttresses the modern American economy. True, he does *attempt* to get in touch with his atavistic androgynous self; when he feels his epic poem of the West "germinating from within" his mind (8), he sounds very much like Annixter giving birth to his love for Hilma or like Vanamee materializing Angéle. Yet his poem never fully makes it to paper. His previous bout of consumption and his overwhelming desire to write verse, Walter Benn Michaels adroitly observes, signals "his consuming desire to be consumed."[23] When Presley finally does produce something, it is a socialist poetic diatribe called "The Toilers." But by now his notion of "the People" has changed dramatically. He sees them not as the bulwark of a nation-state, but as a social body that transcends nation and *Volk*. Presley's only product during the whole course of the novel, then, is a piece of literature that runs counter to the goals of national cohesion under capitalist expansion.

Presley embodies Carroll Smith-Rosenberg's formulation of the androgyne-trickster. This figure, she argues, "demonstrate[s] the contingency of order, [and] the fragility of social custom.... A creative force at war with convention, beyond gender, the Trickster personifies unfettered human potential."[24] True, while recovering from consumption Presley seems to personify anything but boundless potential. Yet the fear that he seems to instill in the narrator time and again attests to his sense of power, which resides more than anything in his erratic ability to embody different forms of governmental or philosophical organization throughout the novel. At first a self-absorbed romantic recovering from illness, he then becomes a nationalist obsessed with writing a "vast, tremendous" epic of the West (9). Disillusioned by the railroad's bullying tactics, he then becomes a socialist who writes a moderately successful proletarian poem. Realizing that socialism is still impotent in the face of capitalist monopolies, he becomes an anarchist and tries to assassinate the railroad's local representative, S. Behrman. Finally, disillusioned to the point of ideological paralysis, he becomes an introspective romantic once again and flees to India aboard a steamer full of wheat for starving children in Calcutta. *The Octopus* betrays the dread that democracy allows its citizens the freedom to shed political and economic skins as quickly and dramatically as gender skins. In other words, in contrast to Vanamee and Annixter, the androgynous Presley shows the radical and transgressive potential of American self-making.

Yet Presley's inability to find the proper balance between production and consumption may provide some significant clues to the logic behind Norris's notions of racial cohesion in early twentieth-century America. Like his former undergraduate evolution professor Joseph Le Conte, Norris was deeply concerned about the changing racial makeup of the republic. Much of this general anxiety can be explained through Le Conte's evolutionary theories, which expressed a tremendous dread over miscegenation. "The mixing of primary races is bad," he explains in "The Genesis of Sex" (1879), "and such mixed races, as weaker varieties in the struggle for life, must perish."[25] In another essay entitled "The Effect of Mixture of Races on Human Progress" (1880), he brought concerns of miscegenation closer to a postbellum American context: "[E]xtreme types" such as the "Teutonic and the negro" are "most certain to produce inferior results by mixture."[26] Up to this point, we have seen that atavistic androgyny has manifested itself most steadfastly in white characters. (Though Vanamee's name evokes a more exotic origin, his college pedigree, his easy access to white communities, and his reciprocated love of the blond Angéle suggest his whiteness.) What this racial consistency may signal, as Bert Bender has suggested, is that only the novel's white characters have evolved enough to be able to achieve a true and abiding love for another (white) person.[27] Bender deftly bases his notion on his reading of Le Conte, who believed that the more a species evolves, the more sexual differentiation increases. With this increase also evolves "our noblest altruistic nature," which is concerned mainly about "the well-being of the race" (177). Le Conte's emphasis on sexual differentiation does not contradict my basic premise, for it is only through a clear sense of sexual differentiation that racially advanced characters such as Annixter, Hilma, Vanamee, and Angéle are able to attain Platonic androgynous wholeness through finding their other-sexed complementary halves.

Thus, Presely's stagnancy and bodily weakness may be explained by what the novel calls his "mixed origin" and his "almost swarthy" face (8). Indeed, if Presley's inability to find a complementary other-sexed half is due in part to his possible racial impurity, we might better understand what Norris is after in making *The Octopus* the first novel in an epic trilogy. At their core, after all, epics are narratives that detail the founding or enduring cohesion of the nation or tribe. As Georg Lukács has famously explained, epics depict a hero's ineradicable "immanence" with his people and his native soil.[28] And though Presley initially desires to write an epic, his plans are aborted soon enough and he ends up writing in an antithetical genre, socialist poetry. But furthermore, he never manages to direct his love through heterosexual channels—suggesting perhaps the same type of "androgyny" that plagues Basil Ransom's view of Verena Tarrant's racial ambiguity. In creating an epic that delineates American cohesion, Frank Norris uses atavistic androgyny to keep the bloodlines clean and the economy strong.

Among the list of those who do not fall in love or who are never mentioned in terms of a monogamous relationship are those who may not fit the appropriate racial or ethnic profile. One such example is Delaney, the inebriated Irishman who is humiliated after challenging Annixter to a duel at the barn dance. The tension between Delaney and Annixter is especially intense because up until the barn dance the novel had suggested Delaney's attraction to the racially pure Hilma. Earlier in the story Presley runs into an old Mexican man, "decrepit beyond belief," whose only known contact with love is the story of De La Cuesta, a Spanish-Mexican landlord whose marriage to a beautiful woman is undercut by the sad fact that he ultimately did not love her (22–23). Even the mighty Jewish railroad magnate Shelgrim, though surprising Presley with his compassion and intelligence, seems incapable of love. Usually working late into the evening, Shelgrim seems to have married the octopus-like corporation itself, and in doing so he has come to resemble an octopus in body.

Always the student of naturalism, Norris subjects Presley to natural selection, though somewhat benignly. Since the "morbidly sensitive" (8) poet does not direct his atavistic impulses toward finding an other-sexed complementary half, and since he will not (re)produce, Norris instead sends him with the wheat on a steamship to Calcutta. Presley's only consolation is that once aboard, he learns the lesson of the elemental Male and Female forces. Russ Castronovo remarks that in going away to India, the poet is able to create an aesthetic unity out of the entire massacre at the irrigation ditch. Noting that the novel cheerfully justifies Annixter's death as a chance to feed starving children, and also how the trip to the far East leads Presley back to the starting point of civilization, Castronovo suggests that "just as 'everything' flows into the formal properties of the artwork, the pressures of globalization force every political tendency from democracy to fascism into alignment."[29] This same reasoning applies to the male-female unity that the novel achieves. These forces of consumption and production, which find unity in Cedarquist's twentieth-century buzzword "The Market," keep America a dominant economic power.

Yet the "America" that clearly most concerns Norris is the white Anglo-Saxon America. While the novel's end does give way to a globalist impulse, a rigid sense of nationalism is never left behind. To Presley, the Anglo-Saxon race will use its capitalist might across the world. America may trade with and produce for other nations, but it will never be corrupted or weakened by cultural or racial exchange. In Norris's calculation, globalism does not interfere with national cohesion; it reinforces it. As the closing lines of the novel reveal, "Greed, cruelty, selfishness, and inhumanity are short lived; the individual suffers, but the race goes on" (652). Through commodity exportation, the Anglo-Saxons who control the wheat markets in America contain the threat of racial mixing. If the starving Indians in Calcutta and elsewhere are fed in their own cities and countries, they find fewer reasons to crowd American shores in search of material gain. Cedarquist's ship full of wheat confirms the altruism that Joseph Le Conte and his pupil Norris see manifested in the white Anglo-Saxon race. Globalism, guided ultimately by production and consumption, sustains the superior Anglo-Saxon *Volk* just as surely as it sustains the inferior and distinctly different peoples in other parts of the world.

Within the context of this study, perhaps the most striking feat that Frank Norris achieves though *The Octopus* is an answer to the many anxieties Henry James perceived when envisioning the racial and sexual makeup of the postbellum and early twentieth-century American body politic. In James's formulation of the androgynous *vox Americana* there still resided the hint of dread that acknowledging the individual body as the origin point of the national voice will undermine the cultural unity of the republic. More than anything for James, the prominence of sexological and evolutionary discourses had made androgyny suspect. Yet in *The Octopus* Norris is able to affirm not only androgyny's role in evolutionary science, but also its presence in the human body as an atavistic trait that serves as the foundation for heteronormative relations and a national economy. Norris's achievement is based in part on extending, and therefore reinforcing, the perception that production and consumption themselves are gendered. At the same time, as we have seen with Presley, androgyny could still operate within evolutionary discourse in much the same way it did for Henry James during the 1880s—as a sign of racial degeneration that more clearly defines the limits of political and social enfranchisement.

Androgyny's sometimes contradictory roles within evolutionary and sexological discourses attest to its elasticity once it became unmoored from a primarily genital-based definition. Ever the student of naturalism, Norris traced androgyny to an earlier moment of evolutionary development and found ways through his fiction to avow its durability. As we shall see in the next portion of this chapter, androgyny's conceptual elasticity could just as easily suggest that it is merely a cultural construct that must be tolerated until human evolution progresses to the point that it renders all gender distinctions—especially those accompanying production and consumption—obsolete.

Utopian Matriarchies and the Deconstruction of Androgyny in Charlotte Perkins Gilman

As Frank Norris has shown us, commercial androgyny has its limits. Whereas men such as Annixter or Vanamee can ironically get in touch with their feminine side in order to enjoy the benefits of market-based consumption, women such as Hilma end up merely redirecting their masculine productive impulses back toward a buttressing of the nation through reproduction. Despite Hilma's miscarriage, the terms of androgyny are clear in *The Octopus:* male appropriation of the feminine is simply another aspect of masculine entitlement. Given this tautological thinking, one wonders why consumption was ever regarded as feminine in the first place. Norris never addresses this concern, but only exposes the need for it to be answered.

The second part of this chapter addresses that need by looking at the works of Norris's literary contemporary Charlotte Perkins Gilman. Indeed, these two authors share several similarities that make them suitable for comparison. For example, both lived most of their adult lives in California—Norris moving to Oakland as a teenager in 1884 and Gilman moving to Pasadena after the 1888 separation from her first husband, Charles Walter Stetson. Both even pursued careers in the visual arts before turning to literature; Norris spent the years 1887–89 at the Académie Julian in Paris, while Gilman attended the prestigious Rhode Island School of Design in the late 1870s. The two also identified themselves with some form of Progressivist or Populist politics, as is evident in Norris's *Octopus* and in Gilman's *Herland*. But perhaps most important, their interest in politics was matched and complemented by their interest in the many (and often conflicting) evolutionary theories of the day. Despite her own interest in Darwinism, Gilman came to regard androgyny not as an atavistic trait that could lead white Americans toward economic ascendancy in the early twentieth century, but as a cultural construct that obviously oppressed women and obfuscated the deeper and more resonating similarities among the different sexes of the same race.

Coming from a broken home, subjected to a peripatetic and financially unstable upbringing, and receiving a spotty formal education, Charlotte Perkins learned from an early age what it meant to be a young woman in postbellum America. A great granddaughter of Lyman Beecher, she was exposed to religion, philosophy, feminism, and ethics at an early age. Some of her earliest life lessons came from her father's abandonment of her mother—an act that left Mary Westcott Perkins with a lifelong sense of inferiority. Unwilling to live the domestic life forced upon her mother by Victorian American society, Gilman, who "wished to help humanity," embarked upon a system of self-education that exposed her to history, sociology, and primitive anthropology.³⁰ Perhaps most famous today for her short story "The Yellow Wallpaper" (1892), during her own day she was best known for her 1898 *Women and Economics: A Study of the Economic Relation between Women and Men*, which was subsequently translated into Japanese, Dutch, Danish, Italian, German, and Russian.³¹ In more recent years Gilman has become equally well known for her feminist utopian novel *Herland*, which was initially published in her magazine *The Forerunner* in 1915 and later republished in 1979.

A closer look at these two latter works suggests that Gilman was attuned to the controversies over androgyny as they were played out in her day in sociological, anthropological, and medical communities. Beyond that, she seemed even more attuned to the ways in which the discourses of androgyny and the liberal subject it strove to produce were deeply predicated on masculine prerogative. In privileging and emphasizing racial distinctions over sex distinctions, she came to the same evolutionary conclusions as fellow sociologist Émile Durkheim. Durkheim's famous *Division of Labor in Society* (1893) sought to understand not only the functions of the division of labor, but also "the causes and conditions on which it is dependent." In explaining his rationale, Durkheim references contemporary evolutionary studies that pointed to the relative lack of sexual distinction between primitive men and women. As civilization developed, he notes, the differences became more pronounced to the point that men and women found solidarity not in their sameness, but in their complementary lack: "One urges on, another consoles; this one advises, that one follows the advice." On the macro level, complementary lack and fulfillment catalyzes "the integration of the social body to assure unity."³²

Unlike Durkheim, however, Gilman did not see modern-day differentiation as working toward a greater social unity. Rather, she regarded the loss of key similarities between men and women at an earlier moment of evolutionary history as most unfortunate, since in her opinion the ability to sustain a healthy Anglo-Saxon race was predicated on gender equality in the home, in politics, and in the workplace. Gilman's plan for future racial development was to recover that earliest primitive moment of equality, which she likened to a prelapsarian time. Her utopian novel *Herland* speculates on how women would have fared had they been able to recover that prelapsarian moment and develop a civilization without men's insistence on unreasonable gender differentiation.

Like Frank Norris, Gilman was especially interested in the gendering of labor and economics. Much of *Herland*'s thematic force is driven by a reimagining of material production and consumption without their respective significations of masculine and feminine. Gilman exposes not only the phallocentric thinking of androgynous discourse at the turn of the century, but also the way in which that discourse embeds itself in nationalist paradigms. At the heart of the tension between Norris's and Gilman's visions is the overall conceptualization of androgyny. Whereas Norris suggests that the blurring of "male" and "female" constitutes a primal human androgyny, Gilman suggests that the many similarities between men and women show just the opposite: an asexual, primal "human" category that precedes the superimposition of culturally constructed gender roles. Yet despite the bold claims Gilman makes about the masculine biases in the various intellectual configurations of androgyny, the question that perpetually looms over *Herland* is whether or not an all-female utopia can ever actually escape—and not just momentarily subvert—a masculine signifying system that encodes not only gendered notions of production and consumption, but also gendered notions of the liberal subject and national destiny.

Also like Norris, Gilman had been interpellated by the larger intellectual current of evolutionary thinking, a point she makes plain in *Women and Economics*. Gilman starts from the premise that the evolution of the Anglo-Saxon race took place in two phases, the first being a type of egalitarian existence in which men and women barely recognized their sexual differences. The "Proem" at the beginning of the book explains this earlier moment of evolution: "In dark and early ages, through the primal forests faring, / Ere the soul came shining into prehistoric night, / Twofold man was equal; they were comrades dear and daring, / Living wild and free together in unreasoning delight."[33] Later in the book Gilman describes this moment by claiming, "Primitive man and his female were animals, like other animals. They were strong, fierce, lively beasts; and she was as nimble and ferocious as he, save for the added belligerence of the males in their sex-competition. . . . [S]he ran about in the forest, and helped herself to what there was to eat as freely as he did" (60).

In many ways, these sentiments echo sexologist Otto Weininger's argument for atavistic androgyny, though Gilman herself does not go so far as to use the term "androgynous" to describe her own primitive man and woman. A few years after the publication of *Women and Economics*, in a 1906 review of Weininger's *Sex and Character*, she does acknowledge the fundamental plausibility of his line of thinking, remarking that the German sexologist "advances a theory much of which seems reasonable and bourne out by facts, namely, that sex is not manifested in two absolutely opposite types, either in humanity or lower forms: but that there is an 'ideoplasm' in all our constituent cells; 'Arrhenoplasm' (male plasm), 'Thelyplasm' (female plasm), and that this distinctive plasm is different in amount not only in different personas, but in different cells of the same body."[34] All told, *Sex and Character* develops an intensely misogynistic theory about women's evolutionary inferiority, but Gilman felt that Weininger's emphasis on primitive sexual similarity was the correct starting point on which to base an understanding of modern human equality. Sounding a call that diverges dramatically from Weininger, she tells her readers at the end of the review, "It is the humanness which Mr. Weininger so wholly fails to grasp. What is human he calls male—with the unavoidable result that the woman—not being male—is not human. We need a new understanding of the immeasurable difference between sex-distinctions, which we share with other animals, and our pre-eminent race distinction, which is beyond sex."[35]

The "humanness" that Weininger's theory fails to acknowledge is what was lost in a prehistoric moment Gilman likens to the biblical Fall of Man. In the "Proem" of *Women and Economics* the Fall occurs as Man eats from "that awful tree" of knowledge and learns to sin. Instead of competing with other men for the right to mate with the female, as was the case in the prelapsarian moment, the fallen man simply takes or even rapes the woman and enslaves her as his wife and concubine: "Close, close he bound her, that she should leave him never; / Weak still he kept her, lest she be strong to flee" (x). The ensuing history of the various races was one of female dependence and of growing sexual differentiation: "The human female was cut off from the direct action of natural selection, that mighty force which heretofore had acted on male and female alike with inexorable and beneficial effect, developing strength, developing skill, developing endurance, developing courage—in a word, developing species" (62). Worth noting here are the attributes she ascribes to women in the prelapsarian stage, attributes that make her not an androgyne or an Amazon, but simply a fellow member of the human "species." Furthermore, Gilman already seems to be aware of how men have appropriated universal characteristics as their own while seeing the female body as marked by its difference from this universality.

But when in her review of Weininger's *Sex and Character* Gilman explains that it is necessary to have a new understanding of "*our* pre-eminent race distinction, which is beyond sex" (italics mine), she reveals not only her intention to speak exclusively to a white audience, but also the extent to which her evolutionary theories are based on racist assumptions. In this sense, she amplifies many of the same concerns voiced by both Frank Norris and Henry James in their brooding over the racial makeup of the modern American body politic. For instance, Gilman believed that blacks were not nearly as evolved as whites; moreover, it would take possibly centuries before blacks would be able to attain the type of civilization whites had attained. As she explained in an 1890 speech to the Los Angles Women's Club:

> Some of you will say again that it is part of the male function in the human race to provide for the family, including under this head all the varied activities of our race, and the female function merely to serve the family. . . . But it is a lie! . . . Race function does not interfere with sex function. . . . The dominant soul—the clear strong accurate brain, the perfect service of a healthy body—those do not belong to sex—but to *race!*[36]

In other words, by challenging her audience to think in terms of a white/black binary instead of a male/female binary, Gilman is able to use blacks as straw men against whom white men and women can find solidarity. Gilman could therefore hold up the figure of the primitive black man as a warning to white men that perpetuating the sins of the "fall" mentioned in the "Proem"—that is, continuing to oppress fellow white women—is tantamount to savagery and a form of race betrayal.

Since this evolutionary "fall," one atavistic trait that has helped define the Anglo-Saxon race is male aggression, which has led not only to the development of industry and civilization, but also to the atrophying of women's minds and bodies. No longer concerned with hunting and gathering alongside their male counterparts, they prefer to augment their sexual differences through material adornment in order to attract men. The Victorian era, steeped in its separate spheres mentality, was bringing the Anglo-Saxon race to an evolutionary crisis: women were becoming too "feminine" and men were becoming too "masculine." But with adult men leaving the childrearing to their wives as they went off into the workforce, male children were potentially growing up too much under the influence of their mothers. Raised under such conditions, these meek young men could threaten the progress of white civilization—if not by learning to oppress women as their fathers had done, then by turning into mama's boys.[37]

In this evolutionary pattern, we see Gilman's implicit insistence on the difference between sex and gender, and the overt recognition that "masculine" production and "feminine" consumption are culturally constructed gender dichotomies. First, Gilman understands that all humans are classified by various breakdowns. Though not using the word "gender," she separates sex difference from "human" difference. While these distinctions pervade *Women and Economics,* their most succinct and direct delineation comes in Gilman's *The Man-Made World: Our Androcentric Culture* (1911):

> It seeks to show that what we have all this time called "human nature" and deprecated, was in great part only male nature, and good enough in its place; that what we have called "masculine" and admired as such, was in large part human, and should be applied to both sexes; that what we have called "feminine" and condemned, was also largely human and applicable to both. Our androcentric culture is so shown to have been, and still to be, a masculine culture in excess, and therefore undesirable.[38]

Like gender traits, human traits are those not related to physiological processes such as birth, ovulation, and menstruation for women, or sperm production and semen ejaculation for men. But the lion's share of all human functions can be done by both men and women, just as hunting and gathering occurred among both sexes in primitive societies. When human traits such as writing or material production are misunderstood as sex distinctions, it is because they are "performed," in Judith Butler's formulation, "in an exterior space through a stylized repetition of acts" to provide the illusion of sexual fixity.[39] As I will show in my discussion of *Herland,* Gilman gropes feverishly to understand the linguistic parameters of the masculine signifying system that seems so obvious to Butler. Yet already Gilman understands that biology is rarely destiny, since men and women have more "human" traits that unite them than they have "sex" traits that divide them.

Secondly, Gilman rejects the traditional genderings of production and consumption, while begrudgingly admitting to their discursive efficacy in the modern industrial world. With men in firm control over economic institutions, shared human traits that operate under the guise of male and female sex traits sustain a rigid and often punitive hierarchy. In *Women and Economics* she states simply that "we find that production and consumption go hand in hand; and production comes first. One cannot consume what has not been produced. Economic production is the natural expression of human energy,—not sex-energy at all, but race energy,—the unconscious functioning of the social organism" (116).

Finally, Gilman once again resorts to racist evolutionary assumptions to seek a sense of solidarity—a relative sense of sameness—with fellow white men. The emphasis on production as a race distinction suggests a great deal about Gilman's confidence in the productive capabilities of American blacks—and especially black men—in the first decade of the twentieth century. This lack of confidence is nowhere more evident than in a 1908 article entitled "A Suggestion on the Negro Problem," which assesses the reasons why almost fifty years after emancipation more African Americans have not become "entirely self-supporting and well behaved." In short, for Gilman the issue comes down to a question of a race's innate ability to produce in a modern industrial economy. In many cases, the essay attributes this inability to the deplorable social and economic conditions most blacks faced at the time. But beyond the cultural obstacles still resides the greater evolutionary obstacle. "We have to consider," she explains, "the unavoidable presence of a large body of aliens, of a race widely dissimilar and in many ways inferior, whose present status is to us a social injury. If we had left them alone in their own country this dissimilarity and inferiority would be, so to speak, none of our business."[40] Cleary, Gilman is setting up an us/them binary, just as she has done in other writings we have seen. Yet what is also remarkable here is her opinion that slavery, though a clear violation of human dignity and liberty, is not really the basis of African American inferiority. Had slavery never occurred, blacks still would have been inferior, just in their own part of the world.

If the production impulse therefore comes naturally to the more advanced Anglo-Saxon race, the widening cultural rift among male and female members of that race stalls their evolutionary progress. Gilman acknowledges that in the modern western world, the white woman "is forbidden to make, but encouraged to take" (*WE* 118), and hence the current misunderstanding that production is masculine and consumption is feminine. Yet it is not just women's culturally enforced propensity for taking that codes consumption as feminine—it is *what* they take:

> To consume food, to consume clothes, to consume houses and furniture and decorations and ornaments and amusements, to take and take and take forever,—from one man if they are virtuous, from many if they are vicious, but always to take and never to think of giving

anything in return except their womanhood,—this is the enforced condition of the mothers of the race. (*WE* 118–19)

In other words, women consume the very things that make them seem most different from men—namely decorations, domestic furnishings, and clothing. The consuming woman then becomes her own worst enemy: "As the priestess of the temple of consumption, as the limitless demander of things to use up, her economic influence is reactionary and injurious" (*WE* 120). Through the years, sex distinctions have increased to the point that they create, in Butler's words, "the illusion of an interior and organizing gender core" that duly and "regularly conceals its own [culturally constructed] genesis."[41] But teaching women to recognize their own humanness would be quite a feat. To make inroads in economic production, as their prelapsarian primitive foremothers had done, women must first realize they have just as much emotional, intellectual, and physical aptitude for production as men.

Gilman spoke with authority on the disadvantages of extreme sexual differentiation. After being courted for sixteen months by Charles Walter Stetson, the twenty-two-year-old Charlotte decided to marry him, even though she was fairly certain at the time that the conventional constraints of wifehood would limit her intellectual growth. Her suspicions turned out to be correct: within two months of marriage, Gilman had fallen into a deep depression.[42] To make matters worse, she sought the help of famed psychologist S. Weir Mitchell, who diagnosed her with neurasthenia and prescribed bed rest with minimal mental exertion. Separated from any form of intellectual exertion—her own form of production—and relegated completely to the domestic sphere, Gilman was certain she would go insane. "The Yellow Wallpaper," which chronicles a new mother's descent into madness while being treated by a rest cure, became the fictional account of her own physical and mental confinement. Confronted with the choice of either "cowering on the floor in the women's sphere" or moving back into the men's professional realm of writing, she opted for the latter.[43] Leaving her husband and daughter in 1888, Gilman moved to California. Once established, she called for her daughter and then began a successful career as a writer, lecturer, and political activist. After trying for four years to be the model wife, Gilman realized that the advancement of the Anglo-Saxon race depended in large part on women being able to break free of the material trappings of the domestic sphere and make their own inroads into various forms of production.

Yet for all of Gilman's frustration with her society's imposition of gender binaries on "human" qualities, she argues in *Women and Economics* that such imposition is the inevitable, albeit temporary, outcome of the necessary domestication of men. Primitive men, she claimed, were highly individualistic, hunting and caring for themselves only. But after taking women by force and claiming a kind of ownership over them, men shed their individualism and started to care for their families. Thus, while women began to exaggerate their femininity under this captivity, men actually became androgynized insofar as they were compelled to use their inherent male strength in the service of nurturing an otherwise defenseless family: "As the male, acting through his natural instincts, steadily encroached upon the freedom of the female until she was reduced to the state of economic dependence, he thereby assumed the position of provider for this creature no longer able to provide for herself. . . . He became, and has remained, a sort of man-mother, alone in creation in his remarkable position" (125).

The "fall" that turned mate selection by the female into a rapacious conquest by the male may therefore have been a *felix culpa* of sorts because it harnessed brute male strength toward communalism and the eventual creation of civilization. But if Anglo-Saxon evolution requires androgyny in the form of maternal men, it is only provisional: "By the action of his own desires, through all its by-products of evil, man was made part mother; and so both man and woman were enabled to become human. It was an essential step in our racial progress, a means to an end" (128). Once women are able to shed their excessive femininity and join men in production, white civilization will not only advance, but the masculine/feminine binary will wither away and men and women will claim their equality based on their shared "human" qualities.

When assessing *Herland*, it is necessary to keep in mind the premise that androgyny has come into Gilman's (and our) current-day existence as a culturally constructed gender concept through the male's evolution into a "man-mother." Therefore, as the three male American explorers enter into Herland for the first time they bring the concept of androgyny with them and try to apply it to capable, strong, and productive women who simply have no understanding of gender constructs. In contrasting the representatives of a gendered society with a utopian "human" society, Gilman provides some fascinating clues as to how her Anglo-Saxon race can make the much anticipated leap into an egalitarian future.

When Gilman published *Herland* in several installments of *The Forerunner* in 1915, she took part in a larger discourse on primitive and extinct cultures. Primitivism had often served the interests of conservative-minded male modernists who sought out ways to reinstate hierarchies that were threatened in the modern age of political, gender, and economic upheaval. Even the dandified and cosmopolitan T. S. Eliot lamented the passing away of certain primitive customs that preserved gender roles and that bound people to each other and to "their" land. His use of Middle English in *East Coker*, one of the long poems making up the *Four Quartets* cycle, suggests as much.[44] But, as Lisa Rado points out, female modernists insisted that primitivism was not just a "naughty game played by insecure white men."[45] Seizing hold of various anthropological studies that relied on the new notion of cultural relativism, scholars such as Gasquoine Hartley looked to primitive matriarchal societies to argue that women in the second decade of the twentieth century were "reclaiming a position that is theirs by natural right—a position which once they held."[46] And while many of the primitive matriarchies invoked in anthropological studies such as Hartley's could not always be supported by hard empirical data, they nevertheless fed a larger need among progressive-minded intellects to develop a utopian ideal for a modern world.[47] Gilman differed from Hartley in that she was not so interested in using the model of a primitive matriarchy to reinscribe a current-day matriarchy. Rather, she used her fictitious all-female nation to question the modern world's irrational need for categories of gender.

In creating *Herland,* Gilman drew from various sources. As mentioned earlier, Weininger's *Sex and Character* certainly made an impact, but so did sociologists Lester Ward and Thorstein Veblen. Ward's *Pure Sociology* (1903) was particularly helpful in supplying Gilman with a "gyneacocentric theory," which suggested that females carried all of a race's traits from generation to generation. Ward also claimed that presexual creatures that reproduced through parthenogenesis should be regarded as female.[48] Parthenogenesis would also appear in *Herland* as the women of the remote fictional country are autonomously able to give birth only to females long after all the men had died out. Thorstein Veblen's *Theory of the Leisure Class* had an equally influential role in forming Gilman's understanding of evolution. Veblen believed that primitive men and women had both cooperative and competitive instincts. The modern-day capitalist, caught up in his aggressive drive for financial domination, was the beneficiary of this atavistic competitiveness, whereas his more peaceful and cooperative instincts were left to languish.[49] As *Women and Economics* suggests, there is another atavistic drive—that of cooperation, which mitigates sex distinction—but it is vastly overshadowed in the modern world. The trick for Gilman is to rehabilitate those cooperative instincts as a way of keeping the Anglo-Saxon race healthy, progressive, and dominant.

Herland was one of the first self-consciously feminist utopias written in America.[50] In it, Gilman challenges her readers to regard the muscular, economically productive, and intellectually cultivated women not as androgynes, but as the prototype for the modern Anglo-Saxon woman once she is able to throw off the shackles of culturally prescribed gender distinctions. The tale begins with three male explorers who venture into uncharted territories to seek out a legendary "Woman Country."[51] Each explorer is representative of a type of conventional American manhood. First there is Terry Nicholson, the wealthy and oversexed playboy of the group, who sees women as little more than romantic conquests. At the other end of the spectrum is Jeff Margrave, the chivalrous physician who "idealized women in the best Southern style" (9). Occupying a middle ground between the two is the narrator Vandyck Jennings, a mild-mannered sociologist by profession. Being the one most open to the Herlanders' way of life, Van attempts to provide the most sympathetic view of the all-women civilization.

From the men's first encounter with the Herlanders, issues of gender, production, and consumption come directly to the fore. In fact, the first evidence the men come upon which suggests the existence of such a people is a manufactured "well-woven" piece of cloth (4). Once the three men reach the outer limits of the lost country, they enact a version of *Women and Economics*'s "Proem," in which Terry plays three roles simultaneously: the producer of commodities, the tempting serpent, and the rapacious Adam. Spotting a Herlander, Alima, for the first time, he tries to lure her down from a tree with a necklace. Van recounts: "Terry's smile was irreproachable, but I did not like the look in his eyes—it was like a creature about to spring" (16). Seeing the grab for the necklace as more of a game than a temptation, Alima snatches it before Terry can capture her. While her agility proves she is every bit as athletic as her male tempter, the bigger issue at hand in this moment of contact is the future of the Herland society. Symbolizing the movement toward greater sex-distinction, the necklace would surely have meant Alima's "fall" from her primitive "human" state to that of an irrational, over-sexed consumer whose lust for ornamentation would make her economically and socially dependent on men.

Having avoided capture, Alima then draws the men into the nearest city, where they are themselves captured after instigating a row with the various women who see them on the street. Though held captive for a time, the men are treated more as students than prisoners, receiving tutoring from three older women who teach them the history of Herland and its egalitarian societal structures. Van, Jeff, and Terry find that several thousand years ago men did exist in the community, but because of wars, sickness, and natural catastrophes, they all died out, leaving the women to fend for themselves. Quite miraculously, one of these early women gave birth to five daughters through parthenogenesis. The current-day citizens of Herland are all descendants of these five daughters, and like those original daughters, can themselves reproduce females autonomously. Given the thousands of years the women have lived without men, they have become nearly oblivious to their own sex traits, seeing themselves quite simply as human; therefore the country itself is not feminized so much as it is humanized. Implicit in this argument, then, is the notion that the modern world has allowed humans' primitive cooperative instincts to atrophy and that a stronger reliance on those very traits would mitigate the need for gender distinction. As Van puts it: "Here you have human beings, unquestionably, but what we were slow in understanding was how these ultra-women, inheriting only from women, had eliminated not only certain masculine characteristics, which of course we did not look for, but so much of what we had always thought essentially feminine" (57). Van, Jeff, and Terry come to realize that these women understand the world without the aid (or hindrance) of binary thinking. Eliminating the binary means eliminating the zero-sum game that often circumscribes the men's understanding of gender; by ridding themselves of certain ostensible feminine characteristics, the Herlanders are not necessarily more androgynous, because their loss of such characteristics does not signal an automatic acquisition of certain elements of masculinity. Women are not understood in relation to men any more than good is understood in relation to evil.

Van remarks that "[t]hey had no theory of the essential opposition of good and evil; life to them was growth: their pleasure was in growing, and their duty also" (102).

Gilman's novel eventually focuses on industry and the Herlanders' methods of production and consumption. But because the women do not live in a world of binary oppositions, there is obviously no arbitrary breakdown between masculine and feminine with regard to economic modes. The men are initially surprised to see that cities and industry had evolved to such a high degree in Herland, and to them it first suggests the existence of men, though they never find any. The Herlanders even have motor cars and finely paved roads, both of which prompt Terry to sneer dubiously to his chums, "No men, eh?" (18). At this point, even Van is in subtle agreement with his oversexed colleague that there must be men somewhere.

Once again, through insistence on the impressive productive capabilities of the Herlanders, Gilman is insisting on the relative sameness of white men and women in the face of larger differences with those of other races. The women of Herland, Van explains, "were of Aryan stock, and were once in contact with the best civilization of the old world" (54). The Aryan lineage of these economically productive women shines in stark contrast to black men and women of her own time and country, who, as Gilman further explains in "A Suggestion on the Negro Problem," are united by their productive incompetence. The only solution Gilman can see for the majority of African Americans who cannot adapt to modern production standards is compulsory enlistment in the army. Even the African American woman would enlist; she would be taught to produce, among other things, crops and textiles, which would then be used for the army's consumption.[52] Thus, when Van exclaims that he and his comrades have stumbled upon a "new race," whatever differences exist between them and the Anglo-Saxon men are slight enough still to include the women as members of an industrious, highly evolved white race.

Clearly Terry, Jeff, and Van have yet to learn that racial similarity trumps sexual difference. When finally coming to grips with the fact that women are the country's only means of production, the three go into an ontological tailspin. Through them Gilman takes issue with her own country's economics by revealing the less-than-desirable facets of American industry. To the Herlanders, the separation of spheres is not so foreign a concept because the country is devoid of men, but because even if men did live there it would simply be illogical to proscribe one sex from economic production. In making these points, Gilman is no doubt recalling her writings from the decade of the 1890s, a time when her support for socialism was as vocal as her support for feminism.[53] Throughout that decade she gave a number of lectures on Nationalism, a non-Marxian socialism developed by Edward Bellamy, whose popular utopian novel *Looking Backward* (1888) propounded a system based not on the dialectics of class struggle, but on a peaceful, ballot-driven evolution toward government ownership of national infrastructure and industry as well as the establishment of farm cooperatives and a uniform salary for all adult citizens. At the heart of this vision was "producerism," the belief that production existed beyond the narrow Marxian confines of commodity production to include all forms of output—intellectual, industrial, or even corporeal. In other words, women are natural producers through their ability to reproduce humans.[54] In fact, in drawing from evolutionist Lester Ward the idea that women carry the race traits, Gilman could show that the production impulse in women is as strong as it is in men.

Yet if left at reproduction alone, women's natural form of production proves to be, as Hilma Annixter has shown in Norris's *Octopus,* another form of patriarchal subjugation. As Gilman herself remarked in *Women and Economics,* "The desire to produce—the distinctive human quality—is no longer satisfied with a status that allows only reproduction" (140). If women can make a human life, they are most certainly capable of other forms of production. Thus, while motherhood is held in the highest esteem in *Herland,* the Herlanders are just as active in all other forms of "production" in the way that producerism had come to define the term in the late 1800s.[55]

The interactions between the men and the Herlanders go to great lengths to deconstruct the notion of commercial androgyny espoused by Norris. Through these exchanges we can see that other-sexed complementarity, which brought Angéle to Vanamee and Hilma to Annixter, is based on fallacious and detrimental social assumptions. The reason why such characters as Hilma and Angéle never break out of their one-dimensionality is that androgynous complementarity is no more than a form of male entitlement. These women are idolized but never allowed true subjectivity. They are simply enveloped by the men who fall in love with them. Given the extensive economy of manufacturing, agriculture, and arts the women of Herland have developed over the years, women are obviously just as capable as men in the realm of production. Even though there are no men in the country, the separation of spheres simply does not make sense for those countries that do have both sexes. Somel, one of the tutors, does not even understand the word "home" because there is no equivalent to it in her language. In Herland, all the women live, and all the children are raised, communally.

Gilman exposes the sexist underpinnings of commercial androgyny most obviously through Terry. A wealthy man whose consumption habits include the acquisition of planes, boats, and automobiles, he is also the alpha male of the group. Through him *Herland* entertains notions of the male quest romance genre, but only to turn it on its head.[56] Terry exemplifies the romance hero in the search to find his other-sexed complementary other; but as his attempted rape of Alima shows, the search is really just a pursuit of base sexual fulfillment and domination. Furthermore, Gilman exposes the contradictory impulses men feel in finding their other-sexed complements. Certainly Terry wants a young seductress to fulfill his need for sexual mastery, but he is an equally strong supporter of traditional marriage. "We do not allow our women to work," he tells his Herlander tutor Zava. "Women are loved—idolized—honored—kept in the home to care for the children" (61). In other words, while he and other men of his class can feel equally at home in the realm of consumption, the women are to redirect any productive drives they may have toward reproduction. The women find the traditional marriage scenario, and the sex act that accompanies it, either undesirable or repulsive. Jeff and Van are only slightly better in this respect. Like Terry, they are deeply confused and frustrated when their Herlander wives will not consent to sexual intercourse, the very act in the Platonic tradition that fuses men and women back into androgynous wholes. Their language of seduction is loaded with images of completeness and fulfillment, as when Van explains to Ellador, "Why, to touch you—to be near you—to come closer and closer—to lose myself in you—surely you feel it too, do you not?" (126). But Ellador indeed does not, just as Van had suspected earlier when observing, "There was no sex feeling to appeal to, or practically none" (92).

Yet if commercial androgyny is at its most basic level the blurring of masculine production and feminine consumption, it actually *does* exist in America beyond the middle-class standard of consuming males and their child-producing wives. Only begrudgingly does Terry admit that women in America *do* participate in other forms of production besides childbearing. To Zava's question of whether or not *any* women in America work outside the home, he responds, "Some have to, of the poorer sort" (61). Much to their dismay, the tutors find that roughly one-third of women in America do participate in production, but only the poor ones who have no other options. The conversation bears out the larger reality of early twentieth-century America. As technology made manufacturing jobs less skilled and less sex-specific, more and more women entered the industrial workforce. Many of them were young, poor, and unmarried—those for whom the term "lady" was never meant. By 1900, roughly 932,000 of these women were employed in clothing trades or textile mills. By 1910, there were over 8,000,000 employed outside the home, mostly working as factory hands or store clerks.[57] From her time as a member of the Equality League of Self-Supporting Women, an organization of some 19,000 women whose aim was political and labor equality, Gilman came to know the plight many of these women faced. In his quasi-Spencerian explanation of social determination, Van acknowledges this reality: "[W]here there was severe economic pressure the lowest classes of course felt it the worst, and . . . the poorest of all women were driven into the labor market by necessity" (63). Thus if commercial androgyny has revealed itself to be at last a form of masculine prerogative, the discussion between the men and the Herlanders has also revealed that being the female component of an androgynous whole also comes with certain class prerequisites.

Nevertheless, childbirth is very much a part of these poor women's lives—but only to their detriment. In fact, a large brood signified not so much a mother's high and revered status in America as it did her abject poverty. Jeff explains that "the poorer [working women] were, the more children they had" (63). A personal friend of Margaret Sanger's, Gilman was a staunch supporter of birth control for women, though given her anxiety over the threat of race suicide, most likely with a white supremacist agenda in mind. With many immigrant women flooding American shores and taking many of the lower-wage manufacturing jobs mentioned by Terry, Jeff, and Van, Gilman felt that birth control was one way to keep nonwhite populations in check.[58] But certainly for these women wage earners mentioned in *Herland*, children are not the telos of a women's existence. Motherhood under the wrong circumstances can be a prison as much as a blessing. In this conversation, poor fathers are nowhere mentioned, suggesting their possible absence from the family altogether. So much for other-sexed complementarity.

Gilman exposes the ways in which not only production and consumption but also the larger discourse of androgyny are fully encapsulated within a masculine signifying system. In her deconstructionist reading of Plato's *Symposium*, Kari Weil sees any attempt to vocalize or envision a unified primordial androgyny as inherently flawed. "The presymbolic and presexual state associated with the androgyne," she states, "can only be envisioned from what [Jacques] Lacan calls the symbolic, and with a language that is already marked by difference."[59] Androgyny too easily and too contradictorily symbolizes that which is dual-sexed *and* nonsexed. The problem with the imagination and the language that gives it voice is that it is riddled with what Derrida famously calls *différence*—which implies both that language is inherently constituted by difference ("I know what a cat is because it is not a dog") and that language interminably defers a word's ultimate meaning. Gilman's *Herland* tries to find a way to look beyond male and female difference or *différence* through Van, who goes to great lengths to comprehend and explain a pre-phallogocentric system of signification. The country of Herland may actually possess this much coveted nongendered language, but when recapitulated by those inscribed within the Symbolic Order such as Van or Terry, the language is lost. Thus the Herlander language can only be described by a language inherently marked by gender, difference, and *différance*. If we readers are never fully able to envision the Herlanders' existence as a pregendered "human" one, it is because we fall prey to the same linguistic traps that the intruding men do.

When scholars Nell Irvin Painter and Dorothy Berkson therefore call these women's culture "androgynous," they miss the point, but in missing the point they show Gilman's larger argument that at this present stage in evolutionary history we are trapped by notions of gendered duality.[60] For the Herlanders, who presumably possess a language outside of the Lacanian symbolic, androgyny is a meaningless term because it denotes difference, even if the difference is amalgamated into one dual-sexed entity. These conclusions amplify the point that the liberal subject as envisioned by Locke, Hobbes, and Rousseau never did exist (even theoretically) before gender—or, for that matter, before the linguistic signification that created and ordered gender.[61] Locke's nongendered tabula rasa may correctly delineate the human mind at birth for Gilman, but the blank slate inevitably encounters masculine inscription. The novel's greatest force, then, is in its determination to address the prophecy she made seventeen years earlier in *Women and Economics* by looking forward to a time when the modern liberal subject could shed its gender and assume its humanness.

Here perhaps is where it is worth comparing Gilman to Henry James, who, as we have seen, attempted in his late career to find a means of transcending racial, sexual, and gender differences in America. Where James sought a dual-gendered national voice that effaced corporeality, Gilman sought out a corporeality that effaced gender. In solely theoretical terms, James's voice was the more expansive of the two, as it presumably included even nonwhites and homosexuals within its linguistic parameters. Gilman's "human" liberal subject could never fully accommodate nonwhites precisely because it did not transcend corporeality. (Her greatest hope, as she explains in "A Suggestion on the Negro Problem," was that continual exposure to Anglo-Saxon civilization—not to mention compulsory military enlistment—would accelerate the evolutionary progress of American blacks.)[62] Rather, nonwhite corporeality helped define the relative sexual sameness of white men and women, especially when the prophecies of *Women and Economics* come to pass and women find the cultural license to increase their bodily strength and stamina.

If Gilman was ultimately unsuccessful in envisioning a feminist utopia, as some critics have argued, she was unable to do so because she could not expunge gendered hierarchies from her thinking and her language.[63] As a result, the novel's true pivotal figure is neither the enlightened Van nor the Herlander Ellador, but the playboy Terry, who both pushes the action forward and gives voice to the novel's greatest thematic and ideological contradictions. Terry reminds the reader, after all, that utopian literature has efficacy only through the articulation of difference, through at least implicit juxtaposition with the "real" world. For Terry—and perhaps for so many readers in 1915 or even now—the women of this mystical country are never simply "human" because of their agility and strength; since his world is circumscribed by the Symbolic Order, the Herlanders must fit into identity categories marked by difference. The Herlanders are, in Terry's nomenclature, "old Colonels," or else they are "neuters, epicenes, bloodless, sexless creatures"—alternative terms for androgynes or hermaphrodites in the early part of the twentieth century. But since we readers are also enclosed within the Symbolic Order—at least for the present evolutionary moment—we run into the same problems as the male characters. Therefore, when Van describes the women as "tall, strong, [and] healthy," we must fight our own tendency to revert back to the image of the androgyne. Given these imaginative difficulties, Terry serves as a pivotal figure. Though we may disapprove of his oversexed and insulting disposition, we unwittingly find him at times to be our hermeneutical ally since he interpellates us with a familiar nomenclature to suit our inescapably phallogocentric imagination.

Is it ever possible to escape the binary thinking inherent in the Symbolic Order? *Herland* seems to want it both ways. On the one hand, it wants to reinscribe a feminine signifying order, but on the other, it wants to transcend all gendered orders. Van himself reflects these contradictions. At first he tries simply inverting his gendered figures of speech: he remarks, "I took the bull by the horns—the cow, I should say!" (81). Van's verbal slip shows evidence of Gilman's larger groping toward a common language without gender distinctions, yet Van nevertheless shows the deep oppression of the Symbolic Order since all he is able to do is invert the binary, not erase it.[64] At a later time he strives to get beyond his gendered thinking: "When we say *men, man, manly, manhood,* and all the other masculine derivatives, we have in the background of our minds a huge vague crowded picture of the world and all its activities" (137).

Gilman's greatest fictional feat in *Herland* may not be her ability to fulfill the prophecy of gender eradication as outlined in *Women and Economics,* but rather implicitly to critique America's overwhelming reliance on gender difference and hierarchy. As a result of their conversation with the Herlanders about the country's modes of production and consumption, Van then interrogates his own national sentiments: "I had always been proud of my country, of course. Everyone is. Compared with the other lands and other races I knew, the United States of America had always seemed to me, speaking modestly, as good as the best of them" (62). Yet as the women ask simple questions about the economics of America, he finds himself "evading" certain discussions (62). Van's sheepishness is countered directly by Terry's brazen chauvinism, as he spouts a typical party line, "Ours is the best country in the world as to poverty.... We do not have the wretched paupers and beggars of the older countries, I assure you" (62). Not only do these sentiments ring false and dissatisfying in light of what the Herlanders learn about America, but they also provide the reader with Gilman's most incisive critique of American nationalist articulation.

Like humans, nations are inextricably bound up in difference. "No nation imagines itself coterminous with mankind," Benedict Anderson explains. "The most messianic nationalists do not dream of a day when all the members of the human race will join their nation."[65] By the end of the novel, only Terry is left among the men pledging his undying love for his homeland, a love intensified by his experience among people who go to great lengths to marginalize arbitrary differences. His attempted rape of Alima near the end of the novel then serves as a last-ditch effort to exhibit his masculine difference/dominance over his wife. For Gilman the rape serves as an implicit commentary on the hypermasculine aggression of America at a time when it had begun its own colonial expansion into the Caribbean and the South Seas. Though she eventually supported America's involvement in World War I, Gilman was at her core a pacifist. In fact, before committing to the war effort, she served on the organizing committee of the Women's Peace Parade along with settlement house reformer Lillian Wald and suffragist leader Carrie Chapman Catt.[66] Perhaps Gilman's most biting line of the novel comes when Van remarks, "Patriotism, red hot, is compatible with the existence of a neglect of national interests, a dishonesty, a cold indifference to the suffering of millions. Patriotism is largely pride, and very largely combativeness. Patriotism generally has a chip on its shoulder" (94). Yet for Terry, patriotism and gender are indelibly linked because each one relies on binary opposition for its existence.

If both *Women and Economics* and *Herland* anticipate a utopian future when Anglo-Saxon men and women will recognize the prevalence of their shared "human" characteristics, they concede nonetheless that Norris and Gilman's present moment was still deeply governed by androgyny and the gendered categories that serve as its ideological foundation. Indeed, as Norris's *Octopus* suggests, androgyny can be used to explain a host of national issues, ranging from economics to white cultural cohesion. Moreover, as we shall see in the next chapter on the critic John Crowe Ransom and novelist Grace Lumpkin, the concept of androgyny could be used to explain not only the country's descent into the Great Depression, but also the welfare state that might emerge to defeat it.

CHAPTER 3

Reactionary and Radical Androgyny: Two Southerners Assess the Depression-Era Body Politic

Frank Norris and Charlotte Perkins Gilman, as we have seen in the previous chapter, were heavily involved in reformulating the paradigm of the modern American liberal subject in ways that took evolutionary science's understanding of androgyny into account. For Norris especially, androgynous atavism could explain the strength and global reach of the United States' economy in the first decade of the twentieth century. Despite her belief that Anglo-Saxon evolution would one day leave behind androgyny and its attendant culturally constructed notions of masculinity and femininity, Gilman was forced to recognize that in her own time the escalation in consumption and production was responsible not only for the success of American industry, but also for the durability of American gender roles. As we shall see in the current chapter, the notion of commercial androgyny, even when stripped of its evolutionary baggage, persisted into the 1920s, and it could be used to assess economic turmoil just as easily as it had been used in previous decades to explain economic triumph.

In following the trajectory of commercial androgyny into the third and fourth decades of the twentieth century, this chapter focuses on the writings of two southerners: the conservative poet-critic John Crowe Ransom and the proletarian novelist Grace Lumpkin. I have chosen to pair them here because their ideological differences show the wide political range of writers affiliated with southern modernism. But just as important, these two authors reveal how the South's economic vulnerabilities during the 1920s and 1930s amplified the whole nation's insecurities when it came to larger questions of gender equality.

By the time Ransom and Lumpkin wrote their most famous works of social criticism, there was already a deep anxiety about what the future held for a region overwhelmed by economic desperation and marked with increasing labor agitation. The South, though having industrialized at a much slower pace than the North, nevertheless has its own unique history of labor unrest. For instance, in 1914, a major walkout at the Fulton Bag and Cotton Mill broke out in Atlanta, led in part by the president of the Ladies Auxiliary of the Order of Railroad Telegraphers, O. (Ola) Delight Smith, dubbed the "Mother Jones of Atlanta." The strike marked the first time both the American Federation of Labor and the United Textile Workers of America deployed their organizing energy into the South.[1] By the late 1920s the Alabama Communist Party had become a major source of agitation, seeking not only economic but also racial equality for workers in local textile mills. The Alabama communists remained active well into the 1940s.[2] And in 1929, the Communist Party of the United States (CPUSA) organized strikes at the Loray textile mill in Gastonia, North Carolina. In this particular instance—one that I will explore later in greater detail—the strike led to violence.

But American industrial capitalism sustained its greatest blow not at the hands of communists, but from the stock market crash of 1929. The years following the crash unleashed a torrent of anxieties that Americans felt in very material, psychological, and imaginative terms—especially in the South. It was the South, after all, that Franklin Delano Roosevelt called "the Nation's No. 1 economic problem" in the famed 1938 *Report on Economic Conditions of the South*, which was compiled by the National Emergency Council at FDR's behest.[3] The *Report* showed, for example, "that 16 percent of [southern] children enrolled in school are in high school as compared with 24 percent in States outside the South." In terms of health, pellagra was the most prominent disease of the day, made worse in the region because of widespread poverty and the subsequent lack of dietary options for many families. In terms of housing, the *Report* was especially blunt: "By the most conservative estimates, 4,000,000 southern families should be rehoused. This is one half of all families in the South."[4]

While both writers clearly sensed that capitalism's present vulnerability signaled the possibility of a radical takeover, they recognized that potential with very different attitudes. In giving voice to both their hopes and concerns, Ransom and Lumpkin regarded the South respectively as a model upon which the rest of the country could base its sense of religious and social tradition, or conversely upon which it could effect radical change. Specifically, whereas the conservative Agrarian Ransom envisioned an organic southern community as the remedy for the encroachment of a Depression-era social welfare state, fellow southerner Grace Lumpkin advocated the social welfare state as the most effective means to put the struggling South and the rest of the nation on sounder economic footing.

Moreover, each writer's notion of an American welfare state evoked the image of an androgynous body politic—a specter that horrified the conservative Ransom while intriguing, at least for a time, the radical Lumpkin. That these writers would conflate androgyny with socialism is by no means unprecedented. As Marxist historian Paul Buhle has shown, this conflation dates back to the Pennsylvania-based Ephrata community of the 1730s. The cloistered community, located west of Philadelphia, was grounded in the spiritual principles of the German mystic Jakob Böhme. Böhme himself believed in an androgynous Christ, whose female aspect he called Sophia. The Ephrata community believed that Christ/Sophia would lead followers to an earthly Eden, where a spiritual androgyny supplanted sexual polarity and where humans would live in harmony with other animals.[5]

While industrialism helped solidify the perception—if not always the reality—of the separation of spheres among the bourgeois classes in America and other western nations in the nineteenth century, it also gave rise to a whole stratum of working class women; and as Marx and Engels famously note in *The Communist Manifesto* (1848), technology in the factory had made capitalist society reassess the "intrinsic" differences between men and women: "The less the skill and exertion of strength implied in manual labour . . . the more modern industry becomes developed, the more is the labour of men superseded by that of women. Differences of age and sex have no longer any distinctive social validity for the working class."[6] The *Manifesto* bears witness to the relative interchangeability of men and women in an industrial framework, something that American writers at times also perceived. Rebecca Harding Davis's "Life in the Iron Mills" (1861), for example, details the life of the "girl-m[a]n" Hugh Wolfe, whose artistic self-representation is an androgynous-looking statue sculpted out of korl, the malleable flesh-colored dross from iron production. Labor, the message is clear, cares little for sex or social propriety. Those who can do the most amount of work for the least amount of pay get the job.[7]

If socialism was merely a theoretical abstraction for Americans and western Europeans, after the Bolshevik Revolution of November 1917, it became a reality to those in Russia. A part of the Bolsheviks' social and economic program was to recognize women's and men's political equality, as well as to employ and educate women alongside men. These measures proved inspirational to such Americans as professor Emanuel Kanter, who in 1929 published *The Amazons: A Marxian Study*. In it Kanter advocated using the legendary women warriors as a model on which to base a current-day sexual and proletarian revolution. "The Amazons," he explains, "symbolize woman's desire for freedom. They signify that there is, latent in womanhood, the primitive spirit of equality; that the warrior in woman is not yet dead; that if she [the working woman] is to attain freedom, she must rally with her class around the standard of the Proletarian Revolution."[8]

Ironically, in attempting to stop this tide of history that conflated socialism with androgyny, John Crowe Ransom sought out an androgynous synthesis of his own masculine intellect and feminine sentiment as the means to create a myth of an organic southern community based on clear social distinctions between men and women as well as whites and blacks. In ordering this community, Ransom's vision finds poetic reification in the diminutive, ultra-feminine white woman. Yet even more ironically, constantly threatening this feminine figure and the South it symbolizes is the androgynously envisioned social body, whose historical development from the economic liberalism of separate spheres to a social welfare state signifies the dissolution of gender and racial boundaries.

In many respects, the trajectory of Lumpkin's life, art, and politics moved in the opposite direction. As a young adult, Lumpkin rejected her patrician southern upbringing in favor of communism. While living in New York and circulating among fellow radicals, she commenced her literary career. *To Make My Bread,* her 1932 novel based on actual labor uprisings in the southern Appalachians, investigates what it means for women workers to envision the American body politic divided first and foremost along class lines, not along gender lines. The novel eventually comes to terms with the fact that a dual-sexed proletarian body politic is circumscribed by the same southern myths of gender polarity found in Ransom's organic southern nationalism. Thus the novel's conclusion, though championing workers' rights, anticipates Lumpkin's own return to southern conservatism by the late 1940s.

The Androgynous Godhead and the Threat of the American Welfare State

In November of 1930, almost exactly one year after the disastrous stock market crash, twelve southern men affiliated either directly or indirectly with Nashville's Vanderbilt University banded together to write a symposium decrying the devastating effects of industrial capitalism. Among the most famous of these men were the poet-critics John Crowe Ransom, Allen Tate, Robert Penn Warren, and Donald Davidson. Calling the symposium *I'll Take My Stand: The South and the Agrarian Tradition,* these self-proclaimed "Southern Agrarians" attacked industrial capitalism from all possible perspectives: economic, artistic, religious, historical, and philosophical. Though virulently anti-Marxist, the Southern Agrarians shared with Marx a terrific anxiety about economic alienation and Taylorism's negative impact on various forms of human expression, especially art, religion, and social custom.

Though the Agrarian moment was relatively short-lived, it has commanded a considerable sphere of influence that lasts to this day.[9] Yet critics have given relatively little attention to the ways in which gender pervades Agrarian thought. Primarily concerned with assessing the Agrarians' defense of the southern economy and traditions, critics have largely overlooked more "peripheral" issues, such as the relations between men and women. The concept of the "representative" southerner as developed by the Agrarians, historian W. J. Cash, and other twentieth-century southern thinkers has come with the presumption of whiteness and maleness.[10]

Yet in avoiding sustained mention of gender in their assessment of southern identity, the Agrarian "brethren" were actually speaking volumes about it. Ransom, especially during the 1930s, was deeply interested in gender constructions in much the same way that Henry James and Frank Norris were at the turn of the century. At the heart of his social criticism, I argue, is a deeper fear of the New Woman, that hallmark of modernity who demanded greater public visibility through both her consumption habits and her demands for education and professional advancement. Capitalism's precarious existence during the 1930s not only sounded a tocsin for those on the Right who feared a communist takeover, but it also exacerbated fears that a more politically active woman-citizen would enter the public arena. In other words, such economic instability would have clear resonance for a larger wave of American women who were either dissatisfied with their traditional roles as wives and mothers, or who wished to ameliorate society's social and economic ills by embracing certain aspects of a Soviet-style welfare state.

The year 1930 was transitional for Ransom. By the beginning of this new decade he had already done more than perhaps any other person to bring literary modernism to the South. This achievement dates at least as far back as 1922, the monumental year in modernism that witnessed among other things the publication of James Joyce's *Ulysses*, T. S. Eliot's *The Waste Land*, and James Weldon Johnson's edited collection *The Book of American Negro Poetry* (largely credited with catalyzing the literary component of the Harlem Renaissance). In that same year in Nashville, Ransom assembled a number of colleagues and students from Vanderbilt's English department to publish the literary magazine *The Fugitive*. The magazine's contributors and coeditors included a number of those featured in *I'll Take My Stand*, Tate, Warren, and Davidson in particular. Ransom was not only the one most responsible for the journal's creation; he also helped craft the first issue's provocative foreword, which anticipated certain gender and nationalist themes he and other Fugitives would later take up: "THE FUGITIVE flees from nothing faster than from the high-caste Brahmins of the Old South. Without raising the question of whether the blood in the veins of its editors runs red, they at any rate are not advertising it as blue; indeed, as to pedigree, they cheerfully invite the most unfavorable inference from the circumstances of their anonymity."[11] In other words, though the male authors—who all published under pseudonyms in the first few issues—might be amused by readers' speculations about their class standing, they were certain to proclaim their red-blooded American virility and their repudiation of the outmoded and effete "moonlight and magnolias" tradition that had influenced earlier generations of southern writers.

But by 1930 Ransom had turned away from publishing poetry and began writing social and religious criticism. Aside from his part in *I'll Take My Stand*, he published a full-length study on Christianity, *God Without Thunder: An Unorthodox Defense of Orthodoxy*. In their own ways, these books brought Ransom's suspicions about modernity and American radicalism face to face with his deeper concerns about the shattering of traditional gender roles. In both, the figure of the androgyne plays a significant yet very different role. Not surprisingly, for the conservative Ransom, the affirmative form of androgyny outlined in *God Without Thunder* was one that actually reinscribed a patriarchal order. The dystopian form described in "Reconstructed but Unregenerate," his contribution to *I'll Take My Stand*, was one that gave women too much control over the nation-state, hence bringing out the chaotic and self-destructive side to democracy.

In *God Without Thunder*, Ransom questions how modern western society—which he calls the Occident—interprets Christianity. In its quest for material acquisition and scientific knowledge, the Occident has chosen to put its faith in a God without thunder—that is, a benevolent God who loves His children so much that He opens up the secrets of the universe for them to exploit for their own scientific and commercial gains: "[T]he new religion," cautions Ransom, "presents God as a Great Man with all the uncertainties left out: a Great Man whose ways are scientific and knowable and whose intention is amiable and constant."[12] Consequently, Ransom argues that the West is bent on self-destruction, and he exhorts his readers to understand God as the "Orientals" (i.e., the premodern Church or the Jews of the Old Testament) once did, as a jealous God of contingency, one who could be capable of "evil as well as good" (301). "When God was pictured in the likeness of a fabulously Great Man, of marvelous technique and uncertain favor," he explains, "it was fairly difficult for one to be at ease in Zion; for his fiat was unaccountable and unpredictable; and man worshiping him was necessarily humble, and for the time being neglectful of the ordinary routine of practical life as a very vain thing" (20). Only by living in fear of God as the Orientals once did can the West reverse the course of industrial capitalism, which had fragmented traditional communities, laid waste to arts and social customs, and brought humans into interminable warfare with the natural world.

The 1925 Scopes "Monkey Trial" in nearby Dayton, Tennessee, exacerbated the social conservatism found in *God Without Thunder*. The trial became a media carnival, with the famous Chicago lawyer Clarence Darrow representing the defendant John T. Scopes and an aged William Jennings Bryan giving national visibility to the prosecution. Ransom and his Vanderbilt colleagues were angered at the press's portrayal of Dayton—and by extension the South—as a breeding ground for illiteracy and ignorance. But more than that, the trial distilled their resentment of the ways in which scientific inquiry threatened the community's religious bonds. At the heart of the matter for Ransom in particular was the fear that positivism and materialism had no limits. Already ravaged by the Civil War, the disastrous Reconstruction, strained race relations, and an economy in transition from agriculture to industry, the South as "The South" might completely dissolve if conservative Protestant religion could not sustain its cultural centrality.

Yet unlike fellow modernist T. S. Eliot, who found personal refuge from the fragmentation of modernity in Anglo-Catholicism, Ransom was not a staunch follower of any religious tradition. Talking with Robert Penn Warren in 1931, Ransom made some very curious remarks about *God Without Thunder:* "I found it very odd that I who am not a religious man, should write such a book; but I had to write it for the truth that was in it."[13] The apparent "truth" for this son and grandson of Methodist preachers was the cultural efficacy, though not the verifiable reality, of religious myth. For Ransom, religion was a social contract of sorts, one that outlined the intellectual and material advancements a community would be willing to give up for the greater good of stasis and tradition. Religious orthodoxy must prevail to prevent humans from using their free will to annihilate one another.[14]

At the center of this book stands a Godhead who has been largely understood in the Occident as implicitly masculine, but who in the author's opinion should be seen as androgynous. Remarkably, the gendered construction of Ransom's irascible Oriental god has gone unnoticed over the years, even though it has everything to do with the book's basic thrust. The God of Thunder that Ransom would like to reinstate is not the Trinitarian deity worshiped in traditional Christianity; Ransom believes that Christ is merely a demigod, and thus the two remaining components of the Trinity are the true and supreme components of the Godhead.[15] Ransom calls these co-equal figures the Mother and the Father:

> God is the Father, the masculine, cosmic, and rational Creator. But the material is the Mother, who is feminine, anarchical, and irrational. (We would add, with Plato's permission: The Father is the personification of Quantity, and the Mother is the personification of Quality.) It is upon such a Mother that God [the Father] must beget his children, the objective creatures which we know on earth as nature. They partake of the being of both the parents; and so far as biology can generalize them, in equal degrees. (300)

The Mother is for Ransom what has otherwise been known as the Holy Ghost. "It is a significant fact," he says, "that the Holy Ghost for the Old Testament authors, and for Christ himself speaking in his native Aramaic, was of the feminine gender. But this was the right gender for defending the demonic and irrational aspect of his being" (304). These musings make for a heady proclamation. In short, Ransom asserts that nature (of which humans are a part) is the metaphysical or cosmological product of a masculine and feminine Godhead. Ironically, the Godhead's phallic thunderbolts come from the feminine, irrational side of its being.

The notion of an androgynous Godhead is not original to Ransom. Elizabeth Cady Stanton, for one, had made the same argument thirty-five years earlier in 1895 with her *Woman's Bible*.[16] But whereas Stanton saw the Godhead as a divine sanctioning of sexual equality, Ransom used it to formulate a type of southern nationalism predicated upon traditional gender roles. The southern soil, which is at the ideological, spiritual, and imaginative core of both *God Without Thunder* and *I'll Take My Stand*, also partakes of the Father and Mother. The soil exists on one level as a certain quantity of atoms that can be represented by the rational—that is, masculine—abstraction of a molecular compound. Yet simultaneously, the soil's materiality (smell, texture, etc.) catalyzes a certain amount of sentiment in its cultivator. Through his daily toils on the farm he establishes a personal relationship with the soil, something that cannot be represented merely by a chemical equation. For example, in the poem "Antique Harvesters," published in the 1927 volume of poetry *Two Gentlemen in Bonds*, Ransom invokes the landscape's feminine aspect. In the first stanza, the poet asks: "what shall this land produce?" The answer, which comes at the end of the poem, is an image of a "Proud Lady" who "hath not stooped."[17] As the poem suggests, physical matter such as the soil possesses its own qualitative likeness that people can experience in infinite varieties. The Proud Lady, though old, *is* the primordial landscape, and the (presumably male) antique harvesters, made in the Godhead's androgynous image, are in touch with their feminine sides enough to experience the soil in more than just scientific or "masculine" ways.

As a mythical object of homage, the Proud Lady becomes what Anne Goodwyn Jones has called the symbolic Confederate woman, who dutifully wears Dixie's diadem. "Rather than a person," Jones remarks, "the Confederate woman is a personification, effective only as she works in others' imaginations. Efforts to join person and personification, to make self into symbol, must fail because the idea of southern womanhood specifically denies the self."[18] Not unlike Frank Norris, Ransom sees androgyny as a form of male prerogative. The male antique harvesters, mystically in touch with both their masculine rationality and feminine sensibility, cultivate from their experiences with the soil a female symbol or art object. As such, she is displaced from politics and the marketplace, standing still eternally, never disrupting the traditional order. In fact, she becomes the very embodiment of that order. In this sense, then, the Proud Lady's advanced age is not a sign of temporal decay, but rather a reminder of the vast sweep of (white) southern myth and tradition.

Ransom arrives at many of the same conclusions about gender polarity in other poems. For example, "Spectral Lovers," a poem from his 1924 volume *Chills and Fever*, presents two lovers whose desire for one another is amplified by nature:

> By night they haunted a thicket of April mist,
> Out of that black ground suddenly came to birth,
> Else angels lost in each other and fallen on earth.

> Lovers they knew they were, but why unclasped, unkissed?
> Why should two lovers be frozen apart in fear?
> And yet they were, they were.[19]

In this opening stanza, the burgeoning April landscape amplifies the virginal lovers, who are too innocently timid to take each other in a passionate embrace. The poem leaves the reader wondering how the lovers will stay "frozen" in honor while the "black ground" all around them becomes warmer and more fertile and will soon burst forth with new life. As the poem unfolds, the association between the young woman and the April landscape becomes even more distilled as the man, having finally made up his mind to seduce his love, advances toward her, "swishing the jubilant grass, / Beheading some field-flowers that had come to pass." Yet these suggestive images of defilement do not presage seduction after all. The man realizes that the aesthetic contemplation of his lover will turn to "an unutterable cinder" if he acts upon his desire.[20] The landscape therefore serves as a reminder that the lovers' relationship can be a source of fascination and pleasure only if it remains unconsummated. Moreover, the self-imposed distance that separates these spectral lovers not only enhances and sustains their love for each other, but also prompts them to endlessly ponder the sexual difference they can never explore in the flesh.

Ransom's desire to wed masculine rationality to feminine sentiment for an overarching poetic theory has its antecedents in none other than fellow cultural conservative T. S. Eliot, whose modernist masterpiece *The Waste Land* sought to "shore against [his] ruins" the "fragments" and "broken images" of an enervated western civilization.[21] Of all the figures to preside over this poem, it is the androgyne Tiresias—the prophet "throbbing between two lives / Old man with wrinkled female breasts"—who in Eliot's opinion is "the most important personage in the poem, uniting all the rest." He further explains in "Notes on 'The Waste Land'" that "[j]ust as the one-eyed merchant, seller of currants, melts into the Phoenician sailor, and the latter is not wholly distinct from Ferdinand Prince of Naples, so all the women are one woman, and the two sexes meet in Tiresias."[22] Embodying the Bergsonian notion of *durée*, the transhistorical, dual-sexed figure symbolizes the sweep of western tradition, which is constantly threatened by the disintegrating forces of modernity. Thus, John Crowe Ransom makes Tiresias's androgyny a guiding principle of his own modernist poetics, even if the Greek prophet him/herself does not ever appear in his poetry.

In "Reconstructed but Unregenerate," his contribution to *I'll Take My Stand*, Ransom barely touches on poetry and religion, but the principles in his poetics and in *God Without Thunder* obviously serve as the essay's philosophical basis. Coming at the opening of the symposium, the essay is in many ways the most general. While he claims not to miss the Old South per se, he at least misses the leisurely approach (white) southerners once took to life—one that allowed them to experience the aesthetic pleasures of the quotidian. Since the Civil War, industrial capitalism had encroached upon the South's traditions and ripped them apart.

Yet underneath Ransom's worry about capitalism was a deeper brooding about socialism. The Agrarians believed, for example, that it was through the crisis in capitalist overproduction that labor would organize to the point of melding government to the modes of production. Ironically, the Agrarians believed in the Marxist dialectical narrative of history but certainly did not condone its ends. Considering that the nation was sinking deeper and deeper into the Great Depression while the Soviet Union was reporting a surge in its economy under the first Five Year Plan, the Agrarians no doubt felt they had legitimate reason for concern. It is little wonder why Allen Tate originally proposed calling the Agrarian manifesto *Tracts Against Communism*. The manifesto's "Statement of Principles," which Ransom had a direct hand in drafting, touches on these threats, arguing that a band of "super-engineers" will "adapt production to consumption and regulate prices and guarantee business against fluctuations: they are Sovietists. . . . [T]he true Sovietists or Communists—if the term may be used here in the European sense—are the Industrialists themselves."[23] Ransom put the matter even more succinctly in a response to a claim by critic Stringfellow Barr that agrarianism was ineffectual and outmoded: "The old Southern instinct which identifies [socialism and communism,] is perfectly right in the long run. . . . Big business, which [Barr] accepts, and which every day becomes bigger business, will call for regulation, which every day will become more regulation. And the grand finale of regulation, the millennium itself of regulated industrialism, is Russian communism."[24] No doubt this threat resonated all the more in the South because it had already experienced a hostile occupation at the expense of its economy and its social and racial hierarchies.[25]

As "Reconstructed but Unregenerate" makes clear in later passages, the modern age of industrial capitalism distorts the "orthodox" view of androgyny *God Without Thunder* delineates in its depiction of the Christian Godhead. In its place is a secular male-female coupling akin to the commercial androgyny we have observed at work in Frank Norris's *The Octopus*. Ransom is afraid, however, that women will ultimately demand more than simply production in the form of reproduction. In particular, Ransom speaks of masculine and feminine forms of ambition that operate symbiotically, yet destructively, in the modern world. The masculine form of ambition manifests itself in a war against nature, and its bottom line is production. Sounding like the recollection of Henry James's visit to Chocorua Mountain in *The American Scene*, Ransom worries that men have used their intellectual grasp of chemistry, physics, and engineering to promote a pioneering spirit of progress that sees no end to this conquest. This war is sustained in large measure by an insatiable need for consumption: "If it is Adam's curse to will perpetually to work his mastery upon nature, it is Eve's curse to prompt Adam every morning to keep up with the best people in the neighborhood in taking the measure of his success. There can never be stability and establishment in a community whose every lady member is sworn to see that her mate is not eclipsed in the competition for material advantages."[26]

Yet these gendered forms never adhere categorically to men and women, an indication of commercial androgyny's centrality to the modern American economy. Their distribution "may not be without the usual exceptions" ("RU" 9). Furthermore, the blurring of the masculine and feminine impulses emerges through the irrational fears of cultural emasculation men feel at their wives' behests. In *God Without Thunder,* as a matter of fact, the impulse to consume so preoccupies men that we easily forget that consumption was once considered the exclusive realm of women. Moreover, the male consumer becomes subject time and again to the irrational sense of lack usually ascribed to women—a lack that leads him to consume more and more right alongside his wife. For Ransom, the pioneering spirit that eventually leads to a crisis in overproduction is symbiotically structured: male production and female consumption remain so dependent upon each other that a reliable gender distinction no longer exists. Whereas in *The Octopus* a man's fulfillment of lack through the acquisition of a wife and commodities signals the "natural" outcome of commercial androgyny, in Ransom's writing it leads at last to economic and social devastation.

The feminine sense of ambition goes well beyond turning men into castrated individuals who fulfill their lack through consumption. As "Reconstructed but Unregenerate" further explains:

> The feminine form is likewise hallowed among us under the name of Service. The term has many meanings, but we come finally to the one which is critical for the moderns; service means the function of Eve, it means the seducing of laggard men into fresh struggles with nature. It has special application to the apparently stagnant sections of mankind, it busies itself with the heathen Chinee, with the Roman Catholic Mexican, with the "lower" classes in our own society. Its motive is missionary. Its watchwords are such as Protestantism, Individualism, Democracy, and the point of its appeal is a discontent, generally labeled "divine." (10–11)

In essence, Ransom suggests that the feminine bourgeois devotion to "Service"—a common theme in the contemporaneous discourse of the New Woman—evolves slowly but surely into the modern welfare state. At first glance one might suspect that Ransom would be relieved if "laggard" men could find work; a strong employment rate, after all, might keep workers from organizing and rebelling. Yet Ransom is also mindful that the industrial economy will always have a surplus labor force that women will thus enjoin the state to employ. "Along with the gospel of Progress goes the gospel of Service," he explains. "They work beautifully as a team" (8). Ransom is undoubtedly referring to Progressive-era reforms, which were largely fueled by women activists such as settlement house founders Jane Addams and Lillian Wald, Women's Christian Temperance Union president Frances Willard, and Florence Kelley, the general secretary of the National Consumers League. Not surprisingly, many of these women not only promoted a broader base of gender and social progressivism (if not outright socialism), but were also women who had often been accused of being mannish and aggressive.[27]

By 1930 the South had certainly experienced its share of "service," so much of which came at the behest of northern New Women. As soon as the Civil War ended, northerners—80 percent of whom were women—went south to educate newly freed slaves under the auspices of the Freedmen's Bureau and the American Missionary Association. Around the turn of the century, northern women directed their philanthropic efforts toward white southerners as well, helping inhabitants in remote locations "preserve" their cultural traditions as well as providing them with a basic education. Vassar graduate Susan Chester, for example, founded her Log Cabin Settlement in Asheville, North Carolina, and Katherine Pettit started the Hindman Settlement School in 1902 and the Pine Mountain Settlement School in 1913. These women's intent to preserve indigenous southern culture was perhaps dubious. As well intentioned as they may have been, they more often than not created their own brand of southern culture that directly or indirectly reflected the urban middle-class values of New England.[28]

It would seem that Ransom had been hailed by cultural currents that regarded social amelioration in general as an oddly gendered ideological construct. Social historian Daniel J. Walkowitz notes:

> The decade of the 1920s is a significant historical "moment" in the production of [women] social workers' professional identities. During this decade and into the early 1930s, they developed new self-definitions in response to conflicting pressures. They had to contend with management's efforts to rationalize work and economize, with their families' expectations of a higher standard of living, and with their desires to participate in the new consumer culture.[29]

Women social workers effected these changes through the adaptation of scientific methods for treating clients. And "because objectivity and rationality were conventionally associated with male professional culture . . . , the scientific model created its own tensions for female social workers." The woman social worker not only had to play the Good Mother; she "had to adopt attributes of passionlessness and objectivity generally associated with men, traits that easily allowed others to stereotype her as desexed or androgynous."[30] By the time *I'll Take My Stand* was published at the start of the new decade, social work had changed so much as a result of the "masculine" scientific principles it accepted that it had adopted its own manual for scientific research. Moreover, the 1930 census reported employment of 31,241 social workers with seventy-six different job titles; 80 percent of the profession was female. By 1932, social work had moved into the university curricula of twenty-five different graduate degree-granting schools.[31]

The service impulse also threatened Ransom because it could abstract the South well beyond the mystical organic community he so devoutly envisioned. Yet the insidiousness of the welfare state makes that cohesive community nearly impossible to imagine because feminine service uses the masculine sense of intellect and rationality to carry out its program of uplift and reform. Under such positivist guises as sociology, history, anthropology, demography, and social work, the encroaching welfare state would demystify the South's cultural "unity," which had relied mainly on myths of white supremacy and religious conservatism to keep the bond strong.

Scholars of southern literature are fond of invoking the ideological rift between the conservative Vanderbilt Agrarians led by Ransom and the liberal academics at the University of North Carolina, led by sociology professor Howard Odum.[32] This rift developed in large part because Odum and his Chapel Hill colleagues attempted to ameliorate the poverty and racism of the South by first assessing them through the use of different empirical and abstract methods. Therefore, industrialism and the various "-ologies" would not only create a proletarian state in Ransom's view, but would also use masculine modes of science to seamlessly connect the North and the South culturally, economically, and racially. Through scientific and economic abstraction, the nascent welfare state would create an androgynous and miscegenated social body by incorporating the worst of modern masculine and feminine ambitions.

The perceived racial implications of feminine service wedded to masculine rationality were far-reaching for Ransom. At the heart of the Agrarian movement, sociologist John Shelton Reed rightly observes, was a cultural nationalism that was very much in keeping with the German romantic Johann Gottfried von Herder, whose theory of national cohesion, as mentioned in the introduction, suggested an organic immanence between the *Volk* and its native land.[33] The Agrarians' emphasis on organicism might explain, for example, Donald Davidson's reluctance to include Robert Penn Warren's essay "The Briar Patch" in *I'll Take My Stand* because it spoke of blacks' participation (albeit segregated) in southern agriculture.[34] Ransom himself is guilty of the same discomfort when it comes to the place of African Americans in the South. His essay awkwardly glosses over the issue of slavery, absurdly suggesting that the peculiar institution was "monstrous enough in theory, but, more often than not, humane in practice" ("RU" 14).

In "Reconstructed but Unregenerate" Ransom concerns himself primarily with the "vegetative aspect" of a person (6), which he asserts is the impulse to settle permanently on a piece of land, but which also implies in true Herderian fashion that white southerners spring up from their native southern soil. Of course he fudges the lines of descent in his assumption, and perhaps Warren's "Briar Patch" met such resistance among his colleagues because it reminded them that white southerners were no more indigenous to the land than the first slaves who arrived in Virginia from west Africa in 1619. Still, the racialized notion of an organic South had gained great currency by 1930. As early as the 1830s and 1840s, as talk of secession gained greater momentum, southern presses went to considerable lengths to show that "aristocratic Norman" southerners were racially distinct not only from their slaves but also from their Anglo-Saxon countrymen in the North.[35] Though making no overt claims as to the nature of northern bloodlines, *I'll Take My Stand* nonetheless stresses a difference between a northern and southern fatherland.

The inherent contradictions in Ransom's views on androgyny are, I argue, a part of his eventual turning away from Agrarianism. On the one hand, androgyny was the dreadful result of modernity, for as the American industrial economy inched closer to a full-scale economic depression by 1930, it necessitated a government intervention that put masculine rationality in the service of feminine uplift. On the other hand, androgyny in its orthodox, spiritual manifestation was the elixir for such a diseased nation-state, providing not only a belief in a Godhead half masculine and half feminine, but also enjoining individuals to see themselves as a part of the Godhead's world; like nature itself, humans are both material and spiritual, intellectual and sentimental. In both forms of androgyny, masculine intellect and feminine sentiment were present, but Ransom could never articulate just how these two constitutive elements veered off in such radically different directions. Could the intellectualizing and sentimentalizing of artistic creation really be all that different from the intellectualizing and sentimentalizing of the welfare state? When does history intercede in the formation of cultural myths? In a sense, citizens, like poetry, are made of abstract quantities and tangible qualities, and in coming to terms with these realities, Ransom seemed to have felt that he had to make a choice: either advocate the organic religious community of the South or pursue a larger query into the realm of aesthetics.

He chose the latter. By the end of the 1930s, as his interest in Agrarianism waned, he no longer even lived in the South. Unable in 1937 to agree on a sufficient salary and contract with the English department at Vanderbilt, Ransom uprooted to Kenyon College in Gambier, Ohio, and took on a dual role as professor and founding editor of the *Kenyon Review*. By this point in his career, Ransom had moved so far away from his previous religious orthodoxy that he often found himself advocating a type of philosophical pragmatism similar to that espoused a few decades earlier by William James.[36]

With this change came a deeper ambivalence about the cultural legitimacy and economic viability of the agrarian South. The shift appears in his 1936 essay entitled "What Does the South Want?," which was included in *Who Owns America? A New*

Declaration of Independence, a companion piece to *I'll Take My Stand.* This essay already marks some acquiescence to the welfare state as it had developed during the first four years of Roosevelt's New Deal. Recognizing forthrightly the incredible devastation the Great Depression had inflicted upon the South, Ransom admits to the need for a number of improvements that only a technologically advanced society and a centrally cohesive federal government could provide. While the essay's concessions do have their limits, Ransom does understand how the central government can lend support to blighted rural regions.[37] Almost as if laughing about his militancy during the earlier Agrarian years, he remarks: "The Agrarians have been rather belabored both in the South and out of it by persons who have understood them as denying bathtubs to the Southern rural population. But I believe they are fully prepared to concede the bathtubs."[38] In fact, he accepts the need for fairer income distribution, back-up employment, hospitals, paved roads, parks, and dependable plumbing, all of which are "urged nowadays by welfare workers."[39] One might be shocked to see just how much Ransom acclimated himself to the idea of the welfare state. Having once derided social scientists for breaking up the organic community, he now admonishes them much more humbly: "But I should be a little wary of the professional welfare workers, and not let them drill the population too hard in playhabits and social functions. I should give the labor community its rights and let it make the most of them."[40] In other words, he exhorts the social workers to shape up the southern laborers, but still to be gentle and let them save face by keeping some of their regional-based leisure habits intact.

In fact, by the summer of 1945, when World War II was winding to a close, Ransom had gone so far adrift from his Agrarian past that he found himself siding with none other than Frankfurt School Marxist Theodor Adorno on many issues of economy, art, and religion. As part of a symposium Ransom held with Adorno and R. P. Southard in the *Kenyon Review,* he remarked in an essay entitled "Art and the Human Economy" that yeoman agrarianism was incompatible with the modern world. Those wishing to return to it did not acknowledge that the division of labor— one of the very things he derided in "Reconstructed but Unregenerate"—was what gave artists the time to explore the "world's body" in all its rich detail. In siding with Adorno's claim that "[a]rtistic production cannot escape the universal tendency of Enlightenment," Ransom remarks that "without consenting to division of labor, and hence modern society, we should have not only no effective science, invention, and scholarship, but nothing to speak of in art."[41]

But androgyny did not disappear from his later writings. In fact, by the late 1930s Ransom had found a way to rechannel it back toward the aesthetic program he had suggested in *God Without Thunder*—only this time he left out the overt religious imperatives. For example, in his essay "The Woman As Poet," a review of Edna St. Vincent Millay's poetry that is included in the 1938 critical volume *The World's Body,* he remarks:

> [a] woman lives for love, if we will but project that term to cover all her tender fixations upon natural objects of sense, some of them more innocent and far less reciprocal than men. Her devotion to them is more than gallant, it is fierce and importunate, and cannot but be exemplary to the hardened male observer. He understands it, from his "recollections of early childhood," or at least of youth, but he has lapsed from it; or rather, in the best case, he has pursued another line of development. The minds of man and woman grow apart, and how shall we express their differentiation? In this way I think: man, at best, is an intellectualized woman. Or, man distinguishes himself from woman by intellect, but he should keep it feminized. He knows he should not abandon sensibility and tenderness, though perhaps he has generally done so.[42]

This distinction gets at the very heart of certain gender dynamics that lay hidden just under the surface of Ransom's earlier writings. Good poets, Ransom suggests, are those who find the right balance of sentiment and intellect. In this case Ransom shows no anxiety about women social workers whose masculine rationality overrides their femininity. Rather, he frets about those such as Millay, who allow their feminine poetic sentiment to override their masculine sense of discipline. Likewise, he expresses concern for the overly rational man, who gets no love from poetry and invests all his energies in the corporate or scientific world: "[N]ow that he is so far removed from the world of the simple senses, he does not like to impeach his own integrity and leave his business in order to recover it. . . . He would much prefer if it is possible to find poetry in his study, or even in his office, and not have to sit under the syringa bush" (77–78).

Ransom takes a parting shot at gender roles in the welfare state, however. In the aptly titled essay "Forms and Citizens," also included in *The World's Body*, he argues that "love" (the quotation marks are his) is only possible when men and women adhere to social customs that heighten gender differences and prevent their sexually undifferentiated animal instincts from dominating them. The male suitor "must approach [his female love object] with ceremony, and pay her a fastidious courtship. We conclude not that the desire is abandoned, but that it will take a circuitous road and become a romance" (33). As an example of a culture that has already "rationaliz[ed] and economiz[ed]" its citizens down to their baser instincts, Ransom cites Soviet Russia, where "there is less sex-consciousness . . . than anywhere in the Western world" (37). While by 1938 Ransom had come to embrace much of the New Deal's welfare programs, he nonetheless reserved some of his earlier Agrarian reticence.

Ransom's fears were no doubt grounded in the advent of the "New Soviet Woman." Soviet feminists such as Alexandra Kollontai and Lenin's wife Nadezhda Krupskaya seriously questioned what within the realm of economic production and civic participation constituted difference between men and women. Kollontai was one of the most vocal of Soviet feminists, even publishing opinions in the *Baltimore Sun* in the early decades of the twentieth century.[43] She was particularly outspoken in her advocacy of a Soviet culture that would abolish the notions of gender distinction promoted by the bourgeois patriarchal family. "In place of the individual and egotistical family," she argued, "there will arise a great universal family of workers, in which all the workers, men and women, will be above all, workers, comrades."[44] Ransom seems to wonder the same thing, though reluctantly. "I suppose," he continues, "that the loyal Russians approach the perfect state of animals, with sex reduced to its pure biological business" (37). In other words, while Ransom may believe that the differences between genders are the result of convention, they are nevertheless necessary for sustaining an enjoyment of life. Here he readily acknowledges the relative inconsequence of sex distinctions between males and females in comparison to their gender distinctions, which are governed by culture and habit. In the absence of divinely or culturally enforced gender codes, men and women must *choose* to be different, just as in an earlier moment Ransom was willing to submit to an irrational god in whom he did not personally believe. In preferring "efficient animality," which recognizes sex but not gender differences, humans are bound for a life of "perfect misery" (38).

His essay "Poets Without Laurels," also included in *The World's Body*, serves as a farewell to his overtly political phase. In it he argues that modern poets, needing to adapt to the alienation of modern life, have chosen to write poetry about subjects that are largely divorced from the political arena. The modern poem "has no moral, political, religious, or sociological values. It is not about 'res publica,' the public thing. The subject matter is trifling" (59). Among the trifles are those Wallace Stevens made famous, such as a blackbird, a Key West seascape, or a jar atop a hill in Tennessee.[45] Not surprisingly, the critical theory that would spring forth from his 1941 book *The New Criticism* was one that would champion such poetry, removed as it was from politics, history, and authorial intention.

The nascent New Critical worldview of John Crowe Ransom therefore relegated androgyny to aesthetics: men might tap into their inner woman, or women such as Edna St. Vincent Millay might tap into their inner man, but it was best done in the service of a poetry that forfeits the laurels of the polis. Given Ransom's emphasis on the need for a balance of masculine intellect and feminine sentiment, would we be correct to assume that he envisioned a gender egalitarianism that existed in the aesthetic realm, if not the political? In a 1922 letter to Allen Tate, he wrote: "I can't help believing more and more . . . that the work of art must be perfectly serious, ripe, rational, mature—full of heart, but with enough head there to govern the heart."[46] One might reasonably conclude that despite Ransom's suggestion that the best male poets are those who can tap into their "feminine" emotions, sentiment is never superior to intellect. And for that matter, femininity is never superior to masculinity.

Grace Lumpkin's Feminist-Proletarian Dilemma: Pseudo-Masculinity or Female Effacement?

When critics discuss the southern literary movements of the 1930s, talk inevitably turns to the Agrarians and/or the artistic ascendancy of William Faulkner. This tendency stems in part from the efforts of the Agrarian brethren themselves, who sought to turn their beloved South into a symbol of cultural authenticity and spiritual wholeness.[47] Critics often overlook the presence of southern writers from the Left, especially those who held out hope that the industrializing of the South might actually spark radical upheaval. Such writers include Grace Lumpkin, Fielding Burke (Olive Tilford Dargan), Myra Page, and Erskine Caldwell. Over the years, Lumpkin, Page, and Burke have fallen into relative obscurity. When literary critics take them up, they do so under the larger rubric of "Proletarian Writers" without much regard for the ways their novels of class struggle provide another dimension to modern southern literature.[48]

But understanding Grace Lumpkin in particular within the broader context of southern political writing helps bring the concerns of the Agrarians—be they legitimate or imagined—into tighter focus. Lumpkin's personal resistance to Agrarianism had far-reaching implications. It is not necessarily overstating the case to claim that she had the single most important hand in Agrarianism's downfall. As the movement gained momentum in the years immediately following the publication of *I'll Take My Stand*, various members of the group struck up a professional association with the editor Seward Collins, whose conservative *American Review* not only provided an additional outlet for the Agrarian cause, but also published favorable articles on Benito Mussolini and Adolf Hitler. In 1936, Lumpkin, by then a well-known leftist literary figure, interviewed Collins under a false identity. In the interview, which was eventually published in the proletarian periodical FIGHT *Against War and Fascism*, Collins both confirmed his ideological affinity for the Agrarians and admitted his unequivocal admiration for fascism. In the same article containing the interview, Lumpkin then concludes: "I do believe after reading a number of books like 'God without Thunder,' 'I Take My Stand' [sic], and copies of the *Southern Review* and the *American Review*, that in those who write for them . . . there is the beginning of a group that is preparing the philosophical and moral shirt-front for Fascism. . . ."[49] Despite the Agrarians' subsequent disavowal of Collins's remarks, the damage had been done.[50] Coupled with Ransom's departure for Ohio the following year, the group's public association with fascism helped sweep Agrarianism into the dustbin of history.

By developing the New Criticism in subsequent years, however, the Agrarians (namely Ransom, Tate, and Warren) may have ultimately gotten the upper hand. Barbara Foley explains that Ransom and other New Critics, in their strict critical focus on the text, "articulat[ed] a mandarin distaste for the unabashedly leftist social commitments guiding much literature and criticism produced and read in the 1930s. ... Anti-Marxism, in short, provided much of the political motivation for the formulaic critical program currently under assault by canon-busting critics."[51] If Foley's hunch is correct, the ascendancy of Ransom's New Critical method within academic circles throughout America during the 1940s, 1950s, and 1960s, may therefore have been one of the single largest factors that led to the marginalizing of the radical novel. For this reason, it is all the more important to revisit the literary contributions of Grace Lumpkin, the focus of the second part of this chapter.

Lumpkin reminds us not only of the breadth of political writing in America during the 1930s, but also that the resistance to the New Critics' apolitical approach found in the canon busting of the past few decades owes a deep debt of gratitude to proletarian literature. Indeed, Lumpkin's fiction provides a sharp counternarrative to male-dominated Agrarianism and New Criticism—and she does so as much through a focus on gender as she does through class. In fact, androgyny appears in her most famous novel, *To Make My Bread*, in ways that implicitly respond not only to Ransom's fears of a welfare state predicated on a dual-sexed body politic, but also to the larger ideological conflation of androgyny and radicalism.

Yet, while Lumpkin sought out a way to fuse feminism with proletarian liberation in her novel, she encountered the daunting complexities involved in giving equal voice to gender and class concerns. The personal difficulty women authors encountered in striking that balance roughly mirrored the larger difficulty the Left (particularly the CPUSA) had in doing so throughout the first half of the twentieth century. Indeed, the American Left's commitment to feminism was very contradictory. On the one hand, it created different literary outlets for proletarian women during the 1930s, such as *Working Woman* and *Woman Today*, but on the other hand, the leadership of the CPUSA was almost entirely male. In fact, Elizabeth Gurley Flynn was one of very few women ever to serve on its central committee.[52] Therefore, while the American Left recognized to some extent the particular circumstances of women's social marginalization and oppression, it tended to subsume these issues under the rubric of class struggle. The Left did so assuming that once class hierarchies dissolved, so would gender hierarchies. Thus during the 1930s the male leadership focused their energies largely on labor organizing at home and opposing the growing threat of fascism in European nations.[53]

Proletarian women faced more than intra-party dilemmas. By subsuming themselves and their personal identities under the larger rubric of class, they risked losing the kinship that they had occasionally established with women of the middle and upper classes in previous decades. For example, socialist women were just as motivated as educated upper-middle-class women to promote the passage of the Nineteenth Amendment allowing universal suffrage.[54] Already we have seen in the earlier part of this chapter how the rise of the female social worker in the Progressive Era was a severe departure from previous domestic models of womanhood. But for all the ways these educated women social workers were perceived to threaten the stability of gender boundaries, they were by and large members of the capitalist-sanctioned middle class. But the proletarian woman, with her commitment to ameliorate society not through social work but through the (possibly violent) overthrow of capitalism, presented a new challenge to inter-class female solidarity. As we shall see in Lumpkin's novel, this lack of inter-class gender solidarity is as menacing to Bonnie McClure as the isolation she begins to experience within her community of strikers.

In *To Make My Bread,* these various conflicts play themselves out through the abstract figure of the proletarian androgyne. In a world in which proletarian women such as Bonnie seek sexual liberation though class liberation, they often find themselves being cast as either pseudo-men or as one-dimensional figures, the Proletarian Mother. In choosing the first option, Bonnie runs the risk of having gendered concerns such as motherhood dismissed, but in the second, she runs the risk of being elevated to myth or symbol—just as women in Ransom's writing so often were—leaving her voiceless and ineffectual upon her proletarian pedestal. For men in the novel such as Bonnie's brother John, androgyny means weakness, not gender equality. Ultimately, the novel shows that androgyny, as it played itself out in radical discourse of the 1930s, signals not state-sanctioned gender equality, but rather male weakness or female effacement.

If the novel, as I have suggested, is conflicted in its aim to portray a strong feminist-proletarian agenda, the woman who created that novel was equally so. Grace Lumpkin came to radicalism from a bourgeois southern background, and after living out most of the 1920s and 1930s as a leftist partisan, she returned to that bourgeois lifestyle and denounced her past affiliation with radicalism. Born in Milledgeville, Georgia, in the early 1890s, she moved with her family to Columbia, South Carolina, around the turn of the century. There the young woman, along with her sister, the famed sociologist Kathrine Du Pre Lumpkin, was raised on the myths of the Confederacy, myths that were no doubt reinforced by her Civil War veteran father and her rearing in high-church Episcopalianism.[55]

After the family fell on hard times and was forced to move to the rural outskirts of Columbia, Lumpkin became more sensitive to the economic plight of the country folk, both black and white. Seizing upon an opportunity in 1925 to move to New York and work for the Quaker-sponsored journal *World Tomorrow,* she became increasingly attracted to the CPUSA. By 1928 she reached new personal heights by becoming a writer for the leading communist journal of the day, the *New Masses.* There she met some of the Left's most prominent voices, including literary editors Granville Hicks and Mike Gold, as well as Josephine Herbst, John Dos Passos, and Sherwood Anderson. In 1929, on the eve of the stock market crash, a group of workers led a walkout at the Loray textile mill in Gastonia, North Carolina. The CPUSA sent organizers there to lend support. The event was no small event in the country. Up until the strike, the Gastonia mill brought significant prosperity to the region and served as a national exemplar of southern industrial progress.[56] By the time the strike was over, the Gastonia police chief had been killed, and in retaliation so had one mill worker, Ella May Wiggins, the strikers' unofficial "balladeer." The Gastonia strike was so controversial that it served as the historical basis for six proletarian novels, including Lumpkin's *To Make My Bread*, which was published in 1932 while the nation was sinking deeper and deeper into economic chaos.[57] It was met with relative warmth among critics on the Left, even garnering the Maxim Gorky Prize for best socialist novel. By 1936, the novel's ending was adapted to the stage and appeared on Broadway for the better part of a year.[58]

Yet by the late 1930s Lumpkin had already started to turn away from communism. The reversal occurred in large part as a result of her relationship with Michael Intrator, a brash radical who was at continual odds with the CPUSA's top ranks.[59] Though Lumpkin had never officially joined the Communist Party, she was a strong believer in its tenets and organization. Yet her relationship with Intrator became so intense that it started to drive a wedge between her and many of the party regulars who despised her lover. Sometime in the late 1930s she became pregnant with Intrator's child, and upon his pressuring, she had an abortion. By the time the 1940s came around, she had joined the anticommunist Moral Re-Armament movement, which sought to achieve social justice through devotion to traditional Christian tenets. By 1953, Lumpkin's anticommunism led her to testify before the Senate Sub-Committee on Government Operations, where she stated, among other things, that the CPUSA threatened to ruin her literary career if she did not toe the official party line. Soon after, she returned to Columbia for good, still as anticommunist as ever, and a committed member of the congregation of her youth, the patrician Trinity Episcopal Church.

As the major events of Lumpkin's life suggest, the enthusiasm that led her to communism during the 1920s and 1930s was the same enthusiasm that led her away permanently by the 1940s. Lumpkin's abrupt sea change by the late 1930s may have had very much to do with her gender. Trying to write according to the demands of a male-dominated Communist Party and having an abortion at the behest of her strong-willed, hot-headed radical lover are both clear signs that for many women on the Left, gender equality was more theory than reality. And in her return to the Episcopalian church, she encountered an organization not unlike the Communist Party: both were very patriarchal, and both outlined a rigorous set of beliefs that required immense commitment.

To Make My Bread portrays the same agon between patriarchy and feminism, tradition and revolution. At the heart of the novel lies a deeper rumination on the androgyne as a mediating symbolic factor in these struggles. The novel's form has been an object of speculation for quite some time, and I argue that even the form makes an implicit commentary on the androgyne's mediating influence. In 1934, Granville

Hicks, literary editor for the *New Masses,* attempted to codify the various types of proletarian novels he had seen spring up through the 1920s and 1930s. He saw in many of these novels an attempt to give voice to a collective body, be it workers, strikers, or even the more abstract body politic. In response, Hicks formulated the parameters of the "collective" and "complex" novels. The collective novel, he maintained, "has no individual hero; some group of persons occupies in it a position analogous to that of the hero in conventional fiction." The complex novel was a little more loose in its configuration: it "has no individual hero, no one central character; but at the same time the various characters do not compose a collective entity; they may or may not have a factual relationship, but they do not have the psychological makeup that would entitle them to be called a group."[60]

Though Barbara Foley has argued that *To Make My Bread* resembles more of the proletarian bildungsroman than anything else, I argue instead that the novel more precisely resembles a combination of the complex and the collective forms.[61] For instance, *To Make My Bread* shows evidence of the complex novel insofar as it lacks a detectable main character. Rather, the novel chronicles the movement of three generations of the McClure family from the Appalachian hinterlands to the mill towns. While the mother Emma remains central to this movement, other family members maintain equal importance, even when their actions go against the family's overarching trajectory from the country to the city. For example, sons Basil and Kirk vie for the same woman, Minnie Hawkins, and then leave the family; whereas Basil moves away to educate himself according to bourgeois standards, Kirk winds up dead after confronting Minnie's other lover.

Yet the collective form still has resonance in the novel through young Bonnie and John. Very close in age, they are often described by the narrator as a single unit. Only later in the novel do they take center stage, and as the reader understands, the only way they can do so is by breaking out of their androgynous collectivity and embracing a world of polarized gender norms. In this sense, then, the novel works within a collective framework only to have that framework undercut. In so doing, *To Make My Bread* undermines the assumption that the triumph of the proletarian leads to a leveling of the sexes along with a leveling of the classes.

The novel opens in gender disarray as the widowed Emma gives birth to John while other members of the family look on in horror. Knowing that there is no other woman there to serve as midwife, Emma implores her father, Grandpap Kirkland, to serve in the midwife's place. Concerned about her father's inadequacy in this role, "she wished in herself there was a woman who would know what to do without telling. And she wished the men were where they belonged when a woman was in travail—somewhere out on the mountains or at a neighbor's."[62] This early scene serves several different purposes. First, it goes to show the McClure family's removal from modernity. Midwives had already begun to be replaced by certified male medical professionals by the time the novel begins in the year 1900.[63] More important, the scene adumbrates the significant struggles the McClure family will have over the course of the novel to come to terms with different gender expectations in a world very much in economic and social transition.

The decreasing availability of land and resources that cause the McClure family's eventual movement from rural self-sustainability to urban factory life is what Marx in *Capital* calls "primitive accumulation." For Marx, interestingly enough, primitive accumulation serves as a kind of biblical fall from innocence: "This primitive accumulation plays approximately the same role in political economy as original sin does in theology. . . . [F]rom this original sin dates the poverty of the great majority who, despite all their labor, have up to now nothing to sell but themselves, and the wealth of the few that increases constantly although they have long ceased to work."[64] Here Marx might be guilty of a certain mythical nostalgia for a precapitalist, agrarian world, and it would seem that acolytes such as Lumpkin have followed in his footsteps. Indeed, such nostalgia prompts one to sense that *To Make My Bread* comes as much from the southern "local color" tradition of Sidney Lanier and Joel Chandler Harris as it does from literary radicalism.[65] John and Bonnie's androgynous pairing during early childhood harks back to an idyllic prelapsarian Eden, a time when neither Adam nor Eve truly understood the implications of sexual distinction. (As Genesis suggests, they presumably recognize their nakedness and their different sexual anatomy only after the Fall.) The novel constantly points out Bonnie and John's collective actions. For example, during most of their Appalachian childhood they sleep together in the same bed. A little later on, they act in tandem when attempting to sacrifice a puppy after hearing a sermon about Abraham and Isaac. Their distance from the towns and factories early in the novel provides John and Bonnie a safe playground, a place where they can be "boy-girls," as Emma once calls them, with relative impunity (24).

But as John grows and becomes more aware of the world about him, he longs to become a man. As he gets older he begins to resent his oldest brother Basil, whose name, religious conservatism, and teetotaling self-righteousness make him, in John's eyes, feminine. "Sometimes, big and strong as he was, Basil seemed almost like a woman. And John felt contemptuous of women and of any kind of womanish ways in a man. He was tired of having Bonnie hang around" (76). Here John realizes just how much he has been paired with Bonnie throughout his youth, yet not even Basil can be a proper masculine role model.

In regarding Basil as "womanish" because he aspires to educated bourgeois civility, John reflects certain assumptions about class and gender that many on the Left held during the first decades of the twentieth century. As the CPUSA and its adjoining proletcult movements picked up steam through the 1920s and 1930s, the codification of a classed gender or a gendered class had begun to solidify. In her astute study of proletarian feminism *Labor and Desire*, Paula Rabinowitz observes that "[t]he prevailing verbal and visual [proletarian] imagery reveled in an excessively masculine and virile proletariat poised to struggle against the effeminate and decadent bourgeoisie. Thus the potentially revolutionary struggles of the working class were recontained within the framework of the eternal battle between the sexes found in domestic fiction."[66] This masculine posturing was part and parcel of *New Masses* editor Michael Gold's directive to fellow proletarian writers to "go left" as a new type of masculine manifest destiny. Gold's description of the ideal proletarian writer was "a wild youth of about twenty-two, the son of working-class parents, who himself works in lumber camps, coal mines, and steel mills." Much of his masculine imagery was forged in contradistinction to writers such as playwright Thornton Wilder, whose bourgeois modernism Gold typified as "a daydream of homosexual figures in graceful gowns moving archaically among the lilies."[67] Attesting to this insecurity among the working class, young John McClure most resents his brother Basil after seeing him in a stuffy, effeminate nightgown.

Though Rabinowitz makes a very cogent argument about the gendering of the proletarian and bourgeois classes, she fails to interrogate fully the larger insecurities embedded within the male proletarian writer's feminizing of the bourgeoisie. Within their own circles these writers might be able to operate on the assumption that the working class is robust and masculine, but the larger capitalist world outside the literary Left operated on a different set of assumptions that coded the managerial class as masculine. Beginning in the late nineteenth century, the telos or ideal of American manhood had become the capitalistic "self-made man" who relied only upon himself for his upward mobility into limitless realms of financial possibility. In resisting industrial capitalism throughout most of the nineteenth century, the South was late to embrace the paradigm of the self-made man. Nevertheless, as the region started to industrialize, the emerging "New South," much to John Crowe Ransom's chagrin, began to rethink its assumptions of masculinity. Therefore, the problem with the proletarian man—a problem Rabinowitz leaves largely unexplored—is that to middle-class white men he has seemed culturally emasculated. In fact, lack seems to best define the proletarian man: lack of access to capital and lack of meaningful political enfranchisement.[68] The Great Depression, while humbling millions of middle-class men who found themselves out of work, also undoubtedly exacerbated the sense of emasculation among the unemployed proletarian classes. Contrary depictions of proletarian men by Gold or others on the Left suggest an overcompensation reflex resulting in part from insecurity and anger at the ways in which capitalist ideology had circumscribed the limits of manhood to exclude the working class.

John's personal trajectory from acting as Bonnie's other half to becoming a manly labor leader therefore reveals as much as it hides—or rather, it reveals a good deal *through* what it hides. At the heart of John's aspiration for full manhood is an insecurity about his lower-class status. Earlier I mentioned that Marx envisioned primitive accumulation as a fall from innocence, and that Lumpkin's narrative envisions this fall as one into recognition of sexual differentiation. Once John moves to the mill town with his mother, Grandpap, and Bonnie, his past connection to his sister shames him. When he goes to school with the sons of the mill managers, the boys taunt John with degrading and emasculating names: "In the morning when the line [to class] was formed they satisfied themselves with such names as 'Baby,' and mimicked a baby crying. But after school they thought up other and more hateful words. 'Baby,' they called, 'you're losing your diaper,' or: 'Doctor is it a boy or a girl" (211). The bourgeois boys' recognition of John's ostensible gender indeterminacy reflects as much on his poverty as it does on his physical appearance or his reticence to brawl with them. From this point on in the novel, he works to shed the androgynous collectivity he had with Bonnie at an earlier age. The manhood he claims by the end of the novel, along with his ascension to the top ranks of labor leaders, suggest a deeper conservatism within the male radical tradition; despite the gender-egalitarian rhetoric of the American Left, the access to capital—whether by the proletariat or the bourgeoisie—was still the dominant benchmark of manhood. Under these conditions, how could proletarian feminism ever exist when it insisted on playing by the bourgeoisie's rules and definitions? Given Grace Lumpkin's movement toward political conservatism that came later in the 1930s, one may not be too surprised to find that she ended up reinscribing many of the same traditional gendered assumptions that guided both male proletarian writers and the patriarchal bourgeoisie.

On the other hand, Bonnie's trajectory from John's other-sexed complementary half to full-fledged woman is one that moves her more and more out of circles of power. Her struggles to make her voice heard magnify a larger difficulty on the part of women who participated in a communist community that continually subsumed issues of gender under those of class. In such a scenario, gender equality would only come after the fruition of a classless society. As I have suggested earlier, these are problems Lumpkin ran up against personally, first when being coerced to abort her child at the insistence of her lover-colleague Michael Intrator, and second as a woman who was coerced into spouting the party line well after she had started to question its values. The issue for Bonnie—and certainly for Lumpkin throughout most of the 1930s—was how to be a communist *and* a woman. She risked being treated by her male radical colleagues as little more than a pseudo-man. Under these assumptions, contraception, pregnancy, birth, child rearing, and child care existed only as marginal issues. The narrative recognizes these "ancillary" issues, for not only does the novel begin with a birth, but the action reaches a dramatic urgency as both agrarian and factory women are unable to care for the children they have. These crises have prompted Sylvia Jenkins Cook to remark that birth control activist Margaret Sanger, not Karl Marx, might be the true hero in radical women's fiction.[69]

It appears, then, that Lumpkin's novel takes issue not just with American radicalism's sexism, but also with a larger discourse that has historically conflated radicalism with androgyny at the expense of female subjectivities. For John, androgyny has obviously meant weakness, as if having any feminine qualities exposes his poverty and social disenfranchisement. For Bonnie, the discourse of androgynous radicalism assumes too much—or perhaps too little—because female subjectivity, as diverse as it is, can never be given full voice whenever women are expected to abide by the same class concerns as proletarian men.

Just as Labor assumes the pseudo-maleness of its constituents, so does Capital. Not long after Bonnie is old enough to start working in the textile factory alongside men, she nearly loses her job for reasons specific to her sex. When she asks for small increments of time off from work each day to nurse her baby, her foreman Mr. Burnett rebuffs her with his explanation that "If I let you, . . . I'd have to let every other woman who's got a young baby do the same" (283). Obviously, being a woman wage earner proves to be a general liability. Having no other option, she leaves her child with her mother Emma knowing full well that Emma's debilitating pellagra may prevent a consistent feeding schedule.

At this point in the novel, just when Bonnie's womanhood becomes most pronounced, John achieves his manhood. Having grown into his body and started working at the mill full time, John finds approval from the most unlikely of sources, his brother Basil. "All along I've thought of you as a child, for that was what you were—then," Basil says. "Now—now I feel that you are a man" (290). His praise proves deeply ironic. After all, John had once imagined Basil to be a prudish and effeminate poseur flopping around in a nightgown. Though his morality remains suspect, Basil has achieved the middle-class lifestyle and respectability he always desired. His marriage to a bourgeois woman has made him the most financially successful member of the McClure family. Basil's success must mean something to John, who has been forced from an early age to understand lower-class status as feminine. Despite the American Left's mockery of bourgeois virility, the bourgeois Basil mediates the bestowal of manhood in this proletarian novel. Bonnie's and John's respective ascensions to womanhood and manhood, which occur within only a few pages of each other, also provide an ironic commentary on Granville Hicks's collective novel form. The two who together make up the collective hero experience their different gender identifications at roughly the same time in the novel; for John, manhood is liberating and empowering, but for Bonnie, womanhood is tantamount to punishment.

At all times in Bonnie's life, the bourgeois gaze figures as the final arbiter of her gender identification. If on the one hand the factory managers expect her to efface all her womanly or motherly distinctions in order to keep her job, the middle-class women of the town criticize her just as harshly for being too manly. By this time in the novel, Bonnie has become increasingly involved with the formation of the textile union. In one scene, she and her aunt Ora encounter the bourgeois busybody Mrs. Fayon, who informs them of the scuttlebutt around town: "People are talking about you two. It's getting around that you want t' be like men. And people say the Bible says the women look to their houses and let men tend to the world. It's what I do"

(336). These suspicions seem especially absurd in light of the many children Bonnie has had and the lengths she goes to just to keep them all fed. Ironically, her specific activity with the union is to serve, like the real-life Ella May Wiggins before her, as the workers' unofficial balladeer, and the song that garners the most attention from the fellow workers is "The Mill Mother's Ballad," which laments the difficult choices proletarian women must make between their jobs and their children.

The exchange with Mrs. Fayon is equally revealing in how it shows the lack of solidarity between women of different classes, even when they are of the same race. In her espousal of immutable, biblically sanctioned gender roles, Mrs. Fayon is a throwback to the "Cult of True Womanhood," to use Barbara Welter's famous term, that dominated nineteenth-century notions of what constituted a "lady."[70] Should we ever expect her to relate to Bonnie based on the clear signs of Bonnie's irrepressible womanhood—that is, her many children—we find that she cannot. For Mrs. Fayon, Bonnie's identity as a woman comes second to her role as an economic producer. Thus this lack of solidarity between women of different classes not only exposes the class bias of the separate spheres doctrine, but it also shows that in the eyes of both Capital *and* Labor, working-class women are not really considered women at all.

In this respect, Lumpkin's novel amplifies certain class themes in Charlotte Perkins Gilman's *Herland*. For example, after hearing about all the industry that thrives in Herland, the playboy Terry explains to his tutor Zava that women in his own country do not as a general rule participate in forms of economic production. "The men do everything, with us," he explains (61). But after deeper probing by the Herlanders he concedes that the poor women of America work—about seven or eight million poor women work, Jeff then adds. But what the concession boils down to is the basic difference between Mrs. Fayon and Bonnie, the difference between a "lady" and a poor working woman. But even more, both novels reveal the historical reality of American industrial capitalism, which began in the early 1800s with the poor women of Lowell, Massachusetts, who became the employees of choice for the growing textile industry because they could be paid less than men. The poor women who populated these mills provided the very profits that made the separation of spheres possible for bourgeois ladies, who could then claim a biblical rationale for their place inside the well-furnished home.

The difficulty Grace Lumpkin encounters in *To Make My Bread*, then, is how, if ever, to reconcile womanhood with production without losing sight of her potential reproductive capabilities and desires. Such difficulties were certainly widespread among women proletarian writers. Yet the American Left's answer to such a dilemma was indeed a curious one. As the radical movement moved from its Third Period around the mid-1930s to the Popular Front era, a certain image of the proletarian woman gained greater iconographic prominence. The Popular Front was characterized, in part, by the Left's willingness to accommodate other, more mainstream movements of American liberalism in an effort to fight Italian, German, and Spanish fascism. The image of woman that came out of this phase was the "Great Mother," a figure who could nurture the nascent (male) working masses and who could symbolically protect them from the totalitarian militancy of fascist regimes abroad.[71] A proletarian poem by H. H. Lewis, deceptively titled "The Man from Moscow," shows the pervasiveness of the Great Mother even before the advent of the Popular Front: "The American workingclass is a big-boned working-woman / Muscled like a man, / Simple-hearted, direct and vulgar, / Sweaty and stinking from the vulgarity of it,— / An Amazon / With great waddling dugs and obscene capabilities."[72] Published in 1932, the same year as *To Make My Bread*, Lewis's poem shares an ideological and imagistic kinship with Frank Norris's "robust, red-armed" female embodiment of The People in his essay "Novelists of the Future." But even more to the point, Lewis's poem hints at the larger challenge: women who attempt to embody the proletarian "People" struggle to exist or resonate beyond the rugged proletarian men who imaginatively constitute or engender them.

No doubt the Great Mother also emerged in the 1930s to combat the suspicion that women socialists were somehow sexually aberrant. Indeed, the conflation between socialism and androgyny that I have briefly charted in the first part of this chapter held specific ramifications for homosexuality, thanks in large part to the famous British sexologist Edward Carpenter, who was openly homosexual (a psychical hermaphrodite) and socialist. American women socialists, regardless of their sexuality, were deeply impacted by Carpenter's 1894 *Love's Coming of Age*, which saw women's sexual oppression linked to their economic oppression and which repudiated the separate spheres ideology that often left women lonely and sexually unfulfilled.[73] Yet even those women who did not subscribe to socialism but who gathered in solidarity with other women to push for universal suffrage ran the risk of being labeled "red" or lesbian or both. As Leslie Petty has observed, "Just as women became reluctant to protest together because they could lose their jobs, America's pervasive homophobia discouraged them from creating large single-sex reform communities. Thus, the threat of association with communism and homosexuality played a large role in the demise of widespread 'acceptable' feminist activism."[74] Given these circumstances, the Great Mother's symbolic (heterosexual) fertility could deflect criticism from both socialist and nonsocialist women who were united by the Popular Front's resistance to European fascism.

As the Great Mother gained greater artistic recognition among leftists, complications plagued her arrival—many of which Lumpkin anticipates in the novel. As I explore these complications, it is worth recalling the various dilemmas John Crowe Ransom faced in maintaining—or more accurately, inventing—an organic community in his beloved South. At the heart of Ransom's religious and social commentary was a fear of the New Women and her ability to abstract the body politic into demographic fragments that threatened racial or sectional cohesion. Even as he moved away from social criticism into aesthetics, he never abandoned the mythical image of the "Proud Lady," one of his central metaphors for cultural, artistic, and spiritual unity.

Though *To Make My Bread* shows no outward sign of antifeminist backsliding, a closer look bears out a different story, one in which the patriarchal Agrarian vision voiced so adamantly by the male contributors of *I'll Take My Stand* is the darker underbelly of the socialist-feminist vision that Lumpkin ostensibly trumpets. This dark underbelly amplifies the paradigm that "[m]yth is already enlightenment, and enlightenment reverts to mythology," voiced a decade later in *Dialectic of Enlightenment* by Max Horkheimer and Ransom's *Kenyon Review* symposium partner Theodor Adorno. "Just as myths already entail enlightenment," they explain further, "with every step enlightenment entangles itself more deeply in mythology. Receiving all its subject matter from myths, in order to destroy them, it falls as judge under the spell of myth."[75] Two episodes in the novel, which convey the striking similarities between conservative southern nationalism and proletarian feminism, bear out this dialectic. These similarities suggest that, although Lumpkin was still years away from her complete rejection of Marxist historical narratives (a component of Horkheimer and Adorno's notion of "enlightenment"), she held strong affinities for images of cultural purity and southern mythology.

The first episode takes place when Grandpap and John attend a Confederate veterans' reunion in the state capital. There they listen to a young teenage girl—similar in age to Bonnie, John notes to himself—who praises the veterans for their past bravery and heroism. More than anything, this young girl functions as a reflection of the preindustrial southern patriarchy, of those men who "saved the South from the black menace" (191). This reflective quality becomes most apparent when the men "leaned forward toward her, and seemed to swallow what she said with their open mouths," suggesting that her words are really their own (188). Far from antagonistic, this girl proves to be little more than a younger manifestation of John Crowe Ransom's Proud Lady, who parrots southern patriarchal rhetoric at the expense of female subjectivity. For example, the girl exclaims, "There are those who say you thought you were right. I say you knew you were right, and through the long years the truth shall be written and remain where it belongs" (188). Apparently this young woman had personal resonance for Lumpkin, who as a child publicly paid homage to the Lost Cause each Memorial Day. Lumpkin has recalled that on that day, "dressed in white with a red ribbon sash about my middle, I would stand beside the iron fence that surrounds the grave of General Wade Hampton in the Trinity Churchyard [in Columbia] and with Daughters of the Confederacy and others looking on, recite 'Furl That Banner,' written by Father Ryan, poet-priest of the Confederacy."[76]

Though the chapter has some stark parallels to Lumpkin's childhood, it has nothing to do with advancing the plot. Rather, it serves to complicate the novel's larger themes of gender and racial cohesion, which John and Bonnie at later ages will try to forge as they lead the strikers at the textile mill. Clearly, the role of southern womanhood serves as a symbol of Herderian volkish purity and racial consolidation under a Confederate banner, much like the women-as-art-objects that Ransom envisioned in one form or another throughout his literary career. As such, the young Confederate girl stands outside the historical process, never actively participating in it. Though still young at this point in the novel, John finds himself an initiate in a prolonged rite of passage that begins with this scene and reaches its culmination later when Basil acknowledges his manhood. In listening to past tales of male heroism in battle, and with his veteran grandfather there at his side, John becomes unwittingly indoctrinated into a fraternity that uses women to symbolize the timelessness of male empowerment and racial cohesion.

It would seem that Bonnie functions in the narrative as this young woman's foil by exposing southern nationalism as little more than a strain of American cultural fascism. Yet in a second episode, which portrays her death in the closing pages of the novel, one wonders if, after all, she is really any different from the girl at the Confederate reunion. Similar to the girl and the Proud Lady, both of whom symbolize a preindustrial mythic South, Bonnie symbolizes the South through her married surname "Calhoun." Moreover, both struggle to find or maintain their own voices. While leading a chorus of workers through one of her songs, Bonnie is shot, which suggests that women labor leaders or the songs they sing cannot withstand a stronger, more determined patriarchy; and, just as the Confederate girl's symbolic value eclipses her own identity, Bonnie's death makes her into a one-dimensional symbol of labor—the Great Mother. As such, she is merely invoked by other men as they live on to lead the working masses. For example, when delivering the eulogy for his sister, John mentions her only as a rhetorical springboard for a longer tirade about the evils of private capital and the dawning of a new day when workers around the world will unite. In mentioning how "our women" (381) get beaten down by mill workers, John evidently addresses his rallying cry to only the men in the crowd. This eulogy signals the complete dissolution of John and Bonnie's androgynous collectivity in almost every sense but one. Recall in "The Woman as Poet" how John Crowe Ransom suggests that poetic creation channels masculine rationality and feminine sentiment in order to produce a balanced and complex aesthetic object. Though New Critic Ransom would no doubt criticize John's (and Lumpkin's) attempt to use Bonnie as art object for political, worldly means, John clearly subscribes to the same principles that would later inform the New Criticism in the late 1930s and early 1940s.

When the Reverend Simpkins shows up at Bonnie's gravesite to offer a prayer, his words reflect the real conundrum women face in joining any revolution that subordinates gender to class: "Death is not an aristocratic event," he proclaims. "It comes to poor and rich alike, in the mansion and in the hovel. This mill woman is not different from the man who owns the mill, for he, too, must come to the same end" (382). Though certainly not meaning to, the preacher points out the larger dilemma that the novel cannot adequately resolve: the only way a woman such as Bonnie can be equal to the "man who owns the mill" is not through socialism or labor struggle, but through death. Like socialism, death achieves democracy by transcending national, racial, and gender boundaries, but of course it does so only through the ability to silence and destroy. Ironically, though death may transcend national boundaries, it delivers Bonnie back to her native soil, an action unmistakably nationalistic, considering the link between Bonnie's fecundity and the South throughout the novel. Reverend Simpkins's words on death's democratizing power belie John's "hope and belief" in a proletarian order in which women will count equally with men (384).

In later life, after she made her "return to God," Grace Lumpkin remarked that she decided to break with the American Left after one of her trips to the South with the CPUSA to organize black sharecroppers. While there she apparently visited the graveyard where many family members were buried. She then visited a local courthouse that housed many of her family members' wills. Her visit to the courthouse to read over old wills would have no doubt reminded Lumpkin that her family, though having hit upon hard times in more recent decades, was very unlike the families depicted in her fiction. Given these differences, we might also wonder whether Lumpkin herself ultimately came to resemble her working class heroine Bonnie, or if she truly resembled the upper-middle-class Mrs. Fayon, whose reading of the Bible gave her clear instructions on how to conduct herself within her southern bourgeois milieu. Presumably under the weight of her family's prestige and tradition, Lumpkin concluded that communism was an abomination that mocked traditional religious and American values. Apparently from that point on, she never regarded radicalism with the same earnestness again.[77]

John Crowe Ransom's southern Agrarianism had already envisioned much of the world that Lumpkin ultimately sought—a world steeped in centuries of hierarchy and ritual. Those looking for Lumpkin's conservatism can find subtle indications of it in *To Make My Bread*. Written at the height of her commitment to radicalism, the novel simultaneously trumpets the future triumph of American communism while also relying heavily on traditional tropes and southern gender roles to sound that trumpet. The notion of the organic community that these two white writers hoped to retain (or really to create) was informed by the nationalism of the romantic theologian Johann Gottfried von Herder. But organic nationalism was not the exclusive ideological property of conservative white southerners—or, for that matter, even German fascist dictators. As the next chapter explains, it could be used with tremendous skill and persuasiveness by male and female progressive black writers of the urban North.

CHAPTER 4

Race, Gender, and Democratic Space in W. E. B. Du Bois and Marita Bonner

Historian Elizabeth Reis has observed that "[t]he unnerving possibility that individuals could suddenly change sex paralleled the early national preoccupation with race, racial categories, and the possibility of changing racial identity."[1] Reis offers the example of one Levi Suydam, a property-holding African American from Salisbury, Connecticut, whose crucial vote in an 1843 local election put the Whig candidate in office. In the days before the election, however, the opposing party had challenged Suydam's intention to vote, claiming he was not male. Yet a subsequent medical examination did in fact declare him male. After the election results found that Suydam's vote had actually changed the outcome of the election, the opposing party demanded another examination. This second investigation, conducted by a different physician, found the citizen to be capable of menstruation, and he was ultimately declared female. While the doctor's declaration of Suydam's distinct female sex anticipated the rejection of genital-based hermaphroditism that pervaded postbellum medical discourse, the historical record unfortunately does not indicate if the vote was invalidated, as one might suspect it would be; but as Reis suggests, the case shows the extent to which race, androgyny, and civic participation were all deeply intertwined with one another in the mid-nineteenth century.[2]

Previous chapters have explained how postbellum developments in racial science and ethnology, concurrent (or even in conjunction) with medical science's dismissal of genital-based hermaphroditism, refigured romantic androgyny into a form of devolution or congenital sickness. But the conflation of blackness and androgyny has its roots before the Civil War in, of all places, early discourses of racial uplift. As I have mentioned in the introduction, the antebellum reformist spirit, trumpeted in part by transcendentalists, held great hope for spiritual androgyny as the means by which individual members of the American nation-state could achieve greater gender and social equality. The reformist spirit, caught up as it was in abolition by the 1840s and 1850s, also saw blackness as fitting within their larger androgynous scheme of the body politic. Throughout the era, social reformers depicted male slaves as "female" insofar as they were placed in a similar subservient position as white women. Margaret Fuller's *Woman in the Nineteenth Century* makes just this case: "As the friend of the negro assumes that one man cannot by right, hold another in bondage, so should the friend of woman assume that man cannot, by right, lay even well-meant restrictions on woman. If the negro be a soul, if the woman be a soul, appareled in flesh, to one Master only are they accountable."[3] Though the passage fails to recognize that black women suffered under slavery just as much as their male counterparts (a failure that was unfortunately all too common in abolitionist rhetoric), it relies on similar transcendentalist tenets voiced ten years later by Whitman's *Leaves of Grass* that individual consciousness—male and female, black and white—was fluid and interpenetrating.

Indeed, the gender models adopted by many northeastern reformers and abolitionists were based largely on a spirit of cooperation and harmony instead of unquestioned male authority. The figure most representative of this model was Christ himself, who, according to Cynthia Griffin Wolff, "united *all* virtues, both male and female, in androgynous harmony."[4] These are the values and traits Harriet Beecher Stowe endowed in the eponymous hero of her 1852 sentimental bestseller *Uncle Tom's Cabin*. In the eyes of most readers in 1850s America, Tom's feminine passivity and religiosity contrasted sharply with the dominant white model of masculinity, which in the tense decade before the Civil War was increasingly regarded as aggressive and competitive.[5] Like Wolff, Laurie Crumpacker shows how Stowe "proposes an androgynous individual and a transformed society which provides the male or female individual with both a public and private role." Though Tom is barrel-chested, deep-voiced, and strong-willed, he also possesses certain feminine virtues such as religiosity, sentimentality, and sympathy. Cassie, Chloe, and Eliza, on the other hand, are all "strong and effective" women who defy traditional womanhood's "cardinal virtues" of passivity and submission.[6] The lesson to be learned from this novel, a sympathetic antebellum reader might surmise, is that the body politic, though increasingly severed by the issue of slavery, could be healed if men and women became more androgynous in their expressions of civic participation, religion, and human freedom.

Whatever benevolent or liberatory intentions guided Margaret Fuller's linking of black men and white women in *Woman in the Nineteenth Century* were lost in the postbellum era, as scientists made that same association when attempting to verify black men's lower place within an evolutionary and social hierarchy. By the late 1800s, scientists had formulated a "recapitulation" theory in which evolutionary trajectories from primitivism to civilization were used to classify race and sex. Such theories could be used, as I have explained in chapter 1, to show through comparisons of the clitorises of black women and white lesbians how lesbianism among white women was a sign of racial degeneracy.[7] In other instances, scientists as early as the 1860s could show that white women's low brain mass and supposed inferior brain structures were similar to those of so-called lower races. White women and black men, they specifically claimed, possessed not only smaller and more delicate crania than white men, but they also had a similar protruding jaw. Both groups were also deemed naturally impulsive and emotional, thus making them relatively incapable of abstract reasoning.[8] Under this scientific rationale, a black man's supposed hypermasculinity evinced his "femininity" insofar as Victorian gender roles encoded masculinity as rationality and self-restraint. With this in mind, the widespread notion of black men's lust for white women could mobilize further disenfranchisement of black communities while also safeguarding white men from the fear that they were somehow comparatively undersexed. Buttressed by "science," white society held the epistemological and linguistic terms under which true manhood was bestowed.[9]

The scientific conflation of blackness and androgyny also held deep implications for black women. In the late 1860s, for example, W. H. Flower and James Murie's inquiries into comparative anatomy obscured the physiological differences between black men and women based on certain bodily features found in some African Bushwomen. Among the features the two anatomists examined was an overdeveloped labia minora, which they labeled somewhat pejoratively as an "appendage."[10] For Flower and Murie, Siobhan B. Somerville argues, the enlarged labia minora "fluttered between genders, at one moment masculine, at the next moment exaggeratedly feminine.... [I]n their characterizations, sexual ambiguity delineated the boundaries of race."[11] These observations fed into later assumptions of biologists Patrick Geddes and J. Arthur Thomson, who argued in *The Evolution of Sex* (1889) that so-called primitive human beings, especially black women and lesbians, were less sexually differentiated than white heterosexual women: "[H]ermaphrodism is primitive," they claimed. "[T]he unisexual state is a subsequent differentiation. The present cases of normal hermaphrodism imply either persistence or revision."[12] These studies also figured significantly into white perceptions of black women's libidos. Whereas hypersexuality in black men often showed signs of femininity, hypersexuality in black women revealed their recidivistic masculinity.[13] This myth of the oversexed black woman resonated well into the 1920s and beyond, for Victorian notions of sexuality assumed that men naturally had strong sexual appetites, while women were naturally frigid.[14] Thus black women were more masculine insofar as they contained the sex drives usually attributed to men.

In both its pre– and post–Civil War forms, androgyny was most certainly a concept that whites—even well-meaning whites—could use to find a "suitable" place for blackness within the American body politic. The troublesome legacy of androgyny that black men and women inherited over the course of the nineteenth century was a key concern among twentieth-century black intellectuals, namely the famed sociologist W. E. B. Du Bois and Harlem Renaissance fiction writer Marita Bonner. As Du Bois attempted to formulate his theories of race, gender, and national belonging for the twentieth century, his project encountered deep contradictions rooted in these nineteenth-century imbrications of androgyny and blackness. Though he strove to provide a definition of black manhood that rejected white epistemological notions of black androgyny, he was also careful not to reject unilaterally the "white" epistemological and cultural assumptions that had comprised much of his own education and identity. The solution was to combine black manhood and nativism into a type of mystical post-Herderian nationalism that made manhood, not blood, the very basis of the black folk identity. For Du Bois, such a mystical configuration explained how certain black men could move from the rural southern fatherland to the city without falling prey to the blighted life of the inner cities, which he encoded as dangerously feminine. As we shall also see, such earnest belief in organic nationalism and male privilege situates Du Bois in much the same intellectual camp as the conservative white southerner John Crowe Ransom.

As the Harlem Renaissance gained momentum throughout the 1920s, however, artists portrayed black urbanites in ways that both affirmed and questioned the bifurcated system Du Bois had been propounding over the previous two decades. Marita Bonner, one of the most prolific short story writers of the Renaissance and post-Renaissance period, focuses her attention on the black masses of the inner city whom Du Bois had depicted as degenerately androgynous. These gender indeterminate characters not only deconstruct the system upon which Du Bois based his paradigm of black manhood, but they also establish the inner city as the true testing ground of twentieth-century democratic expression.

The Gendered Souls of Black Volk:
W. E. B. Du Bois's Curious Urban Chauvinism

In an October 1912 editorial of *Crisis*, the official publication of the National Association for the Advancement of Colored People, editor W. E. B. Du Bois remarked on the need for African American men and women to produce a new generation of educated and committed race leaders, which he famously called the "Talented Tenth": "[H]onest colored men and women" must not "bring aimless rafts of children into the world, but as many as, with reasonable sacrifice, we can train to largest manhood."[15] One of the most curious features in this passage is the implicit narrative of descent in which adult men and women presumably give birth only to male children. Despite the race leader's personal, and at times very vocal, support of women's rights,[16] his editorial nevertheless ignores the possibility that female children might come of these unions; as a result, the wife, by virtue of her gender, becomes marginalized almost to the point of nonexistence.

In Du Bois's configuration, it would seem, males beget males who beget males. Noting this elision of women in *The Souls of Black Folk* specifically, Hazel Carby remarks:

> The map of intellectual mentors [Du Bois] draws for us is a map of male production and reproduction that traces in its form, but displaces through its content, biological and sexual reproduction. It is reproduction without women, and is a final closure to Du Bois's claim to be "flesh of the flesh and bone of the bone," for in the usurpation of the birth of woman from Adam's rib, the figure of the intellectual and race leader is born of and engendered by other males.[17]

Carby's reading is informed by Benedict Anderson's notion of the imagined community, arguing that Du Bois "imagines black people as a race in ways that are conceptually analogous to imagining them as a nation."[18] Given the genealogy the race leader had formulated in *Souls* and in the 1912 editorial in *Crisis,* Carby is justified in wondering if in the imagined black nation women exist—either in theory or in the flesh. Are "woman" and "folk" therefore contradictory terms?

Du Bois implied as much by specifically using the Herderian *Volk* concept to create an ideological trajectory that linked his much-cherished rural black folk to modern city life. But making this trajectory seem plausible was a task in and of itself. A sociologist by training, he was all too aware of the troubles blacks encountered when immigrating from the rural South to the urban industrial North. As his 1899 sociological study of urban black life *The Philadelphia Negro* makes plain, the industrial city offered little for black men looking to improve themselves. In the years following the Civil War, "untrained and poorly educated" black immigrants swarmed "suddenly into the new strange life of [Philadelphia] to mingle with 25,000 of their race already there," Du Bois glumly remarks.[19] Once there, black men became enmeshed in a pattern of not only crime and poverty, but also matriarchal structures that seemed to undercut their ability to achieve political and social ascendancy. Du Bois had to confront a certain paradox: certainly the turn-of-the-century city was inhospitable to black men from the rural South, but without the artistic and intellectual cultivation that the city offered, how would they ever "train to largest manhood" and achieve their place within the ranks of the Talented Tenth? What does it take to move from the impoverished rural South—which Du Bois chauvinistically calls the "common

Fatherland"—to the heights of middle-class civility without first passing through the fire of the blighted inner city?[20]

The answer was predicated on Du Bois's implicit bifurcation of black men into what I call the black *Volk* and the black masses. As I have explained earlier in this study, the *Volk* concept originated with Johann Gottfried von Herder, the German romantic philosopher who regarded people as organically and spiritually tied to their native land and to each other. This formulation, the introduction also explains, was instrumental in the development of Emerson's and Whitman's democratic visions. Like Emerson and Whitman, Du Bois believed in transcendental qualities that served as the building blocks of the Herderian *Volk*. Du Bois, however, does not use linguistic, tribal, or racial purity as its quintessential determinant. For someone as racially mixed as he was, doing so only meant excluding himself from the top ranks of his own classification system. Instead, *untainted manhood* became the mystical, primordial element that figured most prominently in his nationalist system. Whereas the manly *Volk* innately possessed the spiritual and mental strength needed to move into the city and cultivate itself, the black masses consisted of men whose insufficient manliness made them unable to resist the economically and socially feminizing influences of the industrial city.

In order to concentrate on the more pressing distinction between those men destined to be part of the Talented Tenth and those destined for the lower ranks of black life, Du Bois had to construct a genealogy that implicitly excluded, if not women, at least femininity. Such an endeavor carried with it a purification of sorts, for Du Bois's emphasis on the manhood of the black *Volk* implies that the men who comprise the black masses are themselves tainted by femininity; and by implying that femininity is a taint of sorts, Du Bois places gender in a position usually reserved in white-supremacist discourses of evolutionary advancement for race. As Nancy Leys Stepan explains, "just as scientists spoke of races as distinct 'species,' incapable of crossing to produce viable 'hybrids,' scientists analyzing male-female differences sometimes spoke of females as forming a distinct 'species,' individual members of which were in danger of degenerating into psychosexual hybrids when they tried to cross boundaries proper to their sex."[21] In other words, if nineteenth-century evolutionary discourse's linking of black men to white women implied that sexes have races, Du Bois's insistence on making distilled masculinity the basis for his *Volk* implies that races at least have genders. In making these claims, I do not want to conflate sex traits with gender traits, for Du Bois clearly recognizes that producing the next generation of black male leaders must involve women with healthy reproductive organs. But for all the good these female sex traits do in the development of future race men, femininity, a gender trait, is another matter altogether. The ways in which Du Bois would often set up the black masses as the black *Volk*'s foil attest to the strength of the public image of the black androgyne that had developed over the better part of the previous century.

In his writings, Du Bois was as partial to grand, dramatic gestures as his contemporary Frank Norris. As with Norris, many of these gestures were imbued with an epic, nationalist fervor. What gave rise to such nationalism? One must look to Du Bois's early manhood. Having nearly no contact with his biological father, he was raised by his mother in Great Barrington, Massachusetts. He first went south in 1885 at the age of seventeen when enrolling as a student at Fisk University in Nashville, Tennessee. During his summers as an undergraduate, he taught school to the children of impoverished black farmers. These experiences among rural blacks served as the foundation for *The Souls of Black Folk*, which he wrote at the turn of the century while on the faculty as a professor of sociology and economics at Atlanta University.

Undoubtedly, the word "folk" in Du Bois's title is politically and philosophically charged. After completing his undergraduate degree at Fisk, Du Bois studied in Germany at the University of Berlin under the guidance of sociologist Max Weber, political economists Adolf Wagner and Gustav Schmoller, as well as the historian Heinrich von Treitschke, whose nationalism was borne out by his overt bigotry.[22] At the time Du Bois was there in the early 1890s, the university was in the middle of a Hegelian revival, and certainly under von Treitschke he was exposed to the German romantic tradition, which included Herder and his theories of organic nationalism.[23] Coupled with the experience among the black peasantry of the South, the introduction to German romantic nationalism left an indelible mark upon the budding black intellectual.

Du Bois's interest in the *Volk* as it was conceptualized by Herder and others would explain his penchant for speaking of peasant communities as emanating from a local, primordial soil. In *Souls of Black Folk*, for example, he explains, "Like all primitive folk, the slave stood near to Nature's heart" (210). Moreover, the book's title, for all its emphasis on the folk/*Volk*, also references another mystical concept, the soul or *Kraft*, which for Herder was the life force of a community or tribe, the transcendental spirit that gave a people its history, traditions, and sense of destiny.

But while the romantic Herder was indeed opposed to the mixing of different ethnic communities, blood and heredity alone did not constitute the foundation of his *Kraft*. The *Kraft* relied particularly on language to sustain a community's purity or homogeneity.[24] Herder's focus on language and not just biology as the source of volkish purity helps to frame Du Bois in the appropriate light, for just as Herder had to find something other than blood to culturally unite a politically fragmented Germany in the late eighteenth century when he was writing his most important works on cultural cohesion, Du Bois would have to base his black *Kraft* on something other than racial homogeneity since slavery and miscegenation had obscured, if not erased, so many African Americans' knowledge of their own origins. In the vacuum that remained, Du Bois posited manhood as the central element of purity for his black folk.

The tie between Herderian organicism and manhood may have had as much to do with Du Bois's personal experiences in Germany as with his academic study at the University of Berlin. In his autobiography, for example, he comments more than once that his time in Germany gave him the first real taste of the manhood that he felt was denied to him back in the United States: "[In Germany] I found myself on the outside of the American world, looking in," he recalls. "With me were white folk—students, acquaintances, teachers—who viewed the scene with me. They did not always pause to regard me as a curiosity, or something sub-human; I was just a man of the somewhat privileged student rank."[25] While abroad he had a number of affairs with German women, including a shop girl in Berlin named Amalie with whom he lived "more or less regularly," and while living in Eisenbach he nearly married a woman named Dora Marbach. He even grew a moustache to resemble that worn by Kaiser Wilhelm.[26]

Du Bois's masculinist-nationalist fervor carries over into "Of the Wings of Atalanta," the fifth chapter of *Souls of Black Folk*. Here he compares the newly industrialized city Atlanta, Georgia, the capital of the "New South," to the Greek mythological maiden Atalanta, who promised to marry the man who could outrun her. Knowing that the only trait greater than Atalanta's celerity was her insatiable greed, the clever Hippomenes agreed to race her, though having first placed three golden apples along the trail to slow her pace. When Atalanta reached out for the third apple along the trail, Hippomenes was able to catch up and grab her in an all-consuming embrace. "If Atlanta be not named for Atalanta," Du Bois remarks in typical grandiose style, "she ought to have been" (65). The moral of the story is that black men should not, like the female nymph, be seduced by the promise of wealth. The black masses who fall prey to such temptation are not only enveloped by the female city, but in their lack of self-control and greed, they become part female themselves.

Du Bois's penchant for coding the city as female actually has its genesis in *The Philadelphia Negro*. In this 1899 work, the author is astounded by "the growing excess of women" in the city, which he bluntly deems "abnormal."[27] He also frequently scapegoats women, noting that they are largely to blame for everything from the lack of good paying jobs for black men, to the disintegration of the family unit, to the prostitution that threatened to displace the nuclear family and undermine bourgeois values of fidelity and propriety.[28] In the nineteenth-century social imaginary, women's desire for gold and other riches was closely linked to their libidos, and the site of these associations was the metropolis, which itself became increasingly depicted as, in Rita Felski's provocative description, a "demonic femme fatale whose seductive cruelty exemplifies the delights and horrors of urban life."[29] Black men who resemble the lusty Atalanta in their ambition for gold make up the 90 percent left out of the Talented Tenth. Drawing on these familiar assumptions about the perceived prominence of feminine consumption and materialism, Du Bois portrays them as too concerned with the acquisition of goods to realize that they must first labor for them in ways that compromise their manhood.

For Du Bois, true manhood is measured by certain men's inherent aptitude to pursue Goodness, Beauty, and Truth. These three timeless virtues provide the basis for his own figuration of the mystical Herderian *Kraft*. In "Of the Wings of Atalanta," he asks:

> What if the Negro people be wooed from a strife for righteousness, from a love of knowing, to regard dollars as the be-all and end-all of life? . . . Whither, then, is the new-world quest of Goodness and Beauty and Truth gone glimmering? Must this, and that fair flower of Freedom which, despite the jeers of latter-day striplings, sprung from our father's blood, must that too degenerate into a dusty quest of gold,—into lawless lust with Hippomenes? (68)

Here Du Bois comes back to his organic metaphors, linking the abstractions of Goodness, Beauty, Truth, and Freedom to the blood of black American forefathers. At the same time, he casts the black masses' lust for gold as a type of feminine, urban, and perhaps even homosexual degeneration. By looking at Du Bois's fear of unrestrained material consumption among uneducated black men, we can understand more clearly how the commercial androgyny paradigm found in Frank Norris's evolutionary scheme is another form of white prerogative. Male economic producers such as Vanamee and Annixter are able to envelop certain "feminine" characteristics through joining their wives in consumption frenzies. Such activities nevertheless reaffirm their masculine privilege. For Du Bois's black masses, material acquisition reveals a type of androgyny that only exacerbates their cultural marginality and political disfranchisement.

While under better circumstances Du Bois may very well wish that all black men could quest after Truth, Beauty, and Goodness, his system of uplift is largely predicated on making a bogeyman of the black masses:

> [H]ow foolish to ask what is the best education for one or seven or sixty million souls! shall we teach them trades, or train them in liberal arts? Neither and both: teach the workers to work and the thinkers to think; make carpenters of carpenters, and philosophers of philosophers, and fops of fools. Nor can we pause here. We are training not isolated men but a living group of men,—nay a group within a group. And the final product must be neither a psychologist nor a brickmason, but a man. And to make men, we must have ideals, broad, pure, and inspiring ends of living,—not sordid money-getting, not apples of gold. (72)

In one moment Du Bois suggests that only intellectuals in pursuit of Goodness, Beauty, and Truth are volkish men, while in another breath he suggests that the psychologist *as well as* the brick mason are both men. In this instance, I argue, even though the passage speaks of a "group within a group," when it comes to the differences between the brick mason and the psychologist, Du Bois is now making a further distinction *among* the *Volk*. The passage nonetheless reveals a temporal progression of uplift fraught with contingencies: those in full command of their manhood such as the educated psychologist must do everything in their power to uplift other males whose aptitude for the achievement of Goodness, Beauty, and Truth is not strong.

While Du Bois therefore plans to deploy the Talented Tenth to uplift the black masses, he cannot fully assuage his fear that the latter's ambition for material goods might turn them into little more than dandified Wildean "fops." Thus, Du Bois's quarrel with antebellum perceptions of blackness does not stop at the white reformers who viewed androgyny as the gender model to which black men should aspire. In his reference to foppery, Du Bois may be leveling an indirect critique on the antebellum minstrel stage. I speak in particular of the effete character Zip Coon, the northern dandified counterpart to the oversexed southern bumpkin Jim Crow. As Eric Lott explains, "The simultaneous production and subjection of black maleness may have been more than a formal consequence of wearing blackface; it may indeed have been the minstrel show's main achievement, articulating precisely a certain structure of racial feeling."[30] In the early years of minstrelsy (mainly the 1830s), Zip Coon's urbanity and stylish clothing were portrayed as masculine assets when in the pursuit of a black woman character. But Zip Coon became more effeminate in later years, chiefly in response to the increasing tension among the black and white working classes in northeastern cities. After Zip Coon's transformation, whites could look at the character as someone inherently ill-equipped for manhood, thus assuaging their own fears that they were somehow being displaced by blacks in northern class hierarchies.[31]

Moreover, Du Bois fears the black masses might too easily fall into the trap set for them by Booker T. Washington, who, Hazel Carby points out, often comes across in *Souls* as the embodiment of black male effeminacy or "sexual compromise."[32] In Du Bois's account, Washington's 1895 "Atlanta Compromise" speech lays the groundwork for this effeminacy (if not androgyny) by suggesting that the Tuskegee founder's doctrines of accommodation and industrial training are "bound to sap the manhood of any race" (*Souls* 45). As chief accommodator, Washington appears as the photographic negative of the nobly androgynous Uncle Tom: sycophant instead of kindhearted pacifist, a rouged-up prostitute who sells himself for a simulacrum manhood based on material acquisition instead of a humble servant guided by Christian directives of love and compassion.

If Du Bois himself is the embodiment of black manhood, certainly the city must play a role in his making, for without the liberal education a city provides through a university, those who hear the call of Truth, Beauty, and Goodness might never ascend to the Talented Tenth. In the closing pages of "Of the Wings of Atalanta," Du

Bois even apotheosizes the universities of the South—both black and white institutions. His coda carries with it an implicit praise of the cities. He glorifies "Howard, at the heart of the Nation; Atlanta at Atlanta, whose ideal of scholarship has been held above the temptation of numbers. Why not here, and perhaps elsewhere, plant deeply and for all time centres of learning and living . . . ?" (71). Understood in this light, the city is the saving grace that allows volkish manhood to reach its fruition. Once again, Du Bois is taking a page from organic nationalism, specifically from Herder's *Ideas on the Philosophy of the History of Mankind*, which argues that "the difference between enlightened and unenlightened, between cultivated and non-cultivated peoples (*Völkern*) is not in kind, but only in degree."³³ In terms of Du Bois, this "difference in degree" is one not between whites and blacks in America. Instead the difference exists between those black members of the southern peasantry who are the sources of black folktales, spirituals, and dance, and the black elite such as Du Bois himself, who can use the resources of the city to bring to those folk arts a deeper aesthetic appreciation and a wider program of cultural uplift.

Even into the next decade of the twentieth century, Du Bois promoted "civilization" as the more productive rationale for race solidarity among blacks. In a 1911 editorial of *Crisis*, for example, he remarked: "So far at least as intellectual and moral aptitude are concerned, we ought to speak of civilization where we now speak of races. . . . Indeed, even the physical characteristics, excluding the skin color of a people, are to no small extent the direct result of the physical and social environment under which it is living."³⁴ But of course, as Theodore Roosevelt and his Rough Riders would attest, the pillar of civilization, especially in the opening decades of the twentieth century, is an unyielding belief in the solidity of manliness.³⁵

The above remarks from *Crisis* suggest just how uncomfortable Du Bois was in grounding "race" in immutable genetic or phenotypical terms. True, Du Bois never could entirely throw off the shackles of racial essentialism in his thinking; nevertheless, "race" and "ethnicity" had very elastic boundaries that suited Du Bois's pragmatic political needs.³⁶ In his 1940 treatise on race *Dusk of Dawn*, for example, Du Bois goes so far as to claim that what binds a race is not so much physicality, but a common heritage: "But the physical bond is least and the badge of color is relatively unimportant save as a badge; the real essence of this kinship . . . and this heritage binds together not simply the children of Africa, but extends through yellow Asia and into the South Seas. It is this unity that draws me to Africa."³⁷ Bernard R. Boxhill goes so far as to argue that Du Bois "was clear that race was not a classification given by nature or reality, but carved out by human beings to suit their purpose, which . . . was to find laws that could be used to enhance human progress."³⁸

Himself the product of African, Dutch, and French ancestry, Du Bois was in no personal position to promote racial purity as the building block of his *Volk* concept. In fact, his mitigation of racial purity clearly set him apart from prominent intellectuals and leaders such as Marcus Garvey, whose Universal Negro Improvement

Association took a more rigid stance on untainted black blood as a pillar of black nationalism.[39] Indeed, Du Bois was very conscious of his mixed ancestry in the face of racial purists. Recalling in *Dusk of Dawn* his time at the University of Berlin in the 1890s, he explains, "I can never forget that morning in the class of the great Heinrich von Treitschke in Berlin. . . . Clothed in black, big, bushy-haired, peering sharply at the class, his words rushed out in a flood: 'Mulattoes,' he thundered, 'are inferior.' I almost felt his eyes boring into me, although probably he had not noticed me. 'Sie fühlen sich niedriger!' 'Their actions show it,' he asserted. What contradiction could there be to that authoritative dictum?"[40] Once back in America, Du Bois publicly rejected von Treitschke's declarations outright. Implicitly using himself as exemplar in an essay called "Miscegenation," he claimed, "In general, the achievement of American mulattoes has been outstanding."[41] Du Bois simultaneously buys into and challenges white essentialist assumptions of racial purity and manhood; while he agrees with whites such as Theodore Roosevelt that the telos of good breeding is the creation of manhood, he also suggests that the means to that telos is not contingent upon racial purity.

Instead, as his musings on the Talented Tenth suggest, not all men—black or white—are inherently suited for the highest ranks of manhood, based as it is on the ability to cultivate Goodness, Beauty, and Truth. In fact, Du Bois's emphasis on the need for intraracial breeding among black elites stemmed from his deeper anxiety about the threatened state of black manhood.[42] For instance, Du Bois's eugenicist sympathies were evidenced by his unrelenting public advocacy of an intraracial breeding scheme in which biracial members of the Talented Tenth reproduced at a greater rate than that of poor and impoverished blacks in blighted urban areas. But if manhood is the true rationale for the *Volk*, then the lines between black and white folk are relatively inconsequential. No doubt the kinship Du Bois sometimes felt with certain whites must have shocked his fellow race men. For example, he consistently reveals pastoral nostalgia for an organic community in his writings. In *Souls of Black Folk*, as Beverly Guy-Sheftall has pointed out, he even harks back to a set of images shockingly similar to those contained in the southern plantation myth.[43] Just as the (stereo)typical white southerner might have mourned the loss of a manly agrarian ideal, so too does Du Bois: "Atlanta must not lead the South to dream of material prosperity as the touchstone of all success; already the fatal might of this idea is beginning to spread; it is replacing the finer type of Southerner with vulgar money-getters; it is burying the sweeter beauties of Southern life beneath pretence and ostentation" (*Souls* 66). These remarks—complete with the ultra-dignified British spelling of "pretense"—amount to a utopian vision of brotherhood that separates the pan-racial, genteel southern *Volk* from the black and white masses (the "vulgar") who, not in possession of full manhood themselves, find themselves engulfed and feminized by Atalanta/Atlanta.

Yet by favorably invoking the Old South, Du Bois is revealing more than nostalgia for a lapsed manhood; he is also showing the tremendous ideological flexibility of Herder's organic nationalism. Recall, for example, in the previous chapter that I explain how John Crowe Ransom used these paradigms to formulate a southern homeland which in many ways is the direct antithesis of the one envisioned by Du Bois. For Ransom (and at a later date, for Grace Lumpkin as well), organic nationalism helped to imagine southern identity as racially homogenous and guided by white supremacy. Du Bois's organic nationalism made greater allowances for not only intraracial intellectual and cultural exchanges (as his own borrowing from Herder would certainly suggest), but also intraracial coupling. Yet for all their differences, each one managed to evoke androgynous monstrosities as a way of distilling their vision of national belonging—Ransom through the figure of the welfare state and Du Bois through the abstraction of the black masses. And though Ransom propounded belief in an androgynous Godhead as a way of resisting the encroaching welfare state, he nonetheless believed, like his contemporary Du Bois, in the resilience of patriarchy.

Ironically, as the 1920s got under way, Du Bois's figuration of manly black folk met its greatest resistance not in the black masses but in the much-coveted New Negro. In fact, one of the founders of the New Negro movement was Howard University professor Alain Locke, the dandified homosexual editor of the groundbreaking anthology *The New Negro* (1925), who once described himself as "a philosophical mid-wife to a generation of younger Negro poets, writers, and artists."[44] Though Du Bois was glad to see the greater visibility of black artists in urban centers in the 1920s, he held significant reservations about any movement that prioritized art at the expense of educational and social mobility for African Americans: "If Mr. Locke's thesis [in *The New Negro*] is insisted on too much," he once cautioned, "it is going to turn the Negro renaissance into decadence."[45] Here, as in *The Souls of Black Folk*, Du Bois fears that Locke's artistic program, which he sees as guided by the decadent credo of "art for art's sake," threatens to undermine his manly Herderian program of racial uplift.

Yet perhaps the biggest threat to Du Bois's artistic aspirations came not from Wildean aesthetics, but from the disastrous marriage that took place in 1928 between his own daughter Yolande and the poet Countée Cullen. Riveted by the prospect of marrying his daughter off to the Renaissance's unofficial poet laureate, the *Crisis* editor dedicated a significant part of the June 1928 issue to the wedding, which, as Daylanne K. English explains, reads as Yolande's "wedding album, and thus her father's family album."[46] Du Bois was shocked and dismayed to find that only a year into the marriage the couple had decided to divorce for reasons of "abnormality . . . as far as other men were concerned," as Yolande described her husband's homosexuality in a letter to her father dated May 23, 1929.[47] Apparently the androgynous figures and male homoerotic scenes illustrating many of Cullen's volumes of poetry caused

Du Bois little or no concern before Yolande's wedding. Having first taken Cullen's side when news of their troubles spread shortly after the wedding, Du Bois must have been dumbfounded by this information, in no small part because he saw the young poet as the shining example of urban New Negro manhood, a surrogate son to replace the actual son, Burghardt, taken by diphtheria just before his second birthday.[48] More and more, it became evident that the Harlem Renaissance had a broader agenda in mind than cultivating manly black men according to a standard Du Bois had set.

When *The Souls of Black Folk* sought to expose "fops for fools," it seemed to have in mind black men who moved to the city for material gain, not those such as the homosexual Locke and Cullen who benefited from the city's educational and cultural resources. When not linked directly to a university, the city evoked significant dread in Du Bois, a man who was often loath to embrace the many sexual and gendered indeterminacies harbored in places such as Harlem. As Marita Bonner's fiction of the same period would insist, however, the city not only harbored these indeterminacies; it often celebrated them as the very bedrock of democracy.

Democracy and Gender Indeterminacy in Marita Bonner's Urban Spaces

The tremendous flourishing of African American art, literature, music, and dance known as the New Negro Renaissance—or now more commonly as the Harlem Renaissance—lasted throughout the decade of the 1920s and into the early to mid-1930s. The movement gave rise to some of the greatest figures in twentieth-century American literature, including Du Bois's one-time son-in-law Cullen, as well as Langston Hughes, Zora Neale Hurston, and Nella Larsen. These and other artists were indebted in large part to Alain Locke, whose essay "The New Negro" in the groundbreaking 1925 edited collection of the same name, proclaimed their birth:

> In the last decade something beyond the watch and guard of statistics has happened in the life of the American Negro and [the sociologist, the philanthropist, and the race leader] who have traditionally presided over the Negro problem have a changeling in their laps. . . . For the younger generation is vibrant with a new psychology; the new spirit is awake in the masses, and under the very eyes of the professional observers is transforming what has been a perennial problem into the progressive phases of contemporary Negro life.[49]

It is only fitting that Locke, the self-proclaimed "mid-wife" of the Harlem Renaissance, should introduce the New Negro as a "changeling . . . vibrant with a new psychology."[50] Given his direct and intense involvement in catalyzing this new movement, his announcement of a newborn to the world positions him as a dual-gendered figure—as simultaneously the proud papa and adoring, if perhaps labor-weary, mother.

The Harlem of the 1920s and 1930s often provided Locke's "changelings" with a sex-saturated environment. As Steven Watson points out, Harlem's concentration of bars, night clubs, and theaters helped give rise to the perception among both blacks and whites that blacks were "uninhibited, expressive being[s]."[51] Moreover, Harlem remained relatively untouched by various anti-vice organizations, which waged morality campaigns throughout so many other parts of the greater New York area. In 1929, an estimated 380 out of 395 Harlem nightclubs and speakeasies were affiliated with prostitution. Even upstanding members of the white community went to Harlem to find the sexual trysts (be they hetero- or homosexual) that were neither found nor tolerated in their home districts.[52]

For many of the Harlem Renaissance artists, androgyny in particular served as a thematic vehicle for artistic exploration or personal sexual liberation. Countée Cullen's volumes of poetry, for instance, contained illustrations of delicately lithe figures whose sexual distinctions were as varied and vague as their racial distinctions. As James Smethurst explains, "the illustrations seem to set rigid oppositions of black/white, male/female, but they also set up a frame of a racially and sexually androgynous eroticism that is both male and bi-sexual, where racial and sexual difference are displaced into one another or obscure the other."[53] Such figures suggest the type of sexual and gender transgression that Cullen tried so desperately to suppress through his disastrous and short-lived marriage to Du Bois's daughter. In music, blues singer Gladys Bentley—whom Langston Hughes called "large, dark [and] masculine"[54]—was a regular at the drag balls held by the Harlem Renaissance's chief white patron, the homosexual Carl Van Vechten. Her unashamed lesbianism, her subsequent marriage to a woman in a civil ceremony, and her scandalous songs about sex and sexuality made her one of Harlem's most colorful personalities.[55]

Perhaps the most overt appearance of androgyny came in the 1926 avant-garde literary magazine *Fire!!*, which ceased publication after only one issue.[56] As Watson remarks, *Fire!!* "celebrated jazz, paganism, blues, androgyny, unassimilated black beauty, free-form verse, homosexuality—precisely the 'uncivilized' features of Harlem proletarian culture that the Talented Tenth propagandists preferred to ignore."[57] Among the journal's contributors were the painter Aaron Douglas, Langston Hughes, Zora Neale Hurston, and Richard Bruce Nugent. A devotee of Wildean aesthetics, Nugent made androgyny and homosexuality a veritable staple of his writings and illustrations. His prose poem "Smoke, Lilies and Jade" proved to be one of the most striking pieces in the issue. In the story's final scene, which David Levering Lewis calls "a montage of pederasty and androgyny," the protagonist Alex visualizes a love object who morphs back and forth between his fiancée, Melva, and a delicate man he calls Beauty.[58] While the *Baltimore Sun* lambasted *Fire!!* as "Effeminate Tommyrot," the more diplomatic, but certainly disapproving, Du Bois simply limited his most enthusiastic commentary to the journal's fairly benign illustrations, drawn by Aaron Douglas.[59]

Nugent's 1933 poem "Narcissus" describes the same sex-morphing process that made its appearance a few years earlier in "Smoke, Lilies and Jade." The poem states: "And the beauty of it pained him so: / The smile so double sexed and slow: / Faint fair breasts and male torso— / Male into female seemed to flow."[60] The poem "Bastard Song," written around 1930, refers to the speaker's ambiguous sexual identity: "neither true the one nor really true the other, / . . . I must be the third."[61] These lines reveal Nugent's awareness of earlier sexological studies, such as Richard von Krafft-Ebing's *Psychopathia Sexualis,* which as we have seen referred to homosexuality as a type of psychical hermaphroditism.[62]

Marita Bonner, the focus of the second half of this chapter, also used androgyny to explore deeper themes of liberation in black urban life. Born into Boston's black bourgeoisie, Bonner was educated at Radcliffe College. And while she spent her life outside of Harlem (living instead in Boston, Chicago, and Washington, D.C.), she was one of the Renaissance's most prolific writers, having published in both the Du Bois–edited *Crisis* and the Urban League's *Opportunity.* In fact, throughout the 1920s and 1930s, she was the latter journal's most frequently published woman writer.[63] Her connection to Harlem and the New Negro Renaissance was further strengthened by her frequent attendance at Georgia Douglas Johnson's famous "S" Street salon in Washington, where she could have met any number of the movement's most famous participants, from Nugent, Cullen, and Locke to Hughes, Angelina Weld Grimké, and Du Bois himself.

Bonner's writings both accommodate and resist the ideology of the New Negro and the Talented Tenth. While she was a well-educated bourgeois urban artist, she wrote predominantly about the urban working and lower classes, and while she most certainly engages notions of the "folk" in her short stories, she resists the "folk idiom" found in more famous female Renaissance writers such as Zora Neale Hurston.[64] In another sense, her writings go with and against the grain simultaneously. Though they seem to take Du Bois's cue that the urban black masses are indeed ambiguously gendered, which the characters in her short stories show time and again, she also treats that ambiguity as a potential force of personal and communal liberation. Being a woman in an artistic movement often restricted to male cultural and intellectual advancement, Bonner used her outsider status as a springboard for a different understanding, if not dismantling, of Du Bois's nationalist sentiment. Seeing the cosmopolitan as a subset *within* the national space actually throws the privileged status of "the national" into disarray. The gender and racial fluidity that serves so often as her fiction's thematic basis deconstructs the national/global binary that undergirds modern nationalist paradigms.

Bonner's writing career began in 1925 with a short essay she published in *Crisis* entitled "On Being Young—a Woman—and Colored," which is written in the second person and employs the modernist conventions of fragmented sentences, ellipses, and dashes. Past critics have noted the essay's theoretical opposition to Du Bois, but they have largely overlooked the ways in which Bonner directly challenges or modifies the volkish fervor that fuels his paradigms of manhood.[65] At its most fundamental level, the essay is a denunciation of racial and gender stereotypes that perpetuate psychological and material deprivation. Her status as a young, educated black woman already made her a walking contradiction in the eyes of Jim Crow America. As the essay explains, her class and gender have left her painfully alienated from any sense of racial solidarity:

> All your life you have heard of the debt you owe "Your People" because you have managed to have the things they have not largely had. . . . If you have never lived among your own, you feel prodigal. Some warm untouched current flows through them—through you—and drags you out into the deep waters of a new sea of human foibles and mannerisms; of a peculiar psychology and prejudices. And one day you find yourself entangled—enmeshed—pinioned in the seaweed of a Black Ghetto.[66]

In his assessment of the Harlem Renaissance, Houston A. Baker argues that black modernism is based in large part on a "mastery of [white literary] form and a deformation of [white political] mastery."[67] On this basis, Baker readily admits Du Bois into his canon of black modernists. In the above lines, however, Bonner exhibits her own mastery of form and deformation of mastery, using Du Bois's black *Volk* as that upon which she signifies. Certainly a significant demographic change had occurred between the publications of *Souls* in 1903 and "On Being Colored" in 1925, namely the Great Migration, in which over 300,000 blacks left the South for northern and midwestern cities between 1910 and 1920 alone.[68] Yet Bonner's "immersion narrative" reflects more than a simple demographic shift; with the mysticism surrounding her phrase "untouched current" she seems to reference the Herderian *Volksgeist* or *Kraft* that Du Bois alludes to in *Souls of Black Folk*. Strangely enough, however, that spirit takes her not to the South, nor to the upper ranks of the Talented Tenth, but to Du Bois's *bête noir*, the inner city.[69]

Bonner's linking of the black *Kraft* with the inner city provides an implicit attack on Du Bois's penchant for romanticization, suggesting that the "untouched current" of blackness is more a product of an educated imagination than a reality based in the primordial soil. The *Volk*, she implies, is an inherently modern and urban construction, a version of the literary pastoral that is neither by nor about the people it represents.[70] In this sense, the attitude of *noblesse oblige* that Bonner's fellow bourgeois New Englander so ardently professed therefore appears unsound, if not outright absurd.

Critic Jennifer Margaret Wilks has suggested that this essay provides the theoretical basis for Bonner's later works by positioning race "as a contested, conditional identity, one that is socially constructed and imposed rather than biologically fixed" (84). Yet Bonner does even more than that, for "On Being Young" makes similar claims about the socially negotiated space of gender. Attempting to find an "untouched current" between the black elite and the masses is absurd enough to turn educated black women away from urban uplift altogether, yet only to find that they suffer from the same debilitating confines as those packed so tightly in the ghetto. Bonner asks:

> Why [does the world] see a colored woman only as a gross collection of desires, all uncontrolled, reaching out for their Apollos and the Quasimodos with avid indiscrimination?
> Why unless you talk in staccato squawks—brittle as seashells—unless you "champ" gum—unless you cover two yards square when you laugh—unless your taste runs to violent colors—impossible perfumes and more impossible clothes—are you a feminine Caliban craving to pass for Ariel? (5)

Partly through a haughty tone and literary allusions, Bonner decries white stereotypes that reduce black women to "uncontrolled" and indiscriminating desire. The stereotype automatically forecloses any possibility in the white imagination that an educated black woman can exist in her own right, and not as an "empty imitation" of a white woman ("On Being Colored" 5). Bonner longs to transgress societal boundaries in order to live authentically as female, black, and middle class; however, the only time white American culture sanctions these transgressions is when they conform to white notions of racial and sexual degeneration, as the reference to a female Caliban attests. Understandably, Wilks wonders why Bonner chose to reference Caliban instead of his deceased mother Sycorax, "the paradigmatic woman of color in postcolonial readings of *The Tempest*."[71] Yet I argue that the reference to Prospero's dull-witted slave is altogether fitting, considering the series of androgynous stereotypes that have dogged blackness since at least the middle of the nineteenth century. In suggesting that the African American woman is a "feminine Caliban" with uncontrolled sexual "indiscrimination," Bonner ruefully acknowledges the cultural force of the myth of the black seductress whose libido is on par with a man's. This myth of the oversexed black woman resonated well into the 1920s and beyond, for Victorian notions of sexuality assumed that men naturally had strong sexual appetites, while white women were naturally frigid.[72] Thus black women were more masculine insofar as they contained the sex drives usually attributed to men.

Having run up against the claustrophobia of the ghetto and the mental confinement of gender and racial myths, the black woman wishes to live without boundaries: "You wish yourself back where you can lay your dollar down and sit in a dollar seat to hear voices, strings, reeds that have lifted the World out, up, beyond things that have bodies and walls" (4). Notably, the music she wishes to hear is presumably classical, not jazz—attesting once again to Bonner's wish to transgress conventional class and race boundaries. Not unlike Henry James, whose early twentieth-century articles on the *vox Americana* sought out a way to transcend barriers of sexed bodies, Bonner's wish bespeaks a need to experience the larger world without the punitive limitations of a black body that at once marks her as poor, hypersexual, or simply unimportant. Bonner resigns herself to waiting for a better day, invoking a final gender-transgressive image: "Like Buddha—who brown like I am—sat entirely at ease, entirely sure of himself; motionless and knowing, a thousand years before the white man knew there was so very much difference between feet and hands. / Motionless on the outside. But on the inside? / Silent. / Still . . . 'Perhaps Buddha is a woman'" (7). The essay cuts off with this image, suggesting that the mental and physical barriers separating men from women, whites from nonwhites, and rich from poor will surely dissipate over time.

In "Nothing New," a short story published just a year later in *Crisis,* Bonner tests the plausibility of living beyond the limitations of gender and race. Specifically, the story disrupts the Du Boisian narrative of ascent by showing how gender indeterminacy dogs a bright young black man on his way from the rural South to the ranks of the Talented Tenth. At the same time it suggests that the black masses, along with other ethnic and racial masses, hold promise as the purveyors of democratic equality. The story takes place in Chicago's fictional Frye Street district, a locale that would serve as the setting for a great number of Bonner's later stories. Before the action begins, the narrative employs a metaphor that provides an ideological framework for understanding the neighborhood's gender and racial dynamics:

> There was, once on a hillside, a muddy brook. A brook full of yellow muddy water that foamed and churned over a rock bed.
> Halfway down the hillside the water pooled in the clearest pool. All the people wondered how the muddy water cleared at that place. They did not know. They did not understand. They only went to the pool and drank. Sometimes they stooped over and looked into the water and saw themselves.[73]

To make these claims, Bonner has obviously revisited and revised certain themes she had introduced a year earlier in "On Being Young." The image of the muddy water's distillation is a metaphor for the racially and ethnically diverse ghetto. "Frye Street flows nicely together. It is like muddy water. Like muddy water in a brook" (69).

Here Bonner takes the black *Kraft* to another level by first rejecting the racial purity so often embedded in volkishness, and second by acknowledging that the similarities in dwelling spaces and class status unite blacks with their German, Asian, French, and Italian neighbors. Ultimately, the muddy brook metaphor serves to subvert the binary upon which volkish purity and cohesion rests. For if in Herderian and post-Herderian circles race or ethnicity is the staple of the *Volk,* or if for Du Bois specifically, the mystical qualities of manhood are the staple, in Bonner, racial and gender heterogeneity become the basis of human "purity." In terms of the metaphor that opens "Nothing New," the muddy brook gains purity only when it settles in a pool where other muddy brooks have collected. This trajectory runs against the current, so to speak, of traditional narratives of national or tribal origins in which the individual "brooks" or *ethnies* are pure, whereas the "pools" or cities that collect them serve only as sites of contamination. Such sentiments were voiced in one form or another by a number of nativist tomes, including Charles W. Gould's *America, A Family Matter* (1922). Gould exemplifies the type of nationalism that emanated from the 1920s in which the nation is regarded as a family, and family unity therefore structures racial inclusion and attitudes. Gould states that Americanness "must come to us with the mother's milk, the baby's lisping questions, and grow with our nerves and thews and sinews until they become part and parcel of our very being."[74] Bonner's pool therefore flies in the face of the racial homogeneity implied by the family metaphor.

Frye Street is the "muddy" environment that the traditional-minded Reuben and Bessie Jackson find themselves in after having migrated from rural Georgia with their young son Denny. True to the masculinity Du Bois romantically imbues in his southern folk, Reuben worries that in this new place his sensitive son is not growing up to be a proper man. "With his oval clear brown face and his crinkled shining hair, Denny looked too—well as Reuben thought no boy should look." Denny's artistic temperament and "slender little body" project a gender indeterminacy that clearly unsettles his father, who remarks crossly one day, "Why don't you run and wrestle and race with the other boys? You must be a girl. Boys play rough and fight!" (70). Reuben's mind is surely put at ease in the next scene when Denny has his first fight. The reasons for and the consequences of Denny's fight are truly ironic, given the young boy's apparent gender liminality. One day while running along outside—as "young Frye Street, mixed as usual, raced with him" (70)—he stops just beyond the neighborhood's boundary to pick a flower for a little girl. Denny then encounters two white kids from outside the neighborhood who call him "Sissy nigger" and threaten to hurt him if he does not return to his own side (71). This epithet, Carol Allen argues, "acts as a salvo which helps to enforce . . . de facto rather than legal separation."[75] But of course the separation is as much gendered as it is racial. The slurs typify Denny's inescapable double bind in which a gesture of conventional masculinity (i.e., picking a flower for a little girl) is simultaneously, albeit unwittingly, a sign of his femininity.

At this point in the story, it is unclear whether Denny has a romantic interest in the little girl or if he simply picks the flower as a friendly gesture—or if, given his artistic temperament, he is more fascinated by the flower's appearance. Though the reasons for picking the flower may not translate as masculine to the outside world, they are still perfectly acceptable within the boundaries of Frye Street. Therefore, young Denny feels anxiety about "acting like a girl" only when people raised outside the neighborhood, such as his father or the truculent white boys, insist that such behavior is shameful. After all, Frye Street "flows nicely together" (69), as if it were a polymorphous mass riding high on its own "oceanic" exuberance.[76] The neighborhood has ultimately come together as a solid front to oppose the intolerance of the outside world, and thus Denny's subsequent victory over the white kids is not an individual one but one for the community.

Whereas in *Herland* Charlotte Perkins Gilman envisions a utopian world where gender distinctions are reduced, or almost reduced, to sex distinctions, and where any talk of androgyny is evidence of the linguistic imposition of the "outside" androcentric world, the language of gender and racial identity on Frye Street simply does not carry the negative stigma that it does beyond the neighborhood's limits. *Herland* sought a way to escape the confines of the masculine signifying order, while "Nothing New" merely seeks to show how malleable that order can be by enjoining readers to reverse their gaze and see Denny through the eyes of the fluid neighborhood, not through those of the white boys. In this sense, Bonner anticipates the poststructuralist thought of a later generation by suggesting that, at least within the boundaries of Frye Street, signifiers such as "Italian," "black," or "girl" are slippery enough *not* to be necessarily fettered by self-defeating signs.

The consequences of transgressing gender and racial categories are even greater when Denny grows older and moves out of Frye Street to attend art school—despite his father's passionate objections. Reuben feels Denny "ought to go somewhere and do some real man's work. Ain't nothin' but women paddin' up and down, worryin' about paintin'" (73). Such criticism exemplifies the bind a precocious young black man feels in wishing to make his own path in life. On the one hand, his father simply voices the Du Boisian objection that art—or more precisely, art without a political objective—will feminize Denny the way it seemed to have done to some of the Harlem Renaissance's leading male representatives. Yet on the other hand, if in the Du Boisian scheme Denny is finding his manhood through the pursuit of Truth, Beauty, and Goodness at art school, then his own father—fresh from the southern fatherland that Du Bois also praises as manly—sees manhood as bestowed by manual labor found in the cities.

Having known only racial and gender liminality inside the ghetto, Denny is unaware of the repercussions involved in dating Pauline Hammond, a young white woman at the art school. The latter half of the story roughly mirrors the first half, though now Denny does not have the safety of the polyglot neighborhood or its multiethnic children to provide solidarity. Therefore, when Allen Carter, a white art student who used to date Pauline, strikes Denny and Denny retaliates, the state, in the form of the courts and adult correctional facilities, becomes the official arbiter of safety and morality, not the neighborhood that once "sang the song of triumph" when Denny beat the white boys (72). Unleashing the pent-up anger he has felt since the incident involving the flower years earlier, Denny kills Allen and subsequently receives a death sentence. "After that," the narrative says in providing an abrupt ending to the story, "Frye Street unmixed itself. Flowed apart" (76).

While the story implicitly deconstructs the male/female binary that constitutes the basis of Du Bois's *Volk*, it also challenges the legitimacy of the narrative that outlines a black man's ascent into the ranks of the Talented Tenth. In his pursuit of Du Bois's elusive Beauty, Truth, and Goodness, Denny finds that the world beyond Frye Street does not adhere to the same fluidity of gender and racial identity. Moreover, Denny's potential career as an artist highlights Du Bois's anxiety that the Talented Tenth might degenerate into a class of fops and aesthetes.

In a 1933 issue of *Opportunity*, Bonner published "There Were Three," the first vignette in the cycle "A Possible Triad on Black Notes." Also set on Frye Street, the story suggests in its opening that racial and gender indeterminacies create the bedrock of democratic individualism. The foreword to the trilogy states:

> *Now, walking along Frye Street, you sniff first the rusty tangy odor that comes from a river too near a city; walk aside so that Jewish babies will not trip you up; you pause to flatten your nose against discreet windows of Chinese merchants; marvel at the beauty and tragic old age in the faces of the young Italian women; puzzle whether the muscular blond people are Swedes or Danes or both; pronounce old consonant names in Greek characters on shops; wonder whether Russians are Jews, or Jews, Russians—and finally you will wonder how the Negroes there manage to look like all men of every other race and then have something left over for their own distinctive black-browns.*
>
> *There is only one Frye Street. It runs from the river to Grand Avenue where the El is.*
>
> *All the World is there.*
>
> *It runs from the safe solidity of honorable marriage to all of the amazing varieties of harlotry—from replicas of Old World living to the obscenities of latter decadence—from Heaven to Hell.*
>
> *All the World is there.*[77]

Though published seven years after "Nothing New," "There Were Three" begins in a remarkably similar fashion by describing the co-minglings of Frye Street. In her deft analysis of Bonner's urban spaces, Carol Allen makes a key distinction between what she calls the local and the neighborhood: "[T]he local contains newly arrived migrants and immigrants within nuclear families that accept their roles as workers on the lowest rungs of the social ladder; on the other hand, the neighborhood represents all those practices and attitudes that resist this mechanization. What Bonner suggests is that the state directs black and immigrant citizens to certain areas, and out of these physical and psychological boundaries come the neighborhood's resisting strategies."[78] Allen's formulation usefully calls attention to the tension between the state and its various regulated communities. But as the foreword suggests, the relationship between the state and community is even more complex because of a third term, "the World." Just as Bonner deconstructs the pure/impure binary in

"Nothing New" through her metaphor of the muddy brook, she likewise dismantles popular assumptions about the national and the global. Insofar as modern nationalism relies on knowing who one is by knowing who one is not, the privileging of the national disappears in Bonner's fiction when she insists that the national is not forged in contradistinction to the global, but rather that the global constitutes the nation-state. Indeed, her postulation provides the basis of a nationalist formulation in which civic participation, not cultural or racial homogeneity, provides the key to citizenship and prosperity. If, as Frye Street shows, the neighborhood and "the World" are roughly synonymous, the national/global binary dissolves because the binary implies that the neighborhood is antithetical to the state, not a subset of it.

Although "the global" becomes the privileged term in the global/national binary, it proves to be only tentatively privileged. The foreword says as much about racial and ethnic indeterminacy as it does about revisions of nationalism. If the lines demarcating Jews from Russians, blacks from whites, or (as we shall see) men from women remain too blurry for clear demarcation, life exists in the interstices. Bonner's Frye Street inhabitants embody the "hybridity" that, as Homi K. Bhabha asserts, acknowledges a person's constantly shifting subject positions:

> The move away from the singularities of "class" or "gender" as primary conceptual and organizational categories, has resulted in an awareness of the subject positions—of race, gender, generation, institutional location, geopolitical locale, sexual orientation—that inhabit any claim to identity in the modern world. What is theoretically innovative, and politically crucial, is the need to think beyond narratives of originary and initial subjectivities and to focus on those moments or processes that are produced in the articulation of cultural differences. These "in-between" spaces provide the terrain for elaborating strategies of selfhood—singular or communal—that initiate new signs of identity, and innovative sites of collaboration, and contestation, in the act of defining the idea of society itself.[79]

Here we see some differences between Bhabha's concept of "in-between spaces" and the androgyny espoused by critic Carolyn Heilbrun, which, as I have mentioned in the introduction, came under fire during second-wave feminism for its implicit advocacy of essentialism. Whereas Heilbrun attempts to find a harmonious balance between masculine and feminine traits in individual subjects that will eventually lead to a quasi-utopian world, Bhabha figures hybridity in a more poststructuralist fashion, using such abstract poles as "male" and "female" to enact their own deconstruction. It is obvious how Bhabha's postmodern theory complements Derridean and queer theories: because human experience and identity exist in "the overlap and displacement of domains of difference," living within the interstices of national, racial, or gender labels such as "Greek," "black," "male," or "female" are only transcendental signifieds to which no one subject can completely and purely adhere.[80] In other words, one must gauge "true" identity according to one's "queerness," or by the extent to which all subjects are always already alienated from these monolithic abstractions.

Moreover, as we shall see with regard to Lucille, the protagonist of "There Were Three," racial and ethnic hybridity opens up larger questions of gender hybridity, especially for urban populations whose material and social circumstances put them at odds with the bourgeois separation of spheres. Along with her two children Robbie and Lou, Lucille lives on Frye Street, making a living by prostituting herself to men outside the neighborhood. "She was fat, but most certainly shapely and she was a violet-eyed dazzling blonde. But something in the curve of her bosom, in the swell of her hips, in the red fullness of her lips, made you know that underneath this creamy flesh and golden waviness, there lay a black man—a black woman" (102–3). In ways that would most likely abhor Henry James or John Crowe Ransom, Lucille literally embodies the hybridity and indeterminacy of which Bhabha speaks. Even more, she embodies everything that democracy theoretically attempts to embrace and represent within its purview: man and woman, black and white, rich and poor. The bounds of Lucille's gender are fairly limitless; when asked by her children about the identity of their father(s), she simply explains, "You're all mine the both of you" (102), as if to suggest that she is somehow both mother and father in more than just a figurative sense.

Bonner is careful not to idealize the family's lifestyle, which, like Lucille herself, is a mixture of highs and lows: "There were silk sheets on the beds, there was silk underwear in abundance in the bureau drawers, there were toilet waters, perfumes and flashy clothes. But sometimes there was no dinner or no breakfast" (103). This view of Lucille's household in particular and Frye Street in general shows a much more complicated view than "Nothing New," which itself runs the risk of romanticizing ghetto life. In this sense, the Frye Street of "There Were Three" provides a more accurate view of democratic possibilities and vicissitudes. Yet the neighborhood still provides the solidarity through fluidity that was evident in "Nothing New." Fearing that her children might find out what she does after taking a taxi outside of the neighborhood every night, Lucille tells her children never to leave the neighborhood while she is away. The neighborhood, in other words, protects Lucille's two children from the workings of an "outside" world that puts a premium on human exploitation and, as we shall see, boundaries enforced by violence.

The directive to stay within the confines of this fluid community is especially tempting to resist for her son Robbie, an enterprising young man whose "lithe slenderness [and] small features" suggest his inheritance of his mother's androgyny (103). Robbie learns the hard way why he must not leave Frye Street, for in defying his mother and picking up a shift as a bellhop at a posh hotel downtown, he understands that the outside world adheres to stricter gender and racial codes. In responding to a call for room service, Robbie takes a few drinks to a room only to find the man who has requested them is his mother's white john, and Lucille is there in his bed, passing for white. The scene hardens the boundaries of gender and race in Robbie's mind, for far from regarding Lucille as the parent who claims both motherly and fatherly rights over him, he now sees her as a person whose very livelihood is based on singular identities, as being only "white" and only female. At Robbie's shocked exclamation of "Mama!," the john realizes the woman he has solicited is not white, and in a rage he knocks Robbie out of the room's open window on the hotel's seventh floor (107). The story closes bleakly with an announcement of his death in the local papers, Lucille's internment in a whites-only mental asylum, and with no knowledge of Lou's whereabouts.

"Nothing New" and "There Were Three" amplify Klaus Theweleit's larger point about the modern nation-state's regulation of bodies, gender roles, and spaces. His groundbreaking *Male Fantasies* (1977) analyzes the Freikorps, the hypermasculine, anticommunist, and protofascist mercenaries who emerged in Germany after the Central Powers' humiliating capitulation at Versailles in 1919. The Freikorpsmen's anticommunism reflected a deep-seated hatred and fear of the loss of social, gender, and national boundaries. The figure that embodied this amorphousness was the "red nurse," whom the Freikorps often perceived as possessing a "vagina dentata." Simultaneously castrating and penetrating, the red nurse is violently androgynous not only because of her horrifying genitalia, but also because of her phallic rifle, which she wields with the intent of long-range penetration.[81] Most frightening for the Freikorpsmen is the growing multitude of red nurses, who, like members of Bonner's Frye Street, defy clear boundaries. The red nurses and their male cohorts constitute a "red flood" that threaten males' and states' psychic and/or physical boundaries at every turn: "The flood is abstract enough to allow processes of extreme diversity to be subsumed under its image. All they need have in common is transgression of boundaries. Whether the boundaries belong to a country, a body, decency or tradition, their transgression must unearth something that has been forbidden."[82]

As Bonner makes plain, the "outside" world resorts to violence when trying to contain the racial and gender fluidity otherwise tolerated on Frye Street. In such a case, the democratic nation-state contains the seeds of its own undoing by allowing citizens and institutions under certain circumstances to use democratic means for mobocratic ends. In fact, this is precisely Bonner's point in juxtaposing the neighborhood of Frye Street and all its vicissitudes with the "stable" urban world beyond its borders. The ghetto is not the problem in these stories; Frye Street has learned to live within the interstices of singular identities and accept racial and gender fluidity among its inhabitants. The true site of mobocratic governance is the "outside world"—the genteel art institutes, the pleasant whites-only picnic grounds, the posh downtown hotels—where the rule of law is supposed to reign supreme by ensuring a strict code of gender, sexual, racial, and class boundaries.

Bonner's reversal of the civil/mob binary suggests her sensitivity to the prevailing winds of world politics. In fact, in 1933, the same year she published "A Possible Triad on Black Notes," a new regime called the National Socialist German Workers' Party persuaded German president Paul von Hindenburg to appoint its leader, the eloquent and charismatic Adolf Hitler, to the post of chancellor. Not surprisingly, the Nazi Party was largely made up of former Freikorpsmen. For many political scientists and historians, the high tide of nationalism was the rise of the Third Reich under Hitler, the self-proclaimed *Führer des Volkes*. Ironically, the Nazi Party came to power by gaining a plurality of 230 seats in the Reichstag through none other than democratic universal suffrage by a sovereign (albeit economically and politically beleaguered) German public.

With its radical racializing of earlier Herdian nationalist doctrine, Nazi Germany pursued a path leading to the wholesale extermination of those it saw as sexually and racially impure. These actions based on ideologies of violent containment would confirm Bonner's suspicions that the most "ordered" and "pure" in society could use democratic self-determination as a means for mobocracy, just as German citizens had done in 1932. For Bonner, America had its own protofascist poisons circulating throughout the institutions of the body politic, and one cannot help but wonder if Denny, Lucille, and all their fellow hybrids in fiction and reality were her antidote. Ironically, the neighborhood might have proven to be the purest distillation of American democracy at a time when western nationalism was about to draw many nation-states into the bloodiest conflict the world has ever known.

EPILOGUE

Androgyny, Fascism, and Beyond

I began this study with Alexis de Tocqueville, whose *Democracy in America* feared that the interest in androgyny that had spread across the Atlantic Ocean from postrevolutionary France might possibly create "weak men and disorderly women" out of the young republic's male and female citizens. Democracy itself, implied the Frenchman, seemed to hang in the balance. Despite these fears, Tocqueville held out hope that the emerging economic liberalism of the mid-nineteenth century and its attendant ideology of separate spheres would prevent "so preposterous a medley of the works of nature."

Almost one hundred years later, Marita Bonner, the figure whose short stories are assessed in the pages directly preceding this epilogue, had come to radically different conclusions. For her, democracy hung in the balance when the inevitable hybridities of race, class, and especially gender were not allowed expression within the body politic. Yet as we have also seen in the previous chapter, the fascism that developed in Germany while Bonner was publishing her fiction coalesced in part against an androgynous specter, the red nurse, whose figurative vagina dentata threatened a German manhood already made vulnerable by humiliating defeat in the Great War.

Indeed, fascism, a political ideology whose extreme nationalism was predicated on a rejection of the Enlightenment's notion of the inherently rational subject,[1] provided the crescendo of an interwar era that historian Eric Hobsbawm has called the "apogee of nationalism."² In concluding this study, I wish to examine more closely the relationship that has existed between androgyny and fascism, the most extreme and violent form of western nationalism to emerge in the first half of the twentieth century. By looking at this relationship, I suggest that while on its surface androgyny challenges the hypermasculinity that so often informed fascist thought, its unintended reinscription of gender fixity makes it fascism's unwitting ally. These internal conflicts, as we shall see, have haunted androgyny well beyond fascism's demise and have likewise helped frame the debate among second-wave and postmodern feminists about the role of gender in the formulation of nationalist sentiment.

If Marita Bonner only suggests a link between brute masculinity and fascism in her short stories from the 1920s and 1930s, the British modernist Virginia Woolf makes the connection outright. Woolf's *A Room of One's Own* (1929) regarded androgyny as the antidote to the "unmitigated masculinity" ruling the fascist mindset.³ In the book's sixth chapter she recalls a time seeing a man and a woman get into a taxi together. "[W]hen I saw the couple get into the taxi-cab the mind felt as if, after being divided, it had come together again in a natural fusion. The obvious reason would be that it is natural for the sexes to co-operate. One has a profound, if irrational, instinct in favour of the theory that the union of man and woman makes for the greatest satisfaction, the most complete happiness" (101–2). The sight of the taxi and its two passengers becomes an epiphany, making Woolf realize that "in each of us two powers preside, one male and one female; and in the man's brain the man predominates over the woman, and in the woman's brain, the woman predominates over the man" (102). Thus by invoking the kind of gender complementarity also found in Plato's myth of the androgynes and in Carl Jung's contemporaneous concepts of the masculine animus and the feminine anima,⁴ Woolf makes her famous case for the "androgynous mind" (102).

In some critical respects, however, Woolf felt that the modern age had become overwhelmingly masculine. She cites as an example Benito Mussolini's Italy:

> [A]ccording to the newspapers, there is a certain anxiety about fiction in Italy. There has been a meeting of academicians whose object it is "to develop the Italian novel." "Men famous by birth, or in finance, industry or the Fascist corporations" came together the other day and discussed the matter, and a telegram was sent to the Duce expressing the hope "that the Fascist era would soon give birth to a poet worthy of it." We may all join in that pious hope, but it is doubtful whether poetry can come out of an incubator. Poetry ought to have a mother as well as a father. The Fascist poem, one may fear, will be a horrid little abortion such as one sees in a glass jar in the museum of some county town. Such monsters never live long, it is said; one has never

seen a prodigy of that sort cropping grass in a field. Two heads on one body do not make for length of life. (107)

Fascist Italy's attempt to produce a truly national literature will no doubt result in failure, Woolf contends, because male authors in Italy "are now writing with only the male side of their brains" (105). In other words, Woolf can safely surmise that the Fascists will fall short of their goal because their übermasculine, nondemocratic politics will inevitably encourage a flat, one-dimensional, übermasculine national literature.

In making these claims, Woolf both explicitly and implicitly defines masculinity and femininity. For her, masculinity consists primarily of "self-assertion" and "confidence," which, if left unchecked, will turn toward fascism or some other form of egomania (103). Gleaning exactly what Woolf means by the feminine, however, is not nearly as straightforward. Teresa Heffernan, for one, has argued that on the feminine side of Woolf's gender spectrum is death and insanity, which are both held in check by masculine qualities of control and drive.[5] I am not convinced that Woolf holds distilled femininity in quite such low regard, though it seems clear from *A Room of One's Own* that femininity must at least mean either "anonymity" or "subtlety" (her own terms) if either of these is the quality that can effectively temper masculine self-assertion (106).[6]

But Woolf need not look to Italy alone for self-assertive masculine writing; she can find those same impulses embedded in the writings of many British male authors. "The Suffrage campaign was no doubt to blame," she explains in a move that links her discussion of literature more clearly to domestic politics. "It must have roused in men an extraordinary desire for self-assertion; it must have made them lay an emphasis upon their own sex and its characteristics which they would not have troubled to think about had they not been challenged" (103). Woolf's case in point is the author "Mr. A," whose novels protest "against the equality of the other sex by asserting his own superiority" (105). The more British men such as Mr. A resisted the appeal for universal suffrage, the more their gender anxiety was reflected in their novels.

Woolf's *Three Guineas* moves beyond the literary critique of *A Room of One's Own*, denouncing "the tyranny of the Fascist state" by linking it more broadly to "the tyranny of the patriarchal state."[7] By the time this second work was published in 1938, fascism had grown beyond Mussolini's Italy into Germany and Spain, and though sexism manifested itself differently in each fascist country, as George L. Mosse and others have explained, it manifested itself deeply nonetheless.[8] For example, *Three Guineas* decries Italy and Germany's mutual insistence on the separation of spheres. This separation is "a principle which is frequently stated and approved by the dictators. Herr Hitler and Signor Mussolini have both often in very similar words expressed the opinion that 'There are two worlds in the life of the nation, the world of men and the world of women.'"⁹ In taking both of Woolf's books into account, we are able to surmise that her thoughts on androgynous literary creation suggest a more profound political analogue: an enduring national literature must have its antecedents in a nation-state that not only recognizes women's political and social equality, but that also encourages male and female citizens to become "man-womanly" and "woman-manly" respectively (*Room* 108). In other words, the androgynous mind is democracy's best hope for survival in a world increasingly threatened by more extreme versions of nationalism.

But *is* the androgynous mind the antidote to fascism, particularly if fascism and the androgynous mind both inevitably rely on certain gender dichotomies? The seven authors included in this study might provide some clues to this question, even though some of them did not live to see fascism's rise or else they did not comment directly on it. As I have suggested already, Marita Bonner, though not singling out fascism by name in her stories and nonfiction prose, regarded androgyny in much the same way as her contemporary Woolf. Appearing in print in the decades when fascist movements in Italy, Germany, and Spain were gaining tremendous strength, Bonner's writings suggest that hybridity should be the type of "purity" to which the American nation-state should aspire.

Henry James, the first author discussed in this study, died too early to see Mussolini's formation of the Fascist party in 1919 or his rise to power in 1922. Yet Woolf's concern about unbridled masculinity emerging first in Italy and later in Hitler's Germany distantly echoes the concerns James had in the first decade of the twentieth century when he returned to the United States and saw American culture immersed in industry and economic competition. This male-dominated culture compelled James to look toward the educated New Woman, herself frequently perceived as androgynous, to formulate a *vox Americana* comprised in equal measurements of masculine control and feminine charm. Still, James's hope in a disembodied voice suggests his earlier anxiety about androgyny's association with devolutionary homosexuality. In fact, these nineteenth-century sexological studies that so concerned James served as the medical basis for the Nazis' persecution of homosexuals during the 1930s and 1940s.[10]

Though living until the 1930s, Charlotte Perkins Gilman's greatest thoughts on androgyny and national destiny came from her writings of the late nineteenth and early twentieth centuries. As explained in her 1898 *Women and Economics*, androgyny is for Gilman a provisional concept, lasting only during the present evolutionary moment while Anglo-Saxon men continue to shed their primitive individualism and learn to nurture their families in much the same way mothers nurture their young. During this same evolutionary moment, Anglo-Saxon women will learn to drop their excessive and debilitating femininity. Once this evolutionary process is complete, culturally enforced gender characteristics will fall away, leaving only physiological differences between men and women, who otherwise live in complete political equality. Gilman's vision, predicated in large part on non-Marxian socialism, seems to fly in the face of fascism's emphasis on immutable masculinity and femininity. Her similarities with fascist doctrine—especially German fascist doctrine—lie more in her steadfast belief in white superiority. Too often in her writings nonwhites appear as the other against whom Gilman can create a nongendered racial solidarity among white men and women. Thus, even the escape from androgyny is built upon a strict racist hierarchy.

Frank Norris's fiction has long been linked to fascist discourse. Richard Chase, for one, proclaimed in his classic *The American Novel and Its Tradition* that novels such as *The Octopus* expose "the tension between Norris the liberal humanist and ardent democrat and Norris the protofascist, complete with a racist view of Anglo-Saxon supremacy, a myth of the superman, and a portentous nihilism."[11] More recently, Russ Castronovo has argued that *The Octopus*'s ending, which brings Anglo-Saxon wheat around the globe to the starving in India, provides an imperial aesthetics of wholeness that complements a "postfascist" aestheticization of politics. The term "postfascist" here describes not the demise of fascism by liberal democracy or socialism, but Aryan global dominance that accompanies fascism's imperial triumph over other lands. In amending Chase, Castronovo claims, "The *proto*fascist is more properly a *post*fascist who retools the aesthetic politics of unity to a global world where state channels are outmoded by the new connections of world culture."[12] Yet the basis of such connections, the novel tells us, is a life force that provides a cosmic totality linking not only East to West, but also male to female. This life force is reminiscent of Henri Bergson's *élan vital*, a spiritual concept that interested fascists Benito Mussolini and Giovanni Gentile.[13] Yet Norris's life force, for all its androgynous connectivity, privileges men over women just as it does Anglo-Saxons over other peoples.

Like Norris, John Crowe Ransom and his Agrarian brethren have come under fire for promoting pro-fascist sentiments. The charge came in part as the result of the Agrarians' occasional association throughout the early and mid-1930s with the conservative *American Review* and its openly fascist editor Seward Collins.[14] But beyond this guilt by association, the most visible link between Agrarianism and fascism is the mutual insistence on a sense of belonging rooted in the soil. Second-generation Agrarian Richard M. Weaver, for one, even admitted that white southerners, believing in both "the influence of blood and soil" and the "glorification of the martial spirit," often "considered themselves *Herrenvolk* in relation to the Negro."[15] The use of the term *Herrenvolk*—roughly translated as "master race"—is especially apt here because it reminds us (via the prefix *herr*) of the male prerogative embedded in both Agrarianism's and fascism's claim to cultural and political legitimacy. Even Ransom's reformulation of the Christian Godhead, which consists in equal measures of masculine rationality and feminine emotion, is promoted in the service of a strict gendered hierarchy.

Ironically, the one most responsible for publicly linking agrarianism to fascism was Grace Lumpkin. At the time, the mid-1930s, Lumpkin was a devout communist, and her 1932 novel *To Make My Bread* appeared as a public disavowal of southern patriarchy. In one sense, the androgynous creative mind that Virginia Woolf promotes in *A Room of One's Own* finds its communist counterpart in Lumpkin's complex/collective novel, which attempts to give voice to both its male protagonist John and its female protagonist Bonnie. Yet the Agrarians' volkish sense of belonging, which Lumpkin herself eventually embraced by the 1940s, has its antecedents in Bonnie's death and before that in her ironic metaphorical kinship with a young girl who honors Confederate veterans.

W. E. B. Du Bois was also informed by some of the Herderian volkish sensibilities found in southern Agrarianism and German fascism. Yet Du Bois's linkage with fascism resonates at an even deeper level. As George L. Mosse explains, the earliest notions of German fascism developed out of the male camaraderie found among veterans of World War I. Angered by the concessions Germany made at the Treaty of Versailles, this militant league of men, or *Männerbund,* sought redemption through the development of a hypermasculine nation-state, the *Männerstaat*.[16] This attitude found its way into the highest ranks of Nazi leadership. As SS leader Heinrich Himmler explained in a 1937 speech, "[F]or centuries, yea millennia, the Germans . . . have been ruled as a *Männerstaat*."[17] By framing Germany as such, Himmler was not only able to delineate a clear and hierarchical distinction between men and women, but also to classify homosexuality and other forms of sexual "deviancy" as un-German. While it is not my intention here to implicate Du Bois's early twentieth-century writings as somehow protofascist, it is clear nonetheless that his emphasis on a manly black "folk" as outlined in *The Souls of Black Folk* and elsewhere holds some remarkable similarities to the ways in which German fascism brought untainted masculinity to bear on questions of national belonging.

If androgyny, composed as it is of a male-female binary, is the very thing that can save democracy, and yet the male-female binary is inherent in fascist ideology, how is democracy to be a safeguard against fascism or other forms of extreme nationalism? Hitler's Nazi Party, after all, was democratically elected. As we might suspect, Virginia Woolf's faith in androgyny—which she herself calls "irrational"— must ultimately confront the challenge of defining masculinity and femininity while at the same time not allowing those definitions to become immutable categories that can be used against the cause of individual freedom or even against the cause of international peace.

The trick, it would seem, is to make gender distinctions mean something and yet not mean anything at the same time. This is a struggle that confronted Carolyn Heilbrun, who in her 1973 reprisal of Woolf argued that androgyny could once again be used in the cause of peace: "Unless we can check the power of manly men and the women who willingly support them, we will experience new Vietnams, My

Lais, Kent States. . . . So long as we continue to believe the 'feminine' qualities of gentleness, lovingness, and the counting of cost in human rather than national or property terms are out of place among rulers, we can look forward to continued self-brutalization and perhaps even to self-destruction."[18] These and other comments from Heilbrun's *Toward a Recognition of Androgyny,* as I have shown in the introduction, suggest the durability of gendered categories.

Therefore, as we move forward through the postmodern era, we obviously cannot deny nationalism's role in perpetuating the masculine-feminine binary. If Judith Butler's hypothesis is correct, we may never fully escape our "gender trouble," and as long as "man" and "woman"—or especially "masculine" and "feminine"—continue to exist as binary oppositions in the national imaginary, the invocations of androgyny that were so prominent in the late nineteenth and early twentieth centuries will persist well into the future. And for that reason, scholarly studies of androgyny will persist. Assessing the politico-literary deployment of androgyny is, in a sense, like asking the body politic to disrobe. Somehow we dare not look away—for whatever is hidden under those vestments is certain to reflect the democratic principles that we simultaneously exalt and fear.

NOTES

Introduction

1. Alexis de Tocqueville, *Democracy in America*, trans. Henry Reeve, ed. Phillips Bradley (1840; New York: Knopf, 1945), vol. 2: 222.
2. Ibid., 222.
3. Linda M. Shires, "Of Maenads, Mothers, and Feminized Males: Victorian Readings of the French Revolution," in *Rewriting the Victorians: Theory, History, and the Politics of Gender*, ed. Linda M. Shires (New York: Routledge, 1992), 147, 156–57.
4. See Kari Weil, *Androgyny and the Denial of Difference* (Charlottesville: Univ. Press of Virginia, 1992), 69, and A. J. L. Busst, "The Androgyne in the Nineteenth Century," in *Romantic Mythologies*, ed. Ian Fletcher (New York: Barnes and Noble, 1967), 12.
5. Weil, *Androgyny and the Denial of Difference*, 66.
6. Quoted in Robert J. C. Young, *Colonial Desire: Hybridity, Culture, and Race* (London: Routledge, 1995), 39. For more information on Herder's organicism, see F. M. Barnard, *Herder's Social and Political Thought: From Enlightenment to Nationalism* (Oxford: Clarendon Press, 1965).
7. Barnard, *Herder's Social and Political Thought*, 32–39.
8. Ralph Waldo Emerson, in *The Selected Writings of Ralph Waldo Emerson*, ed. Brooks Atkinson (New York: Modern Library, 1992), 13. Emerson remarks: "It is well known to most of my audience that the Idealism of the present day acquired the name of Transcendental from the use of the term by Immanuel Kant, of Königsberg, who replied to the skeptical philosophy of Locke, which insisted that there was nothing in the intellectual which was not previously in the experience of the senses, by showing that there was a very important class of ideas or imperative forms, which did not come by experience, but through which experience was acquired; that these were intuitions

of the mind itself; and denominated them *Transcendental* forms" (86). For Herder's influence on Emerson, see Gene Bluestein, *The Voice of the Folk: Folklore and American Literary Theory* (Amherst: Univ. of Massachusetts Press, 1972).

9. W. G. Gilman et al., eds., *The Journals and Miscellaneous Notebooks of Ralph Waldo Emerson* (Cambridge: Belknap Press of Harvard Univ., 1978), vol. 7: 380.
10. Gilman et al., *The Journals and Miscellaneous Notebooks of Ralph Waldo Emerson* 9: 21.
11. On the "separation of spheres," see Barbara Welter, "The Cult of True Womanhood, 1820–1860," *American Quarterly* 18, no. 2 (1966): 151–74. For Emerson's patriarchal view of androgyny, see Eric Ingvar Thurin, *Emerson as Priest of Pan: A Study in the Metaphysics of Sex* (Lawrence: Regents Press of Kansas, 1981), 189.
12. Gary A. Williams, introduction to *The Hermaphrodite*, by Julia Ward Howe, *The Hermaphrodite* (Lincoln: Univ. of Nebraska Press, 2004), xxxvi–v.
13. Julia Ward Howe, *The Hermaphrodite*, ed. Gary A. Williams (Lincoln: Univ. of Nebraska Press, 2004), 195–96.
14. Quoted in Helen Lefkowitz Horowitz, *Rereading Sex: Battles over Sexual Knowledge and Suppression in Nineteenth-Century America* (New York: Alfred Knopf, 2002), 30.
15. Margaret Fuller, *Woman in the Nineteenth Century*, ed. Larry J. Reynolds (1845; New York: W. W. Norton, 1998), 14, 20.
16. Ibid., 68–69.
17. Bluestein, *The Voice of the Folk*, 41.
18. James E. Miller, Jr., Leaves of Grass: *America's Lyric-Epic of Self and Democracy* (New York: Twayne, 1992), 9.
19. Justin Kaplan, *Walt Whitman: A Life* (New York: Simon and Schuster, 1980), 183.
20. Walt Whitman, *Leaves of Grass*, ed. Michael Moon (New York: W. W. Norton, 2002), 3.
21. Curiously, Whitman struck this line from later editions of *Leaves of Grass*. At the time of the 1855 printing, Whitman had not yet given *Song of Myself* its title.
22. Walt Whitman, *Leaves of Grass: The First (1855) Edition*, ed. Malcolm Cowley (New York: Penguin, 1986), 31, 44, 61.
23. Ibid., 107.
24. Benedict Anderson, *Imagined Communities: Reflections on the Origins and Spread of Nationalism* (London: Verso, 1991), 26.
25. David Leverenz, *Paternalism Incorporated: Fables of American Fatherhood, 1865–1940* (Ithaca: Cornell Univ. Press, 2003), 5.
26. See chapters 1 and 4 of Nina Silber, *The Romance of Reunion: Northerners and the South, 1865–1900* (Chapel Hill: Univ. of North Carolina Press, 1993).
27. Ibid., 29–37.
28. Quoted in Kristin L. Hoganson, *Fighting for American Manhood: How Gender Politics Provoked the Spanish-American and Philippine-American Wars* (New Haven: Yale Univ. Press, 1998), 23.
29. Nancy Leys Stepan, "Race and Gender: The Role of Analogy in Science," in *Anatomy of Racism*, ed. David Theo Goldberg (Minneapolis: Univ. of Minnesota Press, 1990), 39–40.
30. Quoted in Werner Sollors, *Neither White Nor Black Yet Both: Thematic Explorations of Interracial Literature* (New York: Oxford Univ. Press, 1997), 131.
31. Sharon R. Ullman, *Sex Seen: The Emergence of Modern Sexuality in America* (Berkeley: Univ. of California Press, 1997), 3.

32. Michel Foucault, introduction to *Herculine Barbin: Being the Recently Discovered Memoirs of a Nineteenth-Century French Hermaphrodite,* by Herculine Barbin, trans. Richard McDougal (Sussex, England: Harvester Press, 1980), xiii.
33. Alice Domurat Dreger, *Hermaphrodites and the Medical Invention of Sex* (Cambridge: Harvard Univ. Press, 1998), 29.
34. Elizabeth Reis, "Impossible Hermaphrodites: Intersex in America." *Journal of American History* 92, no. 2 (2005): 419.
35. Ibid., 435.
36. Thomas Laqueur, *Making Sex: Body and Gender from the Greeks to Freud* (Cambridge: Harvard Univ. Press, 1990), 62, 35.
37. Judith Butler, *Gender Trouble: Feminism and the Subversion of Identity* (1990; London: Routledge, 1993), 7.
38. See Mark Spilka, *Hemingway's Quarrel with Androgyny* (Lincoln: Univ. of Nebraska Press, 1990); Christophe Den Tandt, "Amazons and Androgynes: Overcivilization and the Redefinition of Gender Roles at the Turn of the Century," *American Literary History* 8, no. 4 (1996): 639–64, and Lisa Rado, *The Modern Androgyne Imagination: A Failed Sublime* (Charlottesville: Univ. Press of Virginia, 2000).
39. Judith Butler, *Bodies That Matter: On the Discursive Limits of "Sex"* (New York: Routledge, 1993), 3.
40. See part 1 of Carolyn Heilbrun, *Toward a Recognition of Androgyny* (New York: W. W. Norton, 1973).
41. Carolyn Heilbrun, "Further Notes Toward a Recognition of Androgyny," *Women's Studies* 2, no. 2 (1974): 146.
42. Nancy Topping Bazin and Alma Freeman, "The Androgynous Vision," *Women's Studies* 2, no. 2 (1974): 193.
43. Cynthia Secor, "Androgyny: An Early Reappraisal," *Women's Studies* 2, no. 2 (1974): 164, 166.
44. Toril Moi, *Sexual/Textual Politics: Feminist Literary Theory* (New York: Routledge, 1985), 13. Moi includes Virginia Woolf in the same conceptual category as Heilbrun.
45. Judith Halberstam, *Female Masculinity* (Durham: Duke Univ. Press, 1998), 28–29.

Chapter 1

1. Leon Edel, *Henry James: The Conquest of London, 1870–1881* (New York: J. B. Lippincott, 1962), 102.
2. Michel Foucault, *The History of Sexuality, Part I: An Introduction,* trans. Robert Hurley (New York: Vintage, 1978), 43.
3. Richard von Krafft-Ebing, *Psychopathia Sexualis,* trans. Charles Gilbert Chaddock (1886; Philadelphia: F. A. Davis, 1908), 279, 304. For a discussion on sexology's link to androgyny, see chapter 1 of Lisa Rado, *The Modern Androgyne Imagination.*
4. Wendy Graham, *Henry James's Thwarted Love* (Stanford: Stanford Univ. Press, 1999), 22.
5. See Heilbrun, *Toward a Recognition of Androgyny,* 58. See also Kelly Cannon, *Henry James and Masculinity: The Man at the Margins* (New York: St. Martin's Press, 1994), 8.
6. Havelock Ellis and John Addington Symonds, *Sexual Inversion* (1897; New York: Arno Press, 1975), x.

7. Siobhan B. Somerville, *Queering the Color Line: Race and the Invention of Homosexuality in American Culture* (Durham: Duke Univ. Press, 2000), 4.
8. Ibid., 27, 270.
9. Ibid., 29.
10. [?] Morris, "Is Evolution Trying to Do Away with the Clitoris?" Paper presented at the meeting of the American Association of Obstetricians and Gynecologists, St. Louis, 21 September 1892, Yale Univ. Medical Library, New Haven, CT.
11. Perry M. Lichtenstein, "The 'Fairy' and the Lady Lover," *Medical Review of Reviews* 27 (1921): 372.
12. F. O. Matthiessen and K. B. Murdock, eds., *The Notebooks of Henry James* (New York: George Brazillier, 1947), 47.
13. Henry James, "The Art of Fiction," in *Tales of Henry James*, ed. Christof Weglin (New York: W. W. Norton, 1984), 352.
14. Henry James, *Henry James: Literary Criticism*, ed. Leon Edel and Mark Wilson (New York: Library of America, 1984), vol. 1: 600.
15. See Carroll Smith-Rosenberg's chapter "The New Woman as Androgyne," in *Disorderly Conduct: Visions of Gender in Victorian America* (New York: Oxford Univ. Press, 1985), 284, 288. Smith-Rosenberg breaks the age of the New Woman into three generations, starting with those who were educated around midcentury and ending with a third generation that, by the third decade of the twentieth century, idealized androgyny and used sexological terms to define itself.
16. See George L. Mosse, *Nationalism and Sexuality: Respectability and Abnormal Sexuality in Modern Europe* (New York: Howard Fertig, 1985), 103, and Laura H. Behling, *The Masculine Woman in the United States, 1890–1935* (Urbana: Univ. of Illinois Press, 2001).
17. Havelock Ellis, "Sexual Inversion in Women," *Alienist and Neurologist* 16 (1895): 155–56.
18. Lisa Duggan, *Sapphic Slashers: Sex, Violence, and American Modernity* (Durham: Duke Univ. Press, 2000), 21.
19. Henry James, "Daisy Miller," in *The Tales of Henry James*, ed. Christof Weglin (New York: W. W. Norton, 1984), 10.
20. Henry James, *The Bostonians* (1886; New York: Penguin, 1986), 85. All subsequent page references to this novel will appear parenthetically in the text.
21. John Carlos Rowe, *The Other Henry James* (Durham: Duke Univ. Press, 1998), 38–41, 41.
22. Quoted in Jonathan Ned Katz, *The Invention of Heterosexuality* (New York: Dutton, 1995), 51.
23. Hubert Kennedy, *Ulrichs: The Life and Work of Heinrich Ulrichs, Pioneer of the Modern Gay Movement* (Boston: Alyson Publications, 1998), 30.
24. Quoted in Duggan, *Sapphic Slashers*, 160.
25. On the similarities between Henry James and his creation Olive Chancellor, see Kristin Boudreau, "Narrative Sympathy in *The Bostonians*," *Henry James Review* 14 (1993): 22.
26. Consult Elisa Tamarkin's "Black Anglophilia; or, The Sociability of Antislavery," in *American Literary History* 14, no. 3 (2002): 444–78.
27. Nina Auerbach, *Communities of Women: An Idea in Fiction* (Cambridge, MA: Harvard Univ. Press, 1978), 127.
28. See Silber, *The Romance of Reunion*, intro. and chap. 1.
29. Lora Romero, *Home Fronts: Domesticity and Its Critics in the Antebellum United States* (Durham, Duke Univ. Press, 1997), 63.

30. Cynthia Griffin Wolff, "'Masculinity' in *Uncle Tom's Cabin*," *American Quarterly* 41, no. 4 (Dec. 1995): 601.
31. Silber, *The Romance of Reunion*, 108, 110, 118–19.
32. Noel Ignatiev, *How the Irish Became White* (London: Routledge, 1995), 2.
33. Eric Lott, *Love and Theft: Blackface Minstrelsy and the American Working Class* (New York: Oxford Univ. Press, 1993), 51–55.
34. David Roediger, *The Wages of Whiteness: Race and the Making of the American Working Class* (London: Verso, 1991), 106.
35. W. T. Lhamon, *Raising Cain: Blackface Performance from Jim Crow to Hip Hop* (Cambridge: Harvard Univ. Press, 1998), 208.
36. Bertram Wyatt-Brown, *Southern Honor: Ethics and Behavior in the Old South* (Oxford: Oxford Univ. Press, 1983), 319.
37. Caroline Field Levander, *Voices of the Nation: Women and Public Speech in Nineteenth-Century American Literature and Culture* (Cambridge: Cambridge Univ. Press, 1998), 15.
38. Somerville, *Queering the Color Line*, 36–37.
39. Levander, *Voices of the Nation*, 29.
40. Shane Phelan, *Sexual Strangers: Gays, Lesbians, and Dilemmas of Citizenship* (Philadelphia: Temple Univ. Press, 2001), 7.
41. Eve Kosofsky Sedgwick, *Epistemology of the Closet* (Berkeley: Univ. of California Press, 1990), 197.
42. See Graham's *Henry James's Thwarted Love* for James's intimate letters (47–48). Others, such as Sheldon M. Novick, are bolder in asserting that "[h]istoric fact . . . supports, or is at least consistent with, a portrait of James as a rather conventional, conservatively inclined man—a man who while closeted was sexually active, who was 'homosexual' in the clinical language that my generation uses for such matters" (11). See Novick's introduction to *Henry James and Homo-Erotic Desire*, ed. John R. Bradley (New York: St. Martin's Press, 1999), 1–23.
43. Henry James, *Letters*, ed. Leon Edel (Cambridge: Harvard Univ. Press, 1984), vol. 4: 53.
44. Terry Castle, *The Apparitional Lesbian: Female Sexuality and Modern Culture* (New York: Columbia Univ. Press, 1993), 170.
45. David Van Leer, "A World of Female Friendship: *The Bostonians*," in *Henry James and Homo-Erotic Desire*, ed. John R. Bradley (New York: St. Martin's Press, 1999), 101, 102.
46. See Charles Caramello, "The Duality of *The American Scene*," in *A Companion to Henry James Studies*, ed. Daniel Mark Fogel (Westport, CT: Greenwood, 1993), 454.
47. Henry James, *The American Scene* (1907; New York: Penguin, 1994), 297. All subsequent page references to this work will appear parenthetically in the text.
48. Sara Blair, *Henry James and the Writing of Race and Nation* (Cambridge: Cambridge Univ. Press, 1996), 202.
49. David Blight, *Race and Reunion: The Civil War in American Memory* (Cambridge: Harvard Univ. Press, 2001), 2.
50. Ibid., 2.
51. Levander, *Voices of the Nation*, 17.
52. Jessica Berman, "Feminizing the Nation: Woman as Cultural Icon in Late James," *Henry James Review* 17 (1996): 60.

53. Henry James, "The Speech of American Women," in *French Writers and American Women: Essays by Henry James,* ed. Peter Buitenhuis (Branford, CT: Compass, 1960), 33. All subsequent page references to this essay will appear parenthetically in the text.
54. Ernest Gellner, *Nations and Nationalism* (Oxford: Blackwell, 1983), 55.
55. Henry James, "The Question of Our Speech," in *French Writers and American Women: Essays by Henry James,* ed. Peter Buitenhuis (Branford, CT: Compass, 1960), 26. All subsequent page references to this essay will appear parenthetically in the text.
56. Berman, "Feminizing the Nation," 64.
57. Anne McClintock, "'No Longer in a Future Heaven': Nationalism, Gender, and Race," in *Becoming National: A Reader,* ed. Geoff Eley and Ronald Grigor Suny (New York: Oxford Univ. Press, 1996), 263. McClintock takes her premise of Janus-faced nationalism from Tom Nairn's *The Faces of Nationalism: Janus Revisited* (London: Verso, 1998).
58. Walter Pater, *Plato and Platonism* (Charleston, SC: Bibliobazaar, 2007), 185.
59. Henry James, *French Poets and Novelists* (New York: Grosset and Dunlap, 1964), 320.
60. Henry James, "The Manners of American Women," in *French Writers and American Women: Essays by Henry James,* ed. Peter Buitenhuis (Branford, CT: Compass, 1960), 78. All subsequent page references to this essay will appear parenthetically in the text.
61. Bederman, *Manliness and Civilization,* 178 (italics in original).
62. Theodore Roosevelt, "The Negro in America," in *The Works of Theodore Roosevelt* (New York: Charles Scribner's Sons, 1925), vol. 14: 194.
63. Theodore Roosevelt, "The Law of Civilization and Decay," in *The Works of Theodore Roosevelt* 13: 345.
64. Theodore Roosevelt, "The Value of an Athletic Training," *Harper's Weekly,* December 23, 1893, 1236.
65. John F. Sears, introduction to *The American Scene,* by Henry James (New York: Penguin, 1994), xii.
66. Rowe, *The Other Henry James,* 30. Sara Blair follows a similar train of thought, asserting that James's late writings "promote an ethos of openness to racial exchange even as they record vivid urges to conduct, and to resist, racial management" (163).
67. Matthiessen, *The Notebooks of Henry James,* 329.

Chapter 2

1. John Locke, *An Essay Concerning Human Understanding,* ed. Kenneth P. Winkler (Indianapolis: Hackett Publishing, 1996), 33 (italics in original).
2. Laqueur, *Making Sex,* 196.
3. Linda K. Kerber, "Separate Spheres, Female Worlds, Woman's Place: The Rhetoric of Women's History," in *No More Separate Spheres!* ed. Cathy N. Davidson and Jessamyn Hatcher (Durham: Duke Univ. Press, 2002), 34.
4. Tocqueville, *Democracy in America,* 2:222–23.
5. See, for example, Lori Merish, *Sentimental Materialism: Gender, Commodity Culture, and Nineteenth-Century American Literature* (Durham: Duke Univ. Press, 2000), 17.
6. See Daniel Horowitz, *The Morality of Spending: Attitudes Toward the Consumer Society in America, 1875–1940* (Baltimore: Johns Hopkins Univ. Press, 1985), xxv, and Stuart M.

Blumin, *The Emergence of the Middle Class: Social Experience in the American City, 1760–1900* (New York: Cambridge Univ. Press, 1989), 187–90.
7. See Merish, *Sentimental Materialism,* chaps. 1 and 2; Rita Felski, *The Gender of Modernity* (Cambridge: Harvard Univ. Press, 1995), chap. 3; and Victoria de Grazia and Ellen Furlough, introduction to *The Sex of Things: Gender and Consumption in Historical Perspective,* ed. Victoria de Grazia and Ellen Furlough (Berkeley: Univ. of California Press, 1996).
8. Merish, *Sentimental Materialism,* 18.
9. Den Tandt, "Amazons and Androgynes," 640.
10. Thorstein Veblen, *The Theory of the Leisure Class* (1899; New York: Penguin, 1994), 75, 74.
11. Frank Norris, "Novelists of the Future: The Training They Need," in *The Literary Criticism of Frank Norris,* ed. Donald Pizer (Austin: Univ. of Texas Press, 1964), 13.
12. See Lon West, *Deconstructing Frank Norris's Fiction: The Male-Female Dialectic* (New York: Peter Lang, 1998). Using a Jungian approach, West claims that Norris "was always concerned with finding a way to fulfill the maternally and paternally-centered sides of himself" (122). Similarly, Den Tandt argues that "[Norris's] awkward similes [for the muse figure] point to the existence of male writers' androgynous fantasies of empowerment in the public sphere" (654).
13. Kevin Starr, introduction to *The Octopus: A Story of California,* by Frank Norris (New York: Penguin, 1994), viii–ix.
14. Frank Norris, *The Octopus* (1901; New York: Penguin, 1994), 36 (italics mine). All subsequent references to this novel will appear parenthetically in the text.
15. Charles Darwin, *On the Origin of the Species: A Facsimile of the First Edition* (Cambridge: Harvard Univ. Press, 1964), 16.
16. Charles Darwin, *The Descent of Man,* in *Darwin: A Norton Critical Edition,* ed. Philip Appleman (New York: Norton, 2001), 226.
17. Otto Weininger, *Sex and Character,* trans. Ladislaus Löb (1901; New York: AMS Press, 1975), 3, 5, 8.
18. Joseph Le Conte, "The Genesis of Sex," *Popular Science Monthly* 16 (1879): 169–70.
19. See Mark Seltzer, *Bodies and Machines* (New York: Routledge, 1992), 33.
20. West, *Deconstructing Frank Norris's Fiction,* 16.
21. Frank Norris, "The Frontier Gone at Last," in *The Literary Criticism of Frank Norris,* ed. Donald Pizer (Austin: Univ. of Texas Press, 1964), 113.
22. For other such attributes associated with the post-1850 androgyne, see Busst, "The Image of the Androgyne in the Nineteenth Century," 39.
23. Walter Benn Michaels, *The Gold Standard and the Logic of Naturalism: American Literature at the Turn of the Century* (Berkeley: Univ. of California Press, 1987), 186.
24. Smith-Rosenberg, *Disorderly Conduct,* 291.
25. Le Conte, "The Genesis of Sex," 178.
26. Joseph Le Conte, "The Effect of Mixture of Races on Human Progress," *Berkeley Quarterly* 1 (1880): 101.
27. Bert Bender, "Frank Norris on the Evolution and Repression of the Sexual Instinct," *Nineteenth-Century Literature* 54, no. 1 (June 1999): 79, 89.
28. Georg Lukács, *The Theory of the Novel: A Historico-Philosophical Essay on the Forms of Great Epic Literature,* trans. Anna Bostock (Cambridge: MIT Press, 1971), 67.

29. Russ Castronovo, "Geo-Aesthetics: Fascism, Globalism, and Frank Norris," *boundary 2* 30, no. 3 (Fall 2003): 184.
30. Quoted in Bederman, *Manliness and Civilization*, 126.
31. Bederman, *Manliness and Civilization*, 135.
32. Émile Durkheim, *The Division of Labor in Society*, trans. George Simpson (New York: Free Press, 1964), 45, 48, 63. Anticipating Norris's *Octopus* in some respects, Durkheim sees personal and communal fulfillment as reciprocal: "The image of the one who completes us becomes inseparable from ours. . . . It thus becomes an integral and permanent part of our conscience, to such a point that we can no longer separate ourselves from it and seek to increase its force. That is why we enjoy the society of the one it represents, since the presence of the object that it expresses, by making us actually perceive it, sets it off more" (61–62).
33. Charlotte Perkins Gilman, *Women and Economics: A Study of the Economic Relation between Women and Men* (1898; Amherst, NY: Prometheus Books, 1994), ix. Subsequent references to this book will appear parenthetically in the text.
34. Charlotte Perkins Gilman, "Dr. Weininger's 'Sex and Character,'" *Critic* 48, no. 5 (May 1906): 414–15.
35. Ibid., 417.
36. Charlotte Perkins Gilman, "Our Place Today," in *Charlotte Perkins Gilman: A Nonfiction Reader*, ed. Larry Ceplair (New York: Columbia Univ. Press, 1991), 55, emphasis in original.
37. Louise Michele Newman, *White Women's Rights: The Racial Origins of Feminism in the United States* (New York: Oxford Univ. Press, 1999), 143.
38. Charlotte Perkins Gilman, *The Man-Made World: Our Androcentric Culture*, in *The Yellow Wallpaper and Other Writings* (1911; New York: Bantam, 1989), 204. Subsequent references to this book will appear parenthetically in the text.
39. Butler, *Gender Trouble*, 140.
40. Charlotte Perkins Gilman, "A Suggestion on the Negro Race," *American Journal of Sociology* 14, no. 1 (July 1908): 80, 78.
41. Butler, *Gender Trouble*, 136, 140.
42. Bederman, *Manliness and Civilization*, 129.
43. Ibid., 132.
44. Also consider the closing lines of Eliot's 1922 *The Waste Land*: "Shantih shantih shantih." The Sanskrit lines, according to Eliot's own notes, are "a formal ending to an Upanishad," and they are translated as "The Peace which passeth understanding." See *The Waste Land and Other Poems* (San Diego: Harcourt, 1971), 46, 54.
45. Lisa Rado, "Primitivism, Modernism, and Matriarchy," in *Modernism, Gender, and Culture: A Cultural Studies Approach*, ed. Lisa Rado (New York: Garland, 1997), 283.
46. Gasquoine Hartley, *The Position of Women in Primitive Society: A Study of the Matriarchy* (London: Eveleigh Nash, 1914), 13.
47. Rado, "Primitivism, Modernism, and Matriarchy," 287.
48. See Lester F. Ward, *Pure Sociology: A Treatise on the Origin and Spontaneous Development of Society* (1903; New York: Macmillan, 1909), 213–23.
49. Newman, *White Women's Rights*, 146.
50. Ann J. Lane, introduction to *Herland*, by Charlotte Perkins Gilman (New York: Pantheon, 1979), xix.
51. Charlotte Perkins Gilman, *Herland* (1915; New York: Pantheon, 1979), 5. All subsequent references to this novel will appear parenthetically in the text.

52. Gilman, "A Suggestion on the Negro Race," 81–82.
53. For more information on Gilman's Nationalism and populism, see Mark W. Van Wienen, "A Rose by Any Other Name: Charlotte Perkins Stetson (Gilman) and the Case for American Reform Socialism," *American Quarterly* 55, no. 4 (2003): 603–34. According to Van Wienen, Gilman's commitment to Nationalism and populism may have even eclipsed her commitment to feminism for most of the 1890s (603–4). Once populism collapsed after the People's Party was co-opted by Democrat William Jennings Bryan in the 1896 presidential election, Gilman began to downplay her Nationalist and populist ties in her writings (616).
54. Van Wienen, "A Rose by Any Other Name," 603, 611.
55. For the link between production and reproduction, also see Naomi B. Zauderer, "Consumption, Production, and Reproduction in the Works of Charlotte Perkins Gilman," in *Charlotte Perkins Gilman: Optimist Reformer*, ed. Jill Rudd and Val Gough (Iowa City: Univ. of Iowa Press, 1999).
56. Aleta Cane, "Charlotte Perkins Gilman's *Herland* as a Feminist Response to Male Quest Romance," *Jack London Journal* 2 (1995): 27.
57. Nell Irvin Painter, *Standing at Armageddon: The United States, 1877–1919* (New York: W. W. Norton, 1987), 235, 242.
58. Lisa A. Long, "Charlotte Perkins Gilman's *With Her in Ourland*: Herland Meets Heterodoxy," in *Charlotte Perkins Gilman and Her Contemporaries: Literary and Intellectual Contexts*, ed. Cynthia J. Davis and Denise D. Knight (Tuscaloosa: Univ. of Alabama Press, 2004), 190–91.
59. Weil, *Androgyny and the Denial of Difference*, 8, 10.
60. Painter, *Standing at Armageddon*, 247; Dorothy Berkson, "'So We All Became Mothers': Harriet Beecher Stowe, Charlotte Perkins Gilman, and the New World of Women's Culture," in *Feminism, Utopia, and Narrative*, ed. Libby Falk Jones and Sarah Webster Goodwin (Knoxville: Univ. of Tennessee Press, 1990), 107–8.
61. Carol Pateman, *The Sexual Contract* (Stanford: Stanford Univ. Press, 1988), 41.
62. Gilman states: "The African race, with the advantage of contact with our more advanced stage of evolution, has made more progress in a few generations than any other race has ever done in the same time, except the Japanese" (80).
63. See, for example, Kathleen Margaret Lant, "The Rape of the Text: Charlotte Gilman's Violation of *Herland*," *Tulsa Studies in Women's Literature* 9 (Fall 1990): 297.
64. See Lou Ann Matossian, "A Woman-Made Language: Charlotte Perkins Gilman and *Herland*," *Women and Language* 10, no. 2 (Spring 1987): 17.
65. Anderson, *Imagined Communities*, 7.
66. Painter, *Standing at Armageddon*, 297.

Chapter 3

1. Jacquelyn Dowd Hall, "Private Eyes, Public Women: Images of Class and Sex in the Urban South, Atlanta, Georgia, 1913–1915," in *Work Engendered: Toward a New History of American Labor*, ed. Ava Baron (Ithaca: Cornell Univ. Press, 1991), 249–59.
2. See Robin D. G. Kelley, *Hammer and Hoe: Alabama Communists during the Great Depression* (Chapel Hill: Univ. of North Carolina Press, 1990).
3. David L. Carlton and Peter Coclanis, eds., *The Report on Economic Conditions in the South with Related Documents* (Boston: Bedford/St. Martin's Press, 1996), 42.

4. Ibid., 58, 61, 63.
5. Paul Buhle, *Marxism in the USA from 1870 to the Present Day: Remapping the History of the American Left* (London: Verso, 1987), 59. For a more complete understanding of the androgyny celebrated among the Ephrata members, see Jeff Bach, *Voices of the Turtledoves: The Sacred World of Ephrata* (University Park, Pennsylvania State Univ. Press, 2003).
6. Karl Marx and Friedrich Engels, *The Communist Manifesto* (1848; New York: Signet, 1998), 59.
7. Rebecca Harding Davis, "Life in the Iron Mills," in *Four Stories by American Women*, ed. Cynthia Griffin Wolff (New York: Penguin, 1990), 11.
8. Emanuel Kanter, *The Amazons: A Marxian Study* (Chicago: Charles Kerr, 1926), 121.
9. See Michael Kreyling, *The Invention of Southern Literature* (Jackson: Univ. Press of Mississippi, 1998) and Paul V. Murphy, *The Rebuke of History: The Southern Agrarians and American Political Thought* (Chapel Hill: Univ. of North Carolina Press, 2001). Kreyling has convincingly argued that the Agrarians were largely responsible for constructing the ideological parameters of the Southern Literary Renaissance. Paul V. Murphy has shown how modern American political and social conservatism sprang from the Agrarians' emphasis on states' rights and resistance to racial cohesion.
10. See Anne Goodwyn Jones and Susan V. Donaldson, "Haunted Bodies: Rethinking the South through Gender," in *Haunted Bodies: Gender and Southern Texts*, ed. Anne Goodwyn Jones and Susan V. Donaldson (Charlottesville: Univ. Press of Virginia, 1997), 4.
11. Foreword, *The Fugitive* 1, no. 1 (1922): 1.
12. John Crowe Ransom, *God Without Thunder: An Unorthodox Defense of Orthodoxy* (1930; Hamden, CT: Archon Books, 1965), 20. All subsequent references to this book will appear parenthetically in the text.
13. Floyd C. Watkins, John T. Hiers, and Mary Louise Weeks, eds., *Talking with Robert Penn Warren* (Athens: Univ. of Georgia Press, 1990), 382.
14. Because of their willingness to forfeit personal intellectual submission in the name of cultural cohesion, the Agrarians were sometimes labeled fascist or fascist sympathizers. See Murphy, *The Rebuke of History*, 71.
15. In Ransom's orthodoxy, Christ plays a different role. Now relegated to the inferior position of "demi-god," he does not command nearly the authority that he does in the Trinitarian tradition. For Ransom, Christ was *"[t]he Demigod who knew he was a Demigod and refused to set up as a God"* (305, italics in original). In other words, Christ, being male and partially divine, was an emanation of the Godhead's rational masculine principle, what Ransom calls the "Logos." (Notice, for example, that the word "logic" and the suffix "-ology," as in "sociology" and "anthropology," come from this Greek word.)
16. Elizabeth Cady Stanton, *The Woman's Bible* (1895; Amherst, NY: Prometheus Books, 1999). Stanton based her conclusions on the first human creation story, recounted in Genesis 1:27: "So God created man in his own image, in the image of God created he him; male and female created he them." To this Stanton responds, "We have in these texts a plain declaration of the existence of the feminine element in the Godhead, equal in power and glory with the masculine. The Heavenly Mother and Father!" (14).
17. John Crowe Ransom, *Two Gentlemen in Bonds* (New York: Knopf, 1927), 50, 51.
18. Anne Goodwyn Jones, *Tomorrow Is Another Day: The Woman Writer in the South, 1859–1936* (Baton Rouge: Louisiana State Univ. Press, 1981), 4.
19. John Crowe Ransom, *Chills and Fever* (New York: Knopf, 1924), 14.

20. Ibid., 15.
21. Eliot, *The Waste Land and Other Poems*, 46, 30.
22. Ibid., 38, 50.
23. Twelve Southerners, "Statement of Principles," in *I'll Take My Stand: The South and the Agrarian Tradition*, by Twelve Southerners (1930; New York: Harper, 1962), xxiii.
24. Quoted in Donald Davidson, "Counterattack, 1930–1940: The South Against Leviathan," in *Southern Writers and the Modern World* (Athens: Univ. of Georgia Press, 1958), 49.
25. George Lewis, *The White South and the Red Menace: Segregationists, Anticommunism, and Massive Resistance, 1945–1965* (Gainesville: Univ. Press of Florida, 2004), 12–13.
26. John Crowe Ransom, "Reconstructed but Unregenerate," in *I'll Take My Stand: The South and the Agrarian Tradition*, by Twelve Southerners (1930; New York: Harper, 1962), 9–10. All subsequent references to this essay will appear parenthetically in the text.
27. Smith-Rosenberg, *Disorderly Conduct*, 254 and following.
28. David E. Whisnant, *All That Is Native and Fine: The Politics of Culture in an American Region* (Chapel Hill: Univ. of North Carolina Press, 1983), 7, 9, and following.
29. Daniel J. Walkowitz, "The Making of a Feminine Professional Identity: Social Workers in the 1920s," *American Historical Review* 95, no. 4 (Oct. 1990): 1052.
30. Ibid., 1051, 1056.
31. Esther Lucille Brown, *Social Work as a Profession* (New York: Russell Sage Foundation, 1935), 142–43.
32. See, for example, Fred C. Hobson, *Tell about the South: The Southern Rage to Explain* (Baton Rouge: Louisiana State Univ. Press, 1983).
33. See John Shelton Reed, "For Dixieland: The Sectionalism of *I'll Take My Stand*," in *A Band of Prophets: The Vanderbilt Agrarians after Fifty Years*, ed. William C. Havard and Walter Sullivan (Baton Rouge: Louisiana State Univ. Press, 1982), 52–53.
34. As central as the "Negro question" was to the development of postbellum and twentieth-century southern society, race was originally marginalized as much as possible in these works. In fact, *God Without Thunder* mentions race only insofar as it suggests that religion must rest on organic racial communities. See John Tyree Fain and Thomas Daniel Young, eds., *The Literary Correspondence of Donald Davidson and Allen Tate* (Athens: Univ. of Georgia Press, 1974). Upon finding out that Robert Penn Warren's contribution to *I'll Take My Stand*, "The Briar Patch," was to address the place of blacks within the agrarian tradition, Donald Davidson wrote to Allen Tate, "I think there are some things [in Warren's essay] that would irritate and dismay the very Southern people to whom we are appealing" (Fain and Young 250).
35. Ritchie Watson, "'The Difference of Race': Antebellum Race and the Development of Southern Nationalism," *Southern Literary Journal* 35, no. 1 (2002): 11.
36. Kieran Quinlan, *John Crowe Ransom's Secular Faith* (Baton Rouge: Louisiana State Univ. Press, 1989), 9, 68, 87.
37. For these limits consult Paul A. Bové, *Mastering Discourses: The Politics of Intellectual Culture* (Durham: Duke Univ. Press, 1992), 121.
38. John Crowe Ransom, "What Does the South Want?" in *Who Owns America? A New Declaration of Independence*, ed. Allen Tate and Herbert Agar (Wilmington, DE: ISI Books, 1999), 248.
39. Ibid., 251.
40. Ibid.

41. T. W. Adorno, "Theses Upon Art and Religion Today," *Kenyon Review* 7 (Autumn 1945): 680, and John Crowe Ransom, "Art and the Human Economy," *Kenyon Review* 7 (Autumn 1945): 686.
42. John Crowe Ransom, *The World's Body* (1938; Baton Rouge: Louisiana State Univ. Press, 1968), 77. All subsequent references to the essays in this book will appear in the text.
43. For a summary of many of these opinions, see Richard Stite's chapter entitled "The Sexual Revolution," in *The Women's Liberation Movement in Russia: Feminism, Nihilism, and Bolshevism, 1860–1930* (Princeton: Princeton Univ. Press, 1991).
44. Quoted in Stites, *The Women's Liberation Movement in Russia*, 351.
45. Mark G. Malvasi, *The Unregenerate South: The Agrarian Thought of John Crowe Ransom, Allen Tate, and Donald Davidson* (Baton Rouge: Louisiana State Univ. Press, 1997), 79.
46. Thomas Daniel Young and George Core, eds., *Selected Letters of John Crowe Ransom* (Baton Rouge; Louisiana State Univ. Press, 1985), 115.
47. See Kreyling, *Inventing Southern Literature*, chap. 1.
48. Two exceptions to this trend are Sylvia Jenkins Cook's *From Tobacco Road to Route 66: The Southern Poor White in Fiction* (Chapel Hill: Univ. of North Carolina Press, 1976), and Barbara Foley's *Radical Representations: Politics and Form in U.S. Proletarian Fiction* (Durham: Duke Univ. Press, 1993). Of these, Cook's book is the most attentive to placing the southern proletarian writers within a larger southern context.
49. Grace Lumpkin, "I Want a King," *FIGHT Against War and Fascism* 3, no. 4 (Feb. 1936): 14.
50. See Allen Tate's objections to Lumpkin and his passionate repudiation of Collins's remarks in "Fascism and the Southern Agrarians," *New Republic*, May 27, 1936, 75–76.
51. Foley, *Radical Representations*, 3, 5.
52. See Foley, *Radical Representations*, 228–31, and Paula A. Rabinowitz, *Labor and Desire: Women's Revolutionary Fiction in Depression America* (Chapel Hill: Univ. of North Carolina Press, 1991), 20.
53. See Alice Kessler-Harris and Paul Lauter, introduction to *Call Home the Heart*, by Fielding Burke (1932; New York: Feminist Press, 1983), ix.
54. See Mary Jo Buhle, *Women and American Socialism, 1870–1920* (Urbana: Univ. of Illinois Press, 1981), chap. 6.
55. Suzanne Sowinska, introduction to *To Make My Bread*, by Grace Lumpkin (1932; Urbana: Univ. of Illinois Press, 1995), ix.
56. Cook, *From Tobacco Road to Route 66*, 85.
57. Lumpkin, Myra Page, Sherwood Anderson, and Fielding Burke, along with Mary Heaton Vorse and William Rollins, based novels on the Gastonia, North Carolina, mill strike. The first of the Gastonia novels was Vorse's *Strike!* (New York: Horace Liveright, 1930), followed in 1932 by Lumpkin's novel, Page's *Gathering Storm: A Story of the Black Belt* (New York: International Publishers), Burke's *Call Home the Heart*, and Anderson's *Beyond Desire* (New York: Liveright). Rollins's *The Shadow Before* (New York: Robert M. McBride and Co.) came out two years later in 1934.
58. Sowinska, introduction, xv.
59. Ibid., xv–xviii.
60. Jack Alan Robbins, ed., *Granville Hicks in The New Masses* (Port Washington, NY: Kennikat Press, 1974), 27, 29.
61. Foley, *Radical Representations*, 321 and following.

62. Grace Lumpkin, *To Make My Bread* (1932; Urbana: Univ. of Illinois Press, 1995), 12. All subsequent references to this novel appear parenthetically in the text.
63. G. J. Barker-Benfield, *Horrors of the Half-Known Life: Male Attitudes toward Women and Sexuality in Nineteenth-Century America* (New York: Routledge, 2000), 61.
64. Karl Marx, *Capital: A Critique of Political Economy,* trans. Ben Fowkes (1867; New York: Penguin, 1990), vol. 1: 873.
65. See, for example, Walter Rideout, *The Radical Novel in the United States, 1900–1954: Some Interrelations between Literature and Society* (Cambridge: Harvard Univ. Press, 1956), 174.
66. Rabinowitz, *Labor and Desire,* 8.
67. Michael Gold, "Go Left Young Writers!" *New Masses* (Jan. 1929): 3–4, and "Wilder: Prophet of the Genteel Christ," *New Republic,* Oct. 22, 1930, 266.
68. Michael Kimmel, *Manhood in America: A Cultural History* (New York: Free Press, 1996), 192, 199.
69. Cook, *From Tobacco Road to Route 66,* 99.
70. Welter, "The Cult of True Womanhood," 151.
71. Rabinowitz, *Labor and Desire,* 61.
72. H. H. Lewis, *The Man from Moscow* (Holt, MN: Haaglund Press, 1932), 19.
73. Buhle, *Women and American Socialism,* 260–61.
74. Leslie Petty, *Romancing the Vote: Feminist Activism in American Fiction, 1870–1920* (Athens: Univ. of Georgia Press, 2006), 190.
75. Max Horkheimer and Theodor Adorno, *The Dialectic of Enlightenment: Philosophical Fragments,* ed. Gunzelin Schmid Noerr and trans. Edmund Jephcott (1947; Stanford: Stanford Univ. Press, 2002), xviii, 8.
76. Quoted in Sowinska, introduction, ix.
77. Ibid., xxi.

Chapter 4

1. Reis, "Impossible Hermaphrodites," 429.
2. Ibid., 430–31.
3. Fuller, *Woman in the Nineteenth Century,* 20.
4. Wolff, "'Masculinity' in *Uncle Tom's Cabin,*" 601, 602.
5. Ibid., 600.
6. Laurie Crumpacker, "Four Novels of Harriet Beecher Stowe: A Study in Nineteenth-Century Androgyny," in *American Novelists Revisited: Essays in Feminist Criticism,* ed. Fritz Fleischmann (Boston: G. K. Hall, 1982), 78, 79.
7. See chapter 1, entitled "Scientific Racism and the Invention of the Homosexual Body," in Somerville, *Queering the Color Line.*
8. Nancy Leys Stepan, "Race and Gender: The Role of Analogy in Science," in *Anatomy of Racism,* ed. David Theo Goldberg (Minneapolis: Univ. of Minnesota Press, 1990), 39–40. Stepan also notes the relative absence of black women in these studies, explaining that because sexual differentiation among lower races was supposedly slight, any mention of black men—even one that compares them to white women—would tacitly include black women. "The [black] male could be taken as representative of both sexes of his race and the black female could be virtually ignored . . ." (47).
9. See Bederman, *Manliness and Civilization,* 49.

10. W. H. Flower and James Murie, "Account of the Dissection of a Bushwoman," *Journal of Anatomy and Physiology* 1 (1867): 208.
11. Somerville, *Queering the Color Line*, 27.
12. Patrick Geddes and J. Arthur Thomson, *The Evolution of Sex* (1889; New York: Scribner's, 1890), 80.
13. See Trudier Harris's introduction and later relevant chapters on black women's sexuality in *Saints, Sinners, Saviors: Strong Black Women in African American Literature* (New York: Palgrave, 2001). Harris explains that the image of the desexed mammy who "looked more like huge slabs of excessively dark ham" was a reaction to the perception of that black woman as a "hot mama" (3, 2).
14. Barker-Benfield, *Horrors of the Half-Known Life*, 112–17, 275.
15. W. E. B. Du Bois, "Editorial," *Crisis* 4 (Oct. 1912): 287.
16. Some of Du Bois's strongest feminist sentiments come from his 1920 "The Damnation of Women," which proclaims, "The future woman must have a life work and economic independence." See *W. E. B. Du Bois: A Reader*, ed. David Levering Lewis (New York: Holt, 1995), 300. For critical discussions of Du Bois's views of women's liberation, see, for example, Beverly Guy-Sheftall, *Daughters of Sorrow: Attitudes toward Black Women, 1880–1920* (New York: Carlson, 1990) and Farah Jasmine Griffin, "Black Feminists and Du Bois: Respectability, Protection, and Beyond," *Annals of the American Academy of Political and Social Science* 568 (Mar. 2000): 28–40.
17. Hazel V. Carby, *Race Men* (Cambridge: Harvard Univ. Press, 1998), 25–26.
18. Ibid., 27.
19. W. E. B. Du Bois, *The Philadelphia Negro: A Social Study* (1899; New York: Schockden Books, 1967), 45.
20. W. E. B. Du Bois, *The Souls of Black Folk* (1903; New York: Penguin, 1996), 47. All subsequent references to this book will appear parenthetically in the text.
21. Stepan, "Race and Gender," 40.
22. David Levering Lewis, *W. E. B. Du Bois: Biography of a Race, 1868–1919* (New York: Henry Holt and Co., 1993), 136. See also Sieglinde Lemke, "Berlin and Boundaries: *sollen* versus *geschehen*," *boundary 2* 27, no. 3 (2000): 52 and following.
23. Sandra Adell, *Double-Consciousness/Double Bind: Theoretical Issues in Twentieth-Century Black Literature* (Urbana: Univ. of Illinois Press, 1994), 12, 22–23.
24. Barnard, *Herder's Social and Political Thought*, 70.
25. W. E. B. Du Bois, *The Autobiography of W. E. B. Du Bois* (New York: International Publishers, 1968), 157.
26. Du Bois, *Autobiography*, 280; Lemke, "Berlin and Boundaries," 51.
27. Du Bois, *The Philadelphia Negro*, 65.
28. For Du Bois's scapegoating of women, see Kevin K. Gaines, *Uplifting the Race: Black Leadership, Politics, and Culture in the Twentieth Century* (Chapel Hill: Univ. of North Carolina Press, 1996), 170, 175, 169, 177.
29. Felski, *Gender of Modernity*, 75. For the relationship between the female libido and wealth, see Bram Dijkstra, *Idols of Perversity: Fantasies of Feminine Evil in Fin-de-Siècle Culture* (New York: Oxford Univ. Press, 1986), 366.
30. Lott, *Love and Theft*, 115.
31. See also Monica L. Miller, "W. E. B. Du Bois and the Dandy as Diasporic Race Man," *Callaloo* 26, no. 3 (2003): 749. Miller argues that Du Bois rehabilitates the dandy figure

by means of investing him with the charge to make art political (743). I disagree with Miller's overall premise, for the educated and well-dressed man whom Du Bois exalts is the volkish culmination of black manhood.

32. Carby, *Race Men,* 38.
33. Quoted in Lemke, "Berlin and Boundaries," 61.
34. W. E. B. Du Bois, "Races," *Crisis* 4 (August 1911): 158.
35. Indeed, this premise is the thrust of Gail Bederman's *Manliness and Civilization,* claiming as well that "manliness" was socially constructed so as to exclude specifically black men.
36. Kwame Anthony Appiah, "The Uncompleted Argument: Du Bois and the Illusion of Race," in *"Race," Writing, and Difference,* ed. Henry Louis Gates, Jr. (Chicago: Univ. of Chicago Press, 1986), 22, 33.
37. W. E. B. Du Bois, *Dusk of Dawn: An Essay Toward an Autobiography of a Race Concept* (New York: Harcourt, Brace and Co., 1940), 117.
38. Bernard R. Boxhill, "Du Bois on Cultural Pluralism," in *W. E. B. Du Bois on Race and Culture: Philosophy, Politics, Poetics,* ed. Bernard W. Bell, Emily Grosholz, and James B. Stewart (New York: Routledge, 1996), 58–59.
39. See Daylanne K. English, *Unnatural Selections: Eugenics in American Modernism and the Harlem Renaissance* (Chapel Hill: Univ. of North Carolina Press, 2004), 60.
40. Du Bois, *Dusk of Dawn,* 98–99.
41. W. E. B. Du Bois, "Miscegenation," in *Against Racism: Unpublished Essays, Papers, Addresses, 1887–1961,* ed. Herbert Aptheker (Amherst: Univ. of Massachusetts Press, 1985), 100.
42. According to Daylanne K. English, such preoccupation suggests that Du Bois was even more of a eugenics advocate than his socially conservative contemporary T. S. Eliot (English, *Unnatural Selections,* 44, 66–67).
43. Guy-Sheftall, *Daughters of Sorrow,* 161.
44. Quoted in Arthur Paul Davis, *From the Dark Tower* (Washington, D.C.: Howard Univ. Press, 1974), 54.
45. Quoted in Steven Watson, *The Harlem Renaissance: Hub of African American Culture, 1920–1930* (New York: Pantheon Books, 1995), 29.
46. English, *Unnatural Selections,* 55.
47. Quoted in Mason Stokes, "Strange Fruits: Rethinking the Gay Twenties," *Transition* 12, no. 2 (2002): 69.
48. Ibid., 72.
49. Alain Locke, "The New Negro," in *The New Negro,* ed. Alain Locke (1925; New York: Simon and Schuster, 1997), 3.
50. Ibid., 3.
51. Watson, *The Harlem Renaissance,* 105.
52. A. B. Christa Schwartz, *Gay Voices of the Harlem Renaissance* (Bloomington: Indiana Univ. Press, 2003), 9–10.
53. James Smethurst, "On Race, Homosexuality, and Visual and Verbal Androgyny in Cullen's Work," *Modern American Poetry: An Online Journal and Multimedia Companion to* Anthology of Modern American Poetry, http://www.english.uiuc.edu/maps/poets/a_f/cullen/androgyny.htm.
54. Langston Hughes, *The Big Sea: An Autobiography* (1940; New York: Hill, 1993), 226.
55. Marjorie Garber, *Vice Versa: Bisexuality and the Eroticism of Everyday Life* (New York: Simon and Schuster, 1995), 120.

56. The first and only issue of *Fire!!* included contributions from a younger generation of artists, including Langston Hughes, Zora Neale Hurston, Countée Cullen, Wallace Thurman (the main editor), Aaron Douglas, Richard Bruce Nugent, Gwendolyn Bennett, Arna Bontemps, Helene Johnson, Waring Cuney, Lewis Alexander, and Edward Silvera.
57. Watson, *The Harlem Renaissance,* 91.
58. David Levering Lewis, *When Harlem Was in Vogue* (New York: Oxford Univ. Press, 1979), 197.
59. Quoted in Chidi Ikonné, *From Du Bois to Van Vechten: The Early New Negro Literature, 1903–1926* (Westport, CT: Greenwood Press, 1981), 110, and David Levering Lewis, *When Harlem Was in Vogue,* 197.
60. Richard Bruce Nugent, "Narcissus," *Trend* 1 (Jan.–Mar. 1933): 127.
61. Quoted in Thomas H. Wirth, ed., *Gay Rebel of the Harlem Renaissance: Selections from the Work of Richard Bruce Nugent* (Durham: Duke Univ. Press, 2002), 89.
62. Schwartz, *Gay Voices of the Harlem Renaissance,* 125.
63. Judith Musser, "African American Women and Education: Marita Bonner's Response to the 'Talented Tenth,'" *Studies in Short Fiction* 34, no. 1 (Winter 1997): 74.
64. Maria Balshaw, "New Negroes, New Women: The Gender Politics of the Harlem Renaissance," *Women: A Cultural Review* 10, no. 2 (Summer 1999): 28.
65. Arguing that Bonner's stories are representative of social realism, Judith Musser argues that the author takes a sociological approach in her fiction, articulating the absence of black fathers (77) and decrying the naive simplicity of "the Harlem Renaissance's call for self-improvement through education" (73). Similarly, Maria Balshaw states, "More critically than any of her New Negro contemporaries Bonner demonstrates the anomalies of the logic of uplift, that the education and refinement deemed requisite for the New Negro are precisely the qualities likely to alienate them from the masses whose lot they are supposed to improve" (133). Bonner's critique of uplift, I speculate, is a critique specifically aimed at Du Bois.
66. Marita Bonner, "On Being Young—a Woman—and Colored," in *Frye Street and Environs: The Collected Works of Marita Bonner,* ed. Joyce Flynn (Boston: Beacon Press, 1987), 3. Subsequent references to this essay will appear parenthetically in the text.
67. Houston A. Baker, *Modernism and the Harlem Renaissance* (Chicago: Univ. of Chicago Press, 1987), 99.
68. Suzanne W. Model, "Work and Family: Blacks and Immigrants from South and East Europe," in *Immigration Reconsidered: History, Sociology, Politics,* ed. Virginia Yans-McLaughlin (New York: Oxford Univ. Press, 1990), 138.
69. I am borrowing the term "immersion narrative" from Robert B. Stepto's *From Behind the Veil: A Study of Afro-American Narrative* (Urbana: Univ. of Illinois Press, 1979). The term describes a narrative recounting a black individual's acquaintance or reacquaintance with "authentic" black culture and folk. The immersion usually serves to reverse a feeling of racial alienation or disfranchisement.
70. See the classic formulation of the pastoral in William Empson, *Some Versions of Pastoral* (New York: New Directions, 1974), 6.
71. Jennifer Margaret Wilks, "Modernist Women of the Black Atlantic: Gender and Intellectual Citizenship in the Harlem Renaissance and Negritude," Ph.D. diss., Cornell Univ., 2003, 87.

72. Barker-Benfield, *Horrors of the Half-Known Life,* 112–17, 275.
73. Marita Bonner, "Nothing New," in *Frye Street and Environs: The Collected Works of Marita Bonner,* ed. Joyce Flynn (Boston: Beacon Press, 1987), 69. Subsequent references to this short story will appear parenthetically in the text.
74. Charles W. Gould, *America, A Family Matter* (New York: Scribner's, 1922), 163.
75. Carol Allen, *Black Women Intellectuals: Strategies of Nation, Family, and Neighborhood in the Works of Pauline Hopkins, Jessie Fauset, and Marita Bonner* (New York: Garland, 1998), 92.
76. Here I mean "oceanic" in the context Freud made most famous in the first chapter of *Civilization and Its Discontents,* trans. James Strachey (1930; New York: Norton, 1961). He defines this term as "a sensation of 'eternity,' a feeling as of something limitless, unbounded" (11).
77. Marita Bonner, "There Were Three," in *Frye Street and Environs: The Collected Works of Marita Bonner,* ed. Joyce Flynn (Boston: Beacon Press, 1987), 102, italics in original. Subsequent references to this short story will appear parenthetically in the text.
78. Allen, *Black Women Intellectuals,* 105–6.
79. Homi K. Bhabha, *The Location of Culture* (New York: Routledge, 1994), 1–2.
80. Ibid., 2.
81. Klaus Theweleit, *Male Fantasies, Volume 1: Women, Floods, Bodies, History,* trans. Stephan Conway (Minneapolis: Minnesota Univ. Press, 1977), 201.
82. Ibid., 232–33.

Epilogue

1. For a general definition of fascism, including the ideology's rejection of Enlightenment principles, see Mark A. Neocleous, *Fascism* (Minneapolis: Minnesota Univ. Press, 1997), chap. 1.
2. Eric Hobsbawm, *Nations and Nationalism since 1780: Programme, Myth, Reality* (Cambridge: Cambridge Univ. Press, 1983), 131.
3. Virginia Woolf, *A Room of One's Own* (1929; San Diego: Harcourt Brace Jovanovich, 1957), 106. All subsequent references to this book will appear parenthetically in the text.
4. Freud's one-time disciple Carl Jung based his theories of the anima, animus, and persona on a human's supposedly innate androgyny. Jung felt that in order to obtain a total and unified "self," men and women needed to search their unconscious to find their female gendered anima and male gendered animus respectively. See "The Psychology of the Child Archetype," in *The Archetypes and the Collective Unconsciousness,* 2nd ed., trans. R. F. C. Hull (Princeton: Princeton Univ. Press, 1968). In it he declares, "The hermaphrodite means nothing less than a union of the strongest and most striking opposites" (173). Jung's theory is heavily reliant on balance; for example, males could temper their aggressive and acquisitive masculine personae with the help of their gentler, softer anima, should they take the time to find her.
5. Teresa Heffernan, "Fascism and Madness: Woolf Writing Against Modernism," in *Virginia Woolf Miscellanies: Proceedings on the First Annual Conference on Virginia Woolf,* ed. Mark Hussey and Vara Neverow-Turk (New York: Pace Univ. Press, 1992), 24.
6. At a later point in the chapter Woolf states: "The truth is, I often like women [writers], I like their unconventionality. I like their subtlety. I like their anonymity" (115).

7. Virginia Woolf, *Three Guineas* (1938; San Diego: Harcourt Brace Jovanovich, 1966), 102–3.
8. Mosse, *Nationalism and Sexuality*, 156–57. Mosse also shows that the hypermasculine literature found in Mussolini's Italy carried over into Germany. For Gunther d'Alquen, a leading Nazi editor, countries that reinforced the differences between men and women were sure to produce good art and literature (163). For differences between the various fascisms' views of gender, see also Victoria de Grazia, *How Fascism Ruled Women: Italy, 1922–1945* (Berkeley: Univ. of California Press, 1992) and Erin G. Carlston, *Thinking Fascism: Sapphic Modernism and Fascist Modernity* (Stanford: Stanford Univ. Press, 1998).
9. Woolf, *Three Guineas*, 180 n31.
10. See Jane Marcus, *Hearts of Darkness: White Women Writing Race* (New Brunswick, NJ: Rutgers Univ. Press, 2004), chap. 4.
11. Richard Chase, *The American Novel and Its Tradition* (Baltimore: Johns Hopkins Univ. Press, 1957), 198.
12. Castronovo, "Geo-Aesthetics," 164.
13. See Roger Griffin, *Modernism and Fascism: The Sense of a Beginning under Mussolini and Hitler* (New York: Palgrave, 2007), 192.
14. Murphy, *The Rebuke of History*, 71.
15. Richard M. Weaver, "The South and the Revolution of Nihilism," in *The Southern Essays of Richard M. Weaver*, ed. George M. Curtis III and James J. Thompson, Jr. (Indianapolis: Liberty Press, 1987), 183.
16. Mosse, *Nationalism and Sexuality*, 154, 167.
17. Quoted in Mosse, *Nationalism and Sexuality*, 167.
18. Heilbrun, *Toward a Recognition of Androgyny*, xvi.

BIBLIOGRAPHY

Adell, Sandra. *Double-Consciousness/Double Bind: Theoretical Issues in Twentieth-Century Black Literature.* Urbana: Univ. of Illinois Press, 1994.
Adorno, T. W. "Theses upon Art and Religion Today." *Kenyon Review* 7 (Autumn 1945): 677–82.
Allen, Carol. *Black Women Intellectuals: Strategies of Nation, Family, and Neighborhood in the Works of Pauline Hopkins, Jessie Fauset, and Marita Bonner.* New York: Garland, 1998.
Anderson, Benedict. *Imagined Communities: Reflections on the Origin and Spread of Nationalism.* London: Verso, 1991.
Anderson, Sherwood. *Beyond Desire.* New York: Liveright, 1932.
Appiah, Kwame Anthony. "The Uncompleted Argument: Du Bois and the Illusion of Race." In *"Race," Writing, and Difference,* ed. Henry Louis Gates Jr., 21–37. Chicago: Univ. of Chicago Press, 1986.
Auerbach, Nina. *Communities of Women: An Idea in Fiction.* Cambridge: Harvard Univ. Press, 1978.
Bach, Jeff. *Voices of the Turtledoves: The Sacred World of Ephrata.* University Park: Pennsylvania State Univ. Press, 2003.
Baker, Houston A. *Modernism and the Harlem Renaissance.* Chicago: Univ. of Chicago Press, 1987.
Balshaw, Maria. "New Negroes, New Women: The Gender Politics of the Harlem Renaissance." *Women: A Cultural Review* 10, no. 2 (Summer 1999): 127–38.
Barker-Benfield, G. J. *Horrors of the Half-Known Life: Male Attitudes toward Women and Sexuality in Nineteenth-Century America.* New York: Routledge, 2000.
Barnard, F. M. *Herder's Social and Political Thought: From Enlightenment to Nationalism.* Oxford: Clarendon Press, 1965.

Bazin, Nancy Topping, and Alma Freeman. "The Androgynous Vision." *Women's Studies* 2, no. 2 (1974): 185–216.

Bederman, Gail. *Manliness and Civilization: A Cultural History of Gender and Race in the United States, 1880–1917.* Chicago: Univ. of Chicago Press, 1995.

Behling, Laura. *The Masculine Woman in the United States, 1890–1935.* Urbana: Univ. of Illinois Press, 2001.

Bender, Bert. "Frank Norris on the Evolution and Repression of the Sexual Instinct." *Nineteenth-Century Literature* 54, no. 1 (June 1999), 73–103.

Berkson, Dorothy. "'So We All Became Mothers': Harriet Beecher Stowe, Charlotte Perkins Gilman, and the New World of Women's Culture." In *Feminism, Utopia, and Narrative*, ed. Libby Falk Jones and Sarah Webster Goodwin, 100–115. Knoxville: Univ. of Tennessee Press, 1990.

Berman, Jessica. "Feminizing the Nation: Woman as Cultural Icon in Late James." *Henry James Review* 17 (1996): 58–76.

Bhabha, Homi K. *The Location of Culture.* New York: Routledge, 1994.

Blair, Sara. *Henry James and the Writing of Race.* Cambridge: Cambridge Univ. Press, 1996.

Blumin, Stuart M. *The Emergence of the Middle Class: Social Experience in the American City, 1760–1900.* New York: Cambridge Univ. Press, 1989.

Bluestein, Gene. *The Voice of the Folk: Folklore and American Literary Theory.* Amherst: Univ. of Massachusetts Press, 1972.

Bonner, Marita. "Nothing New." In *Frye Street and Environs: The Collected Works of Marita Bonner*, ed. Joyce Flynn, 69–77. Boston: Beacon Press, 1987.

———. "On Being Young—a Woman—and Colored." In *Frye Street and Environs: The Collected Works of Marita Bonner*, ed. Joyce Flynn, 3–8. Boston: Beacon Press, 1987.

———. "There Were Three." In *Frye Street and Environs: The Collected Works of Marita Bonner*, ed. Joyce Flynn, 102–8. Boston: Beacon Press, 1987.

Boudreau, Kristin. "Narrative Sympathy in *The Bostonians*." *Henry James Review* 14 (1993): 17–33.

Bové, Paul A. *Mastering Discourse: The Politics of Intellectual Culture.* Durham: Duke Univ. Press, 1992.

Boxhill, Bernard R. "Du Bois on Cultural Pluralism." In *W. E. B. Du Bois on Race and Culture: Philosophy, Politics, Poetics*, ed. Bernard W. Bell, Emily Grosholz, and James B. Stewart, 57–85. New York: Routledge, 1996.

Bradley, John R. *Henry James's Permanent Adolescence.* New York: Palgrave, 2000.

Brown, Esther Lucile. *Social Work as a Profession.* New York: Russell Sage Foundation, 1935.

Buhle, Mary Jo. *Women and American Socialism, 1870–1920.* Urbana: Univ. of Illinois Press, 1981.

Buhle, Paul. *Marxism in the USA from 1870 to the Present Day: Remapping the History of the American Left.* London: Verso, 1987.

Burke, Fielding [Mary Tilford Dargan]. *Call Home the Heart.* New York: Longmanns, Green, and Co., 1932.

Busst, A. J. L. "The Androgyne in the Nineteenth Century." In *Romantic Mythologies*, ed. Ian Fletcher, 5–95. New York: Barnes and Noble, 1967.

Butler, Judith. *Bodies That Matter: On the Discursive Limits of "Sex."* New York: Routledge, 1993.

———. *Gender Trouble: Feminism and the Subversion of Identity.* New York: Routledge, 1990.

Cane, Aleta. "Charlotte Perkins Gilman's *Herland* as a Feminist Response to Male Quest Romance." *Jack London Journal* 2 (1995): 25–38.
Cannon, Kelly. *Henry James and Masculinity: The Man at the Margins*. New York: St. Martin's Press, 1994.
Caramello, Charles. "The Duality of *The American Scene*." In *A Companion to Henry James Studies*, ed. Daniel Mark Fogel, 453–86. Westport, CT: Greenwood, 1993.
Carby, Hazel V. *Race Men*. Cambridge: Harvard Univ. Press, 1998.
Carlston, Erin G. *Thinking Fascism: Sapphic Modernism and Fascist Modernity*. Stanford: Stanford Univ. Press, 1998.
Carlton, David L., and Peter Coclanis, eds. *The Report on Economic Conditions of the South with Related Documents*. Boston: Bedford/ St. Martin's Press, 1996.
Castle, Terry. *The Apparitional Lesbian: Female Sexuality and Modern Culture*. New York: Columbia Univ. Press, 1993.
Castronovo, Russ. "Geo-Aesthetics: Fascism, Globalism, and Frank Norris." *boundary 2* 30, no. 3 (Fall 2003): 157–84.
Chase, Richard. *The American Novel and Its Tradition*. Baltimore: Johns Hopkins Univ. Press, 1957.
Cook, Sylvia Jenkins. *From Tobacco Road to Route 66: The Southern Poor White in Fiction*. Chapel Hill: Univ. of North Carolina Press, 1976.
Crumpacker, Laurie. "Four Novels of Harriet Beecher Stowe: A Study in Nineteenth-Century Androgyny." In *American Novelists Revisited: Essays in Feminist Criticism*, ed. Fritz Fleischmann, 78–106. Boston: G. K. Hall, 1982.
Curtis, George M., and James J. Thompson Jr., eds. *The Southern Essays of Richard M. Weaver*. Indianapolis: Liberty Press, 1987.
Darwin, Charles. *The Descent of Man*. In *Darwin: A Norton Critical Edition*, ed. Philip Appleman, 175–254. New York: Norton, 2001.
———. *On the Origin of Species: A Facsimile of the First Edition* Cambridge: Harvard Univ. Press, 1964.
Davidson, Donald. "Counterattack, 1930–1940: The South Against Leviathan." In *Southern Writers in the Modern World*, 31–62. Athens: Univ. of Georgia Press, 1958.
Davis, Arthur Paul. *From the Dark Tower*. Washington, DC: Howard Univ. Press, 1974.
Davis, Rebecca Harding. "Life in the Iron Mills." In *Four Stories by American Women*, ed. Cynthia Griffin Wolff, 1–40. New York: Penguin, 1990.
Den Tandt, Christophe. "Amazons and Androgynes: Overcivilization and the Redefinition of Gender Roles at the Turn of the Century." *American Literary History* 8, no. 4 (Winter 1996): 639–64.
Derrida, Jacques. "Sign, Structure, and Play in the Discourse of the Human Sciences." In *Writing and Difference*, translated and ed. Alan Bass, 278–94. Chicago: Univ. of Chicago Press, 1978.
Dijkstra, Bram. *Idols of Perversity: Fantasies of Feminine Evil in Fin-de-Siècle Culture*. New York: Oxford Univ. Press, 1986.
Dreger, Alice Domurat. *Hermaphrodites and the Medical Invention of Sex*. Cambridge: Harvard Univ. Press, 1998.
Du Bois, W. E. B. *The Autobiography of W. E. B. Du Bois*. New York: International Publishers, 1968.

———. "The Damnation of Women." In *W. E. B. Du Bois: A Reader*, ed. David Levering Lewis, 299–312. New York: Holt, 1995.

———. *Dusk of Dawn: An Essay Toward an Autobiography of a Race Concept*. New York: Harcourt, Brace and Co., 1940.

———. "Editorial." *Crisis* 4 (October 1912): 287–90.

———. "Miscegenation." In *Against Racism: Unpublished Essays, Papers, Addresses, 1887–1961*, ed. Herbert Aptheker, 90–102. Amherst: Univ. of Massachusetts Press, 1985.

———. *The Philadelphia Negro: A Social Study*. 1899. New York: Schockden Books, 1967.

———. "Races." *Crisis* 4 (August 1911): 157–58.

———. *The Souls of Black Folk*. 1903. New York: Penguin, 1996.

Duggan, Lisa. *Sapphic Slashers: Sex, Violence, and American Modernity*. Durham, NC: Duke Univ. Press, 2000.

Durkheim, Émile. *The Division of Labor in Society*. Translated by George Simpson. New York: Free Press, 1964.

Edel, Leon. *Henry James: The Conquest of London, 1870–1881*. New York: J. B. Lippincott, 1962.

Edwards, Rebecca. *Angels in the Machinery: Gender in American Party Politics from the Civil War to the Progressive Era*. New York: Oxford Univ. Press, 1997.

Eliot, T. S. *Four Quartets*. 1943. San Diego: Harcourt, Brace and Co., 1971.

———. *The Waste Land and Other Poems*. 1930. San Diego: Harcourt, Brace and Co., 1962.

Ellis, Havelock. "Sexual Inversion in Women." *Alienist and Neurologist* 16 (1895): 147–56.

Ellis, Havelock, and John Addington Symonds. *Sexual Inversion*. 1897. New York: Arno Press, 1975.

Emerson, Ralph Waldo. *The Journals and Miscellaneous Notebooks of Ralph Waldo Emerson*. ed. W. G. Gilman et al. 16 vols. Cambridge: Belknap Press of Harvard Univ., 1960–82.

———. *Nature*. In *The Selected Writings of Ralph Waldo Emerson*, ed. Brooks Atkinson, 3–39. New York: Modern Library, 1992.

———. "The Transcendentalist." In *The Selected Writings of Ralph Waldo Emerson*, ed. Brooks Atkinson, 81–95. New York: Modern Library, 1992.

Empson, William. *Some Versions of Pastoral*. New York: New Directions, 1974.

English, Daylanne K. *Unnatural Selections: Eugenics in American Modernism and the Harlem Renaissance*. Chapel Hill: Univ. of North Carolina Press, 2004.

Fain, John Tyree, and Thomas Daniel Young, eds. *The Literary Correspondence of Donald Davidson and Allen Tate*. Athens: Univ. of Georgia Press, 1974.

Felski, Rita. *The Gender of Modernity*. Cambridge: Harvard Univ. Press, 1995.

Flower, W. H., and James Murie. "Account of the Dissection of a Bushwoman." *Journal of Anatomy and Physiology* 1 (1867): 189–208.

Foley, Barbara. *Radical Representations: Politics and Form in U. S. Proletarian Fiction, 1929–1941*. Durham: Duke Univ. Press, 1993.

Foucault, Michel. Introduction to *Herculine Barbin: Being the Recently Discovered Memoirs of a Nineteenth-Century French Hermaphrodite*, by Herculine Barbin, translated by Richard McDougall. Sussex, England: Harvester Press, 1980.

———. *The History of Sexuality, Volume 1: An Introduction*. Translated by Robert Hurley. New York: Vintage, 1978.

Freud, Sigmund. *Civilization and Its Discontents*. 1930. Translated by James Strachey. New York: Norton, 1961.

———. "The Psychology of Women." In *New Introductory Lectures on Psychoanalysis*, translated by W. J. H. Sprott, 153–85. New York: W. W. Norton, 1933.

———. *Three Essays on the Theory of Sexuality*. 1905. Translated by James Strachey. London: Image, 1949.

Fugitive. Vol. 1, no. 1 (1922): 1.

Fuller, Margaret. *Woman in the Nineteenth Century*. 1845. Ed. Larry J. Reynolds. New York: W. W. Norton, 1998.

Gaines, Kevin K. *Uplifting the Race: Black Leadership, Politics, and Culture in the Twentieth Century*. Chapel Hill: Univ. of North Carolina Press, 1996.

Garber, Marjorie. *Vice Versa: Bisexuality and the Eroticism of Everyday Life*. New York: Simon and Schuster, 1995.

Geddes, Patrick, and J. Arthur Thomson. 1889. *The Evolution of Sex*. New York: Scribner's, 1890.

Gellner, Ernest. *Nations and Nationalism*. Oxford: Blackwell, 1983.

Gilbert, Sandra M., and Susan Gubar. *No Man's Land: The Place of the Woman Writer in the Twentieth Century*. 2 vols. New Haven: Yale Univ. Press, 1989.

Gilman, Charlotte Perkins. "A Suggestion on the Negro Problem." *Journal of American Sociology* 14, no. 1 (July 1908): 78–85.

———."Dr. Weininger's 'Sex and Character.'" *Critic* 48, no. 5 (May 1906): 414–17.

———. *Herland*. 1915. New York: Pantheon, 1979.

———. *The Man-Made World: Our Androcentric Culture*. 1911. In *The Yellow Wallpaper and Other Writings*. New York: Bantam, 1989.

———. "Our Place Today." In *Charlotte Perkins Gilman: A Nonfiction Reader*, ed. Larry Ceplair, 53–61. New York: Columbia Univ. Press, 1991.

———. *Women and Economics: A Study of the Economic Relation between Men and Women*. 1898. Amherst, NY: Prometheus Books, 1994.

Gold, Michael. "Go Left Young Writers!" *New Masses*, Jan. 1929, 3–4.

———. "Wilder: Prophet of the Genteel Christ." *New Republic*, Oct. 22, 1930, 266–67.

Gould, Charles W. *America, A Family Matter*. New York: Scribner's, 1922.

Graham, Wendy. *Henry James's Thwarted Love*. Stanford: Stanford Univ. Press, 1999.

Grazia, Victoria de. *How Fascism Ruled Women: Italy, 1922–1945*. Berkeley: Univ. of California Press, 1992.

Grazia, Victoria de, with Ellen Furlough, eds. *The Sex of Things: Gender and Consumption in Historical Perspective*. Berkeley: Univ. of California Press, 1996.

Griffin, Farah Jasmine. "Black Feminists and Du Bois: Respectability, Protection, and Beyond." *Annals of the American Academy of Political and Social Science* 568 (March 2000): 28–40.

Griffin, Roger. *Modernism and Fascism: The Sense of a Beginning under Mussolini and Hitler*. New York: Palgrave, 2007.

Guy-Sheftall, Beverly. *Daughters of Sorrow: Attitudes toward Black Women, 1880–1920*. New York: Carlson, 1990.

Halberstam, Judith. *Female Masculinity*. Durham: Duke Univ. Press, 1998.

Hall, Jacquelyn Dowd. "Private Eyes, Public Women: Images of Class and Sex in the Urban South, Atlanta, Georgia, 1913–1915." In *Work Engendered: Toward a New History of American Labor*, ed. Ava Baron, 243–72. Ithaca: Cornell Univ. Press, 1991.

Harris, Trudier. *Saints, Sinners, Saviors: Strong Black Women in African American Literature*. New York: Palgrave, 2001.

Hartley, Gasquoine. *The Position of Women in Primitive Society: A Study of the Matriarchy*. London: Eveleigh Nash, 1914.

Heffernan, Teresa. "Fascism and Madness: Woolf Writing Against Modernism." In *Virginia Woolf Miscellanies: Proceedings on the First Annual Conference on Virginia Woolf*, ed. Mark Hussey and Vara Neverow-Turk, 19–27. New York: Pace Univ. Press, 1992.

Heilbrun, Carolyn. "Further Notes Toward a Recognition of Androgyny." *Women's Studies* 2, no. 2 (1974): 143–50.

———. *Toward a Recognition of Androgyny*. New York: Norton, 1973.

Hobsbawm, Eric. *Nations and Nationalism since 1780: Programme, Myth, Reality*. Cambridge: Cambridge Univ. Press, 1990.

Hoganson, Kristin L. *Fighting for American Manhood: How Gender Politics Provoked the Spanish-American and Philippine-American Wars*. New Haven: Yale Univ. Press, 1998.

Horkheimer, Max, and Theodor Adorno. *The Dialectic of Enlightenment: Philosophical Fragments*. Ed. Gunzelin Schmid Noerr and translated by Edmund Jephcott. Stanford: Stanford Univ. Press, 2002.

Horowitz, Daniel. *The Morality of Spending: Attitudes Toward the Consumer Society in America, 1875–1940*. Baltimore: Johns Hopkins Univ. Press, 1985.

Horowitz, Helen Lefkowitz. *Rereading Sex: Battles over Sexual Knowledge and Suppression in Nineteenth-Century America*. New York: Alfred Knopf, 2002.

Howe, Julia Ward. *The Hermaphrodite*. Ed. Gary Williams. Lincoln: Univ. of Nebraska Press, 2004.

Hughes, Langston. *The Big Sea: An Autobiography*. 1940. New York: Hill, 1993.

Ignatiev, Noel. *How the Irish Became White*. London: Routledge, 1995.

Ikonné, Chidi. *From Du Bois to Van Vechten: The Early New Negro Literature 1903–1926*. Westport, CT: Greenwood Press, 1981.

Irigaray, Luce. *The Sex Which Is Not One*. Translated by Catherine Porter. Ithaca, NY: Cornell Univ. Press, 1985.

James, Henry. *The American Scene*. 1907. New York: Penguin, 1994.

———. *The Bostonians*. 1886. New York: Penguin, 1986.

———. *French Poets and Novelists*. Ed. Leon Edel. New York: Grosset and Dunlap, 1964.

———. *Henry James: Literary Criticism*. Ed. Leon Edel and Mark Wilson. New York: Library of America, 1984.

———. *Letters*. Ed. Leon Edel. 4 vols. Cambridge: Harvard Univ. Press, 1974–84.

———. "The Manners of American Women." In *French Writers and American Women: Essays by Henry James*, ed. Peter Buitenhuis, 54–81. Branford, CT: Compass, 1960.

———. "The Question of Our Speech." In *French Writers and American Women: Essays by Henry James*, ed. Peter Buitenhuis, 18–31. Branford, CT: Compass, 1960.

———. "The Speech of American Women." In *French Writers and American Women: Essays by Henry James*, ed. Peter Buitenhuis, 32–53. Branford, CT: Compass, 1960.

———. *Tales of Henry James*. Ed. Christof Weglin. New York: Norton, 1984.

Jones, Anne Goodwyn. *Tomorrow Is Another Day: The Woman Writer in the South*. Baton Rouge: Louisiana State Univ. Press, 1981.

Jones, Anne Goodwyn, and Susan V. Donaldson. "Haunted Bodies: Rethinking the South through Gender." In *Haunted Bodies: Gender and Southern Texts,* ed. Anne Goodwyn Jones and Susan V. Donaldson, 1–19. Charlottesville: Univ. Press of Virginia, 1997.
Jung, Carl. *The Archetypes and the Collective Unconsciousness.* Translated by R. F. C. Hull, Princeton, NJ: Princeton Univ. Press, 1968.
Kanter, Emmanuel. *The Amazons.* Chicago: Charles Kerr, 1926.
Kaplan, Justin. *Walt Whitman: A Life.* New York: Simon and Schuster, 1980.
Katz, Jonathan Ned. *The Invention of Heterosexuality.* New York: Dutton, 1995.
Kelley, Robin D. G. *Hammer and Hoe: Alabama Communists During the Great Depression.* Chapel Hill: Univ. of North Carolina Press, 1990.
———. *Race Rebels: Culture, Politics, and the Black Working Class.* New York: Free Press, 1994.
Kennedy, Hubert. *Ulrichs: The Life and Work of Heinrich Ulrichs, Pioneer of the Modern Gay Movement.* Boston: Alyson Publications, 1988.
Kerber, Linda K. "Separate Spheres, Female Worlds, Woman's Place: The Rhetoric of Women's History." In *No More Separate Spheres!* ed. Cathy N. Davidson and Jessamyn Hatcher, 29–65. Durham: Duke Univ. Press, 2002.
Kessler-Harris, Alice, and Paul Lauter. Introduction to *Call Home the Heart,* by Fielding Burke, vii–xvi. Old Westbury, CT: Feminist Press, 1983.
Kimmel, Michael. *Manhood in America: A Cultural History.* New York: Free Press, 1996.
Krafft-Ebing, Richard von. *Psychopathia Sexualis.* Translated by Charles Gilbert Chaddock. 1886. Philadelphia: F. A. Davis, 1908.
Kreyling, Michael. *Inventing Southern Literature.* Jackson: Univ. Press of Mississippi, 1998.
Lant, Kathleen Margaret. "The Rape of the Text: Charlotte Gilman's Violation of *Herland.*" *Tulsa Studies in Women's Literature* 9 (Fall 1990): 291–308.
Laqueur, Thomas. *Making Sex: Body and Gender from the Greeks to Freud.* Cambridge: Harvard Univ. Press, 1990.
Le Conte, Joseph. "The Effect of Mixture of Races on Human Progress." *Berkeley Quarterly* 1 (1880): 81–104.
———. "The Genesis of Sex." *Popular Science Monthly* 16 (1879): 167–79.
Lemke, Sieglinde. "Berlin and Boundaries: *sollen* versus *geschehen.*" *boundary 2* 27, no. 3 (2000): 45–78.
Levander, Caroline. *Voices of the Nation: Women and Public Speech in Nineteenth-Century American Literature and Culture.* Cambridge: Cambridge Univ. Press, 1998.
Leverenz, David. *Paternalism Incorporated: Fables of American Fatherhood, 1865–1940.* Ithaca, NY: Cornell Univ. Press, 2003.
Lewis, David Levering. *W. E. B. Du Bois: Biography of a Race, 1868–1919.* New York: Henry Holt and Co., 1993.
———. *When Harlem Was in Vogue.* New York: Oxford Univ. Press, 1979.
Lewis, George. *The White South and the Red Menace: Segregationists, Anticommunism, and Massive Resistance, 1945–1965.* Gainesville: Univ. Press of Florida, 2004.
Lewis, H. H. *Thinking of Russia.* Holt, MN: Haaglund Press, 1932.
Lichtenstein, Perry M. "The 'Fairy' and the Lady Lover." *Medical Review of Reviews* 27 (1921): 369–74.

Lhamon, W. T., Jr. *Raising Cain: Blackface Performance from Jim Crow to Hip Hop.* Cambridge: Harvard Univ. Press, 1998.

Locke, Alain. "The New Negro." In *The New Negro,* ed. Alain Locke, 3–16. New York: Simon and Schuster, 1997.

Locke, John. *An Essay Concerning Human Understanding.* Ed. Kenneth P. Winkler. Indianapolis: Hackett Publishing, 1996.

Long, Lisa A. "Charlotte Perkins Gilman's *With Her in Ourland:* Herland Meets Heterodoxy." In *Charlotte Perkins Gilman and Her Contemporaries: Literary and Intellectual Contexts,* ed. Cynthia J. Davis and Denise D. Knight, 171–93. Tuscaloosa: Univ. of Alabama Press, 2004.

Lott, Eric. *Love and Theft: Blackface and the American Working Class.* New York: Oxford Univ. Press, 1993.

Lukács, Georg. *The Theory of the Novel: A Historico-Philosophical Essay on the Forms of Great Epic Literature.* Translated by Anna Bostock. Cambridge: MIT Press, 1971.

Lumpkin, Grace. "I Want a King." *FIGHT against War and Fascism* 3, no. 4 (1936): 3, 14.

———. *To Make My Bread.* 1932. Urbana: Univ. of Illinois Press, 1995.

Malvasi, Mark G. *The Unregenerate South: The Agrarian Thought of John Crowe Ransom, Allen Tate, and Donald Davidson.* Baton Rouge: Louisiana State Univ. Press, 1997.

Marcus, Jane. *Hearts of Darkness: White Women Writing Race.* New Brunswick, NJ: Rutgers Univ. Press, 2004.

Marx, Karl. *Capital: A Critique of Political Economy.* Vol. 1. 1867. Translated by Ben Fowkes. New York: Penguin, 1990.

Marx, Karl, and Friedrich Engels. *The Communist Manifesto.* Ed. Martin Malia. New York: Signet, 1998.

Matossian, Lou Ann. "A Woman-Made Language: Charlotte Perkins Gilman and *Herland.*" *Women and Language* 10, no. 2 (1987): 16–20.

Matthiessen, F. O., and K. B. Murdock, eds. *Notebooks of Henry James.* New York: George Braziller, 1947.

McClintock, Anne. "'No Longer in a Future Heaven': Nationalism, Gender, and Race." In *Becoming National: A Reader,* ed. Geoff Eley and Ronald Grigor Suny, 260–84. New York: Oxford Univ. Press, 1996.

Merish, Lori. *Sentimental Materialism: Gender, Commodity Culture, and Nineteenth-Century American Literature.* Durham: Duke Univ. Press, 2000.

Michaels, Walter Benn. *The Gold Standard and the Logic of Naturalism: American Literature at the Turn of the Century.* Berkeley: Univ. of California Press, 1987.

Miller, James E. *Leaves of Grass: America's Lyric-Epic of Self and Democracy.* New York: Twayne Publishing, 1992.

Miller, Monica L. "W. E. B. Du Bois and the Dandy as Diasporic Race Man." *Callaloo* 26, no. 3 (2003): 738–65.

Model, Suzanne W. "Work and Family: Blacks and Immigrants from South and East Europe." In *Immigration Reconsidered: History, Sociology, Politics,* ed. Virginia Yans-McLaughlin, 130–59. New York: Oxford Univ. Press, 1990.

Moi, Toril. *Sexual/Textual Politics: Feminist Literary Theory.* New York: Routledge, 1985.

Morris, [?]. "Is Evolution Trying to Do Away with the Clitoris?" Paper presented at the meeting of the American Association of Obstetricians and Gynecologists, St. Louis, MO. 21 September 1892. Pamphlet, Yale Univ. Medical Library, New Haven, CT.

Mosse, George L. *Nationalism and Sexuality: Respectability and Abnormal Sexuality in Modern Europe.* New York: Howard Fertig, 1985.
Murphy, Paul V. *The Rebuke of History: The Southern Agrarians and American Conservative Thought.* Chapel Hill: Univ. of North Carolina Press, 2001.
Musser, Judith. "African American Women and Education: Marita Bonner's Response to the 'Talented Tenth.'" *Studies in Short Fiction* 34, no. 1 (1997): 73–85.
Nairn, Tom. *Faces of Nationalism: Janus Revisited.* London: Verso, 1998.
Neocleous, Mark A. *Fascism.* Minneapolis: Minnesota Univ. Press, 1997.
Newman, Louise Michele. *White Women's Rights: The Racial Origins of Feminism in the United States.* New York: Oxford Univ. Press, 1999.
Norris, Frank. "The Frontier Gone at Last." In *The Literary Criticism of Frank Norris,* ed. Donald Pizer, 111–17. Austin: Univ. of Texas Press, 1964.
———."Novelists of the Future: The Training They Need." In *The Literary Criticism of Frank Norris,* ed. Donald Pizer, 10–14. Austin: Univ. of Texas Press, 1964.
———. *The Octopus: A Story of California.* 1901. New York: Penguin, 1994.
Novick, Sheldon M. Introduction to *Henry James and Homo-Erotic Desire,* ed. John R. Bradley, 1–23. New York: St. Martin's Press, 1999.
Nugent, Richard Bruce. "Narcissus." *Trend* 1 (January–March 1933): 127.
Page, Myra. *The Gathering Storm. A Story of the Black Belt.* New York: International Publishers, 1932.
Painter, Nell Irvin. *Standing at Armageddon: The United States, 1877–1919.* New York: W. W. Norton, 1987.
Pateman, Carol. *The Sexual Contract.* Stanford: Stanford Univ. Press, 1988.
Pater, Walter. *Plato and Platonism.* Charleston, SC: Bibliobazaar, 2007.
Petty, Leslie. *Romancing the Vote: Feminist Activism in American Fiction, 1870–1920.* Athens: Univ. of Georgia Press, 2006.
Phelan, Shane. *Sexual Strangers: Gays, Lesbians, and Dilemmas of Citizenship.* Philadelphia: Temple Univ. Press, 2001.
Quinlan, Kieran. *John Crowe Ransom's Secular Faith.* Baton Rouge: Louisiana State Univ. Press, 1989.
Rabinowitz, Paula A. *Labor and Desire: Women's Revolutionary Writing Fiction in Depression America.* Chapel Hill: Univ. of North Carolina Press, 1991.
Rado, Lisa. *The Modern Androgyne Imagination: A Failed Sublime.* Charlottesville: Univ. Press of Virginia, 2000.
———. "Primitivism, Modernism, and Matriarchy." In *Modernism, Gender, and Culture: A Cultural Studies Approach,* ed. Lisa Rado, 283–300. New York: Garland, 1997.
Ransom, John Crowe. "Art and the Human Economy." *Kenyon Review* 7 (Autumn 1945): 683–88.
———. *God Without Thunder: An Orthodox Defense of Orthodoxy.* 1930. Hamden, CT: Archon Books, 1965.
———. "Reconstructed but Unregenerate." In *I'll Take My Stand: The South and the Agrarian Tradition,* by Twelve Southerners, 1–27. New York: Harper, 1962.
———. *Two Gentlemen in Bonds.* New York: Knopf, 1927.
———. "What Does the South Want?" In *Who Owns America? A New Declaration of Independence,* ed. Herbert Agar and Allen Tate, 233–52. Wilmington, DE: ISI Books, 1999.
———. *The World's Body.* 1938. Baton Rouge: Louisiana State Univ. Press, 1968.

Reed, John Shelton. "For Dixieland: The Sectionalism of *I'll Take My Stand.*" In *A Band of Prophets: The Vanderbilt Agrarians after Fifty Years*, ed. William C. Havard and Walter Sullivan, 41–64. Baton Rouge: Louisiana State Press, 1982.
Reis, Elizabeth. "Impossible Hermaphrodites: Intersex in America, 1620–1960." *Journal of American History* 92, no. 2 (2005): 411–41.
Rideout, Walter B. *The Radical Novel in the United States 1900–1954: Some Interrelations of Literature and Society.* Cambridge: Harvard Univ. Press, 1956.
Robbins, Jack Alan, ed. *Granville Hicks in The New Masses.* Port Washington, NY: Kennikat Press, 1974.
Roediger, David. *The Wages of Whiteness: Race and the Making of the American Working Class.* New York: Verso, 1991.
Rollins, William, Jr. *The Shadow Before.* New York: Robert M. McBride and Co., 1934.
Romero, Lora. *Home Fronts: Domesticity and Its Critics in the Antebellum United States.* Durham: Duke Univ. Press, 1997.
Roosevelt, Theodore. "The Value of an Athletic Training." *Harper's Weekly,* December 23, 1893, 1236.
———. *The Works of Theodore Roosevelt.* 14 vols. New York: Charles Scribner's Sons, 1925.
Roses, Lorraine Elena, and Ruth Elizabeth Randolph. "Marita Bonner: In Search of Our Mothers' Gardens." *Black American Literature Forum* 21 (Spring–Summer 1987): 165–83.
Rowe, John Carlos. *The Other Henry James.* Durham: Duke Univ. Press, 1998.
Schwartz, A. B. Christa. *Gay Voices of the Harlem Renaissance.* Bloomington: Indiana Univ. Press, 2003.
Sears, John F. Introduction to *The American Scene,* by Henry James, vii–xxii. New York: Penguin, 1994.
Secor, Cynthia. "Androgyny: An Early Reappraisal." *Women's Studies* 2, no. 2 (1974): 161–69.
Sedgwick, Eve Kosofsky. *Epistemology of the Closet.* Berkeley: Univ. of California Press, 1990.
Seltzer, Mark. *Bodies and Machines.* New York: Routledge, 1992.
Smethurst, James. "On Race, Homosexuality, and Visual and Verbal Androgyny in Cullen's Work." *Modern American Poetry: An Online Journal and Multimedia Companion to Anthology of Modern American Poetry.* http://www.english.uiuc.edu/maps/poets/a_f/cullen/androgyny.htm.
Smith-Rosenberg, Carroll. *Disorderly Conduct: Visions of Gender in Victorian America.* New York: Oxford Univ. Press, 1985.
Sollors, Werner. *Neither Black nor White yet Both: Thematic Explorations of Interracial Literature.* New York: Oxford Univ. Press, 1997.
Somerville, Siobhan B. *Queering the Color Line: Race and the Invention of Homosexuality in American Culture.* Durham, NC: Duke Univ. Press, 2000.
Sowinska, Suzanne. Introduction to *To Make My Bread,* by Grace Lumpkin, vii–xliii. Urbana: Univ. of Illinois Press, 1995.
Stanton, Elizabeth Cady. "Educated Suffrage." *Colliers Weekly,* April 12, 1902, 9
———. *The Woman's Bible.* 1895. Amherst, NY: Prometheus Books, 1999.
Starr, Kevin. Introduction to *The Octopus: A Story of California,* by Frank Norris, vii–xxxi. New York: Penguin, 1994.
Stepan, Nancy Leys. "Race and Gender: The Role of Analogy in Science." In *Anatomy of Racism,* ed. David Theo Goldberg, 38–57. Minneapolis: Univ. of Minnesota Press, 1990.

Stepto, Robert B. *From Behind the Veil: A Study of Afro-American Narrative.* Urbana: Univ. of Illinois Press, 1979.

Stites, Richard. *The Women's Liberation Movement in Russia: Feminism, Nihilism, and Bolshevism, 1860–1930.* Princeton: Princeton Univ. Press, 1991.

Stokes, Mason. "Strange Fruits: Rethinking the Gay Twenties." *Transition* 12, no. 2 (2002): 56–77.

Tamarkin, Elisa. "Black Anglophilia; or, The Sociability of Antislavery." *American Literary History* 14, no. 3 (2002): 444–78.

Tate, Allen. "Fascism and the Southern Agrarians." *New Republic,* May 27, 1936, 75–76.

Theweleit, Klaus. *Male Fantasies, vol. 1: Women, Floods, Bodies, History.* Translated by Stephan Conway. Minneapolis: Univ. of Minnesota Press, 1977.

Thurin, Erik Ingvar. *Emerson as Priest of Pan: A Study in the Metaphysics of Sex.* Lawrence: Regents Press of Kansas, 1981.

Tocqueville, Alexis de. *Democracy in America.* 2 vols. Trans. Henry Reeve and ed. Phillips Bradley. New York: Knopf, 1945.

Twelve Southerners. "Statement of Principles." In *I'll Take My Stand: The South and the Agrarian Tradition,* by Twelve Southerners, xix–xxx. New York: Harper, 1962.

Ullman, Sharon, R. *Sex Seen: The Emergence of Modern Sexuality in America.* Berkeley: Univ. of California Press, 1997.

Van Leer, David. "A World of Female Friendship: *The Bostonians.*" In *Henry James and Homo-Erotic Desire,* ed. John R. Bradley, 93–109. New York: St. Martin's Press, 1999.

Van Wienen, Mark W. "A Rose by Any Other Name: Charlotte Perkins Stetson (Gilman) and the Case for American Reform Socialism." *American Quarterly* 55, no. 4 (2003): 603–34.

Veblen, Thorstein. *The Theory of the Leisure Class.* 1899. New York: Penguin, 1994.

Vorse, Mary Heaton. *Strike!* New York: Horace Liveright, 1930.

Walkowitz, Daniel J. "The Making of a Feminine Professional Identity: Social Workers in the 1920s." *American Historical Review* 95, no. 4 (October 1990): 1051–75.

Wall, Cheryl A. *Women of the Harlem Renaissance.* Bloomington: Indiana Univ. Press, 1995.

Walters, Ronald G. *American Reformers, 1815–1860.* New York: Hill and Wang, 1978.

Ward, Lester F. *Pure Sociology: A Treatise on the Origin and Spontaneous Development of Society.* New York: Macmillan, 1909.

Warmington, Eric H., and Philip G. Rouse. *Great Dialogues of Plato.* Translated by W. H. D. Rouse. New York: Mentor, 1984.

Watkins, Floyd C., John T. Hiers, and Mary Louise Weaks, eds. *Talking with Robert Penn Warren.* Athens: Univ. of Georgia Press, 1990.

Watson, Ritchie. "'The Difference of Race': Antebellum Race and the Development of Southern Nationalism." *Southern Literary Journal* 35, no. 1 (2002): 1–13.

Watson, Steven. *The Harlem Renaissance: Hub of African American Culture, 1920–1930.* New York: Pantheon Books, 1995.

Weil, Kari. *Androgyny and the Denial of Difference.* Charlottesville: Univ. Press of Virginia, 1992.

Weininger, Otto. *Sex and Character.* Translated by Ladislaus Löb. 1901. New York: AMS Press, 1975.

Welter, Barbara. "The Cult of True Womanhood, 1820–1860." *American Quarterly* 18, no. 2 (1966): 151–74.

West, Lon. *Deconstructing Frank Norris's Fiction: The Male-Female Dialectic.* New York: Peter Lang, 1998.

Whitman, Walt. *Leaves of Grass and Other Writings.* Ed. Michael Moon. New York: W. W. Norton, 2002.

———. *Leaves of Grass: The First (1855) Edition.* Ed. Malcom Cowley. New York: Penguin, 1986.

Wilks, Jennifer Margaret. "Modernist Women of the Black Atlantic: Gender and Intellectual Citizenship in the Harlem Renaissance and Negritude." Ph.D. diss., Cornell Univ., 2003.

Williams, Gary. Introduction to *The Hermaphrodite,* by Julia Ward Howe, x–xliv. Lincoln: Univ. of Nebraska Press, 2004.

Wilt, Judith. "Desperately Seeking Verena: A Resistant Reading of *The Bostonians.*" *Feminist Studies* 13, no. 2 (1987): 293–316.

Wirth, Thomas H., ed. *Gay Rebel of the Harlem Renaissance: Selections from the Work of Richard Bruce Nugent.* Durham: Duke Univ. Press, 2002.

Whisnant, David E. *All That Is Native and Fine: The Politics of Culture in an American Region.* Chapel Hill: Univ. of North Carolina Press, 1983.

Wolff, Cynthia Griffin. "'Masculinity' in *Uncle Tom's Cabin.*" *American Quarterly* 47, no. 4 (1995): 595–618.

Woolf, Virginia. *A Room of One's Own.* 1929. San Diego: Harcourt Brace Jovanovich, 1957.

———. *Three Guineas.* 1938. San Diego: Harcourt Brace Jovanovich, 1966.

Wyatt-Brown, Bertram. *Southern Honor: Ethics and Behavior in the Old South.* Oxford: Oxford Univ. Press, 1983.

Young, Robert J. C. *Colonial Desire: Hybridity in Theory, Culture and Race.* London: Routledge, 1995.

Young, Thomas Daniel, and George Core, eds. *Selected Letters of John Crowe Ransom.* Baton Rouge: Louisiana State Univ. Press, 1985.

Zauderer, Naomi B. "Consumption, Production, and Reproduction in the Works of Charlotte Perkins Gilman." In *Charlotte Perkins Gilman: Optimist Reformer,* ed. Jill Rudd and Val Gough, 151–72. Iowa City: Univ. of Iowa Press, 1999.

INDEX

Abolition, 4, 8, 21, 23, 25, 27–28, 112
Académie Julian, 62
Adam. *See* Eden
Addams, Jane, 90
Adorno, Theodor, 93, 107
Agassiz, Louis, 8
"Age of Gonads," 9–10
Agrarianism, 15, 80, 82–83, 88, 91–94, 96–7, 107, 109, 141–42, 154n9, 154n14, 155n34
Alabama Communist Party, 80
Alexander, Lewis, 160n56
Allen, Carol, 130, 132
Ambassadors, The. *See* James, Henry
America: A Family Matter (Gould), 130
American Anti-Slavery Society, 25, 27
American Federation of Labor, 80
American Missionary Association, 90
American Novel and Its Tradition, The (Chase), 141
American Review, The, 96, 141
American Scene, The. *See* James, Henry
Anderson, Benedict, 7, 77, 115
Anderson, Sherwood, 98, 156n57
androgyny: and atavism, 49–50, 52, 79; and body politic, 5–8, 61, 81–82, 97, 99, 112, 114, 136–37, 143; in Christ, 4, 15, 28, 81, 154n15; in Christian Godhead, 85–86, 88, 92, 123, 141, 154n15, 154n16; and commercialism, 47 *passim*; and conflation with homosexuality, 9, 18–21, 23–24, 106; and conflation with socialism, 81, 106; in evolutionary science, 49–50, 52, 79; and fascism, 16, 137–43; and racial science, 8, 19–20, 113–14; and racial uplift, 111–12; in sexological discourse, 9, 18–19, 21, 23–24, 52, 64–65, 70, 148n15; in transcendentalism, 3–7, 116
Anglo-Catholicism, 85
anticommunism, 88, 99, 109, 135
anti-Marxism, 82, 97
"Antique Harvesters." *See* Ransom, John Crowe
Appomattox, 12, 27
Aristotle (pseudonym), 4
"Art and the Human Economy." *See* Ransom, John Crowe
"Art of Fiction, The." *See* James, Henry
Asheville, North Carolina, 90
Atalanta, 118, 122
"Atlanta Compromise" speech (Washington), 120
Atlanta, Georgia, 80, 118, 121–22
Atlanta University, 117, 121
Auerbach, Nina, 27

Baker, Houston A., 127
Ballanche, Pierre-Simon, 2, 4, 6, 31
Balshaw, Maria, 160n65
Baltimore Sun, The, 95, 125
Barbin, Herculine, 9

Barr, Stringfellow, 88
"Bastard Song" (Nugent), 126
"Battle Hymn of the Republic" (Howe), 4
Bazin, Nancy Topping, 12
"Beast in the Jungle, The." *See* James, Henry
Bederman, Gail, 43, 159n35
Beecher, Lyman, 62
Bellamy, Edward, 72
Bender, Bert, 59
Bennett, Gwendolyn, 160n56
Bentley, Gladys, 125
Bergson, Henri, 87, 141
Berkson, Dorothy, 75
Berman, Jessica, 37, 39
Beyond Desire (Anderson), 156n57
Bhabha, Homi K., 133–34
blackface. *See* minstrelsy
Blair, Sara, 150n66
Blight, David, 34–35
Böhme, Jakob, 81
Bolsheviks, 81
Book of American Negro Poetry, The (Johnson, ed.), 83
Bonner, Marita, 11, 15–16, 111–14 *passim*, 137–8, 140; education of, 126; and literary salon in Washington, D.C., 126; "Nothing New," 129–35; "On Being Young—a Woman—and Colored," 126–29; "A Possible Triad on Black Notes," 132, 136; and published stories in journals, 126; "There Were Three," 132, 134–35
Bontemps, Arna, 160n56
Boston Marriage, 20
Boston, Massachusetts, 23–26, 32–33, 36, 126
Bostonians, The. See James, Henry
Bowery Theater, 29
Boxhill, Bernard R., 121
"Briar Patch, The" (Warren), 91–92, 155n34
Bryan, William Jennings, 84, 153n53
Bryn Mawr College, 37–39, 41, 44–45
Buhle, Paul, 81
Burke, Fielding (Olive Tilford Dargan), 96, 156n57
Butler, Judith, 10–11, 66, 68, 143

Caldwell, Erskine, 96
Call Home the Heart (Burke), 156n57
Cannon, Kelly, 19
Capital (Marx), 101
capitalism, 8, 11, 14–15, 28, 38, 54, 56, 58–59, 61, 70, 80–84, 88, 98, 101–5, 108
Carby, Hazel, 115, 120

Carpenter, Edward, 18–19, 106
Cash, W. J., 83
Casper, J. L., 18
Castle, Terry, 33
Catt, Carrie Chapman, 77
Central Powers, 135
Charleston, South Carolina, 33, 42
Chase, Richard, 141
Chester, Susan, 90
Child, Lydia Maria, 25
Chills and Fever. See Ransom, John Crowe
Chocorua Mountain, 40, 88
Christ, 4, 28, 81, 85, 112, 154n15
Civil War, 6–10, 13–14, 16–17, 21, 25, 34, 42, 44, 48, 84, 88, 90, 98, 112, 114–15
Cleveland, Grover, 8
Cloak, B., 10
collective novel, 100, 104, 142
Collins, Seward, 96, 141
Columbia, South Carolina, 98–99, 107
communism, 82, 88, 99, 106, 109, 135
Communist Manifesto, The (Marx and Engels), 81
Communist Party of the United States of America (CPUSA), 80, 97–99, 101, 109
Compleat Master-piece, The (Aristotle), 4–5
complex novel, 100, 142
Cook, Sylvia Jenkins, 103, 156n48
Crisis, 114–15, 121, 123, 126, 129
Crumpacker, Laurie, 112
Cullen, Countée, 123, 125, 160n56
Cuney, Waring, 160n56

Daisy Miller. See James, Henry
d'Alquen, Gunther, 162n8
"Damnation of Women, The." *See* Du Bois, W. E. B.
Darrow, Clarence, 84
Darwin, Charles, 52–54, 62
Daughters of the Confederacy, 107
Davidson, Donald, 82
Davis, Jefferson, 8
Davis, Rebecca Harding, 81
De Forest, John, 28
Delacroix, Eugène, 50
democracy, 8–10, 13, 16–17, 48, 50, 59, 84, 89, 124; and androgyny in Emerson, 3–4, 116; and androgyny in Fuller, 5; and androgyny in Whitman, 5–7, 116; and androgyny in Woolf, 138–40; and blending of genders, 1–3, 11, 114, 132, 134, 137; and race relations, 34, 45–46, 65, 111–12, 129, 134–36; and similarities to

fascism, 60, 135–36, 139–42; and women's liberation, 5, 20, 24–25, 31, 109, 143
Democracy in America (Tocqueville), 1–2, 48, 137
Democratic Party, 8
Den Tandt, Christophe, 49
Derrida, Jacques, 75
devolution, 43, 112, 140
Dial, The, 5
Dialectic of Enlightenment (Horkheimer and Adorno), 107
District of Columbia, 42, 126
Dos Passos, John, 98
Douglas, Aaron, 125, 160n56
Douglass, Frederick, 25, 27
Dreger, Alice Domurat, 9
Du Bois, Burghardt, 124
Du Bois, W. E. B., 11, 15–16, 111 passsim, 142, 159n42; childhood of, 117; "The Damnation of Women," 158n16; *Dusk of Dawn*, 121–22; and editorship of *Crisis*, 114–15, 121, 123; education of, 117–18; as father, 123–24; Herderian influence on, 114–17, 119, 121, 123; "Miscegenation," 122; Old South nostalgia of, 122–23; *The Philadelphia Negro*, 115, 118; *The Souls of Black Folk*, 115, 117–24, 127, 142; support of women's rights by, 115; and time in Berlin, 117–18
Du Bois, Yolande, 123–24
Duggan, Lisa, 21–22
durée, 87
Durkheim, Émile, 63, 152n32
Dusk of Dawn. *See* Du Bois, W. E. B.

Eden, 2, 31, 81, 101
"Effect of Mixture of Races on Human Progress, The" (Le Conte), 59
Egypt, 21
Eisenbach, Germany, 118
élan vital, 141
Eliot, T. S., 69, 83, 85, 87, 152n44, 159n42
Ellis, Havelock, 18–19, 21
Emerson, Ralph Waldo, 3–5, 9, 14, 116, 145n8
Engels, Friedrich, 81
English, Daylanne K., 123, 159n42
Ephrata, 81
epic (literary genre), 5–7, 49–51, 54–57, 60, 117
Episcopalianism, 98–99
Equality League of Self-Supporting Women, 74
Essay Concerning Human Understanding (Locke), 48
Eve. *See* Eden

evolution, 10, 14–15, 18–20, 23, 43–44, 46–47, 49–54, 59, 61–67, 69–70, 72–73, 75–76, 79, 113, 116, 119, 140, 153n62
Evolution of Sex (Thomson and Geddes), 113

fascism, 13, 16, 60, 96–97, 106, 108, 137–42, 161n1, 162n8
Faulkner, William, 96
Felski, Rita, 118
feminism, 10, 62, 72; in antebellum era, 5, 25, 28, 112–13; and Gilman's Nationalism, 72; and homosexuality, 9, 106; and MLA session on *Toward a Recognition of Androgyny*, 12; in postbellum era, 12, 22, 27; in postmodern era, 12–13; and radicalism, 97, 99, 101–3, 106–7; in second-wave era, 12–13, 133, 142–43; and sexological discourse, 9, 13–14, 21, 23–24, 148n15
Fifteenth Amendment, 20
Fifty-Fourth Massachusetts Colored Regiment, 35
FIGHT Against War and Fascism, 96
Firell, 125, 160n56
Fisk University, 117
Five Year Plan, 88
Flower, W. H., 113
Flynn, Elizabeth Gurley, 97
Foley, Barbara, 96–97, 100, 156n48
Forerunner, The, 63, 69
"Forms and Citizens." *See* Ransom, John Crowe
Foucault, Michel, 9, 18
Four Quartets (Eliot), 69
Four Thousand Miles of African Travel (Southworth), 21
Fourteenth Amendment, 20
Frankfurt School, 93
Freedmen's Bureau, 90
Freeman, Alma, 12
Freikorps, 135–36
French Revolution, 1–2, 137
Freud, Sigmund, 10–11, 30, 161n4, 161n76
frontier (American), 12, 43, 57
"Frontier Gone at Last, The." *See* Norris, Frank
Fugitive, The, 83
Fuller, Margaret, 5, 23, 112–13
Fulton Bag and Cotton Mill, 80
"Furl That Banner" (Ryan), 107

Garrison, William Lloyd, 25
Garvey, Marcus, 121–22
Gastonia, North Carolina, 15, 80, 98–99, 156n57

Gathering Storm, The (Page), 156n57
Geddes, Patrick, 113
Gellner, Ernest, 38
"Genesis of Sex, The" (Le Conte), 59
Gentile, Giovanni, 141
Georgia, 8, 98, 118, 126, 130
Germany, 4, 117–18, 135–37, 139–40, 142, 162n8
Gilded Age, 21, 35
Gilded Age, The (Twain and Warner), 42
Gillette, William, 28
Gilman, Charlotte Perkins, 11, 14, 47, 49–50 *passim*, 79, 105, 131, 140–41; and divorce, 62, 68; education of, 62–63; *Herland*, 14, 62–64, 66, 69–78, 105, 131; *The Man-Made World*, 66; and marriage, 62, 68; as patient of S. Weir Mitchell, 68; politics and activism of, 62, 72–73, 77, 153n53; and racial attitudes, 50, 63–70, 72, 76, 78, 153n62; and relationship to daughter, 62, 68; "A Suggestion on the Negro Problem," 67, 72, 76; *Women and Economics*, 14, 63–71, 73, 76–78, 140
God Without Thunder. See Ransom, John Crowe
Gold, Mike, 98
Gould, Charles W., 130
Graham, Wendy, 18
Grand, Sarah (Frances Bellenden Clarke), 21
Great Barrington, Massachusetts, 117
Great Depression, 11, 13, 15, 78, 80, 82, 87, 92–93, 98, 102
"Great Lawsuit, The" (Fuller). See *Woman in the Nineteenth Century*
Great Migration, 127
Great War. See World War I
Grimké, Angela Weld, 126
Guy-Sheftall, Beverly, 122

Hall, Thomas/Thomasine, 9–10
Hampton, Wade, 107
Harlem Renaissance, 15, 83, 114, 124–27, 131, 160n65
Harper's Bazaar, 37
Harris, Joel Chandler, 101
Harris, Trudier, 158n13
Hartley, Gasquione, 69–70
H. D. (Hilda Doolittle), 11
Heffernan, Teresa, 139
Heilbrun, Carolyn, 12–13, 19, 133, 142–43, 147n44
Held by the Enemy (Gillette), 28
Hemingway, Ernest, 11
Herbst, Josephine, 98
Herder, Johann Gottlieb von, 2–5, 15, 91, 108–9, 114–17, 119, 121, 123, 127, 129, 142

Herland. See Gilman, Charlotte Perkins
Hermaphrodite, The (Howe), 4–5
Herrick, Robert, 11
hermaphroditism, 4–5, 21, 76, 161n4; as distinct from androgyny, 11; and electoral politics, 8, 111–12; medical dismissal of, 9–11; in primitive life forms, 18, 49, 51–53, 59
Hicks, Granville, 98, 104
Hindenburg, Paul von, 136
Hindman Settlement School, 90
Hippomenes, 118–19
Hitler, Adolf, 96, 136, 139–40, 142
Hobbes, Thomas, 75
Holy Ghost, 15, 85
homosexuality: and conflation with androgyny, 9, 18–21, 23–24, 106; and conflation with feminism, 9, 106; in relation to Harlem Renaissance, 123–126; in women, 19–23, 27–28, 30, 32–33, 58, 106, 113, 125
Howard University, 123
Howe, Julia Ward, 4–5
Howe, Samuel Gridley, 8
Hughes, Langston, 124–25, 160n56
Hurston, Zora Neale, 124–26, 160n56

Ideas on the Philosophy of the History of Mankind (Herder), 121
I'll Take My Stand (Twelve Southerners), 15, 82–84, 86–87, 90–93, 96, 107, 155n34
Intrator, Michael, 99, 103
inversion. See homosexuality
"Is Evolution Trying to Do Away with the Clitoris?", 20

Jacobs, Harriet, 27
James, Henry, 11, 13–14 *passim*, 47, 58, 61, 65, 76, 83, 88, 128, 134, 140; *The Ambassadors*, 22; *The American Scene*, 14, 33, 36–37, 40, 45–46, 88; "The Art of Fiction," 20–21, 42; "The Beast in the Jungle," 32; *The Bostonians*, 13, 17–18, 20–38, 40, 44–46, 58; *Daisy Miller*, 22; and homosexuality, 18–22, 32, 149n42; and insistence on privacy, 32–33; "The Manners of American Women," 14, 37, 41; *The Portrait of a Lady*, 19, 46; "The Question of Our Speech," 36–38, 41, 44–45; "The Speech of American Women," 14, 36–38; and thoughts on father's career, 17–18; and thoughts on Oscar Wilde, 32; and trip to America in 1904, 33–34, 37, 42, 45–46

James, Henry (Sr.), 17–18
James, William, 18, 46, 92
Jespersen, Otto, 31
Jim Crow, 29, 120, 127
Johnson, Georgia Douglas, 126
Johnson, Helene, 160n56
Johnson, James Weldon, 83
Jones, Anne Goodwyn, 86
Joyce, James, 83
Jung, Carl, 138, 151n12, 161n4

Kant, Immanuel, 3, 145n8
Kanter, Emanuel, 81
Kaplan, Justin, 5–6
Kelley, Florence, 90
Kent State University, 143
Kenyon College, 92
Kenyon Review, The, 92–93, 107
Kerber, Linda K., 48
Kollontai, Alexandra, 94–95
Krafft-Ebing, Richard, 18, 126
Kraft, 117, 119, 127, 129
Kristeva, Julia, 11
Krupskaya, Nadezhda, 94–95

La Liberté guidant le peuple (Delacroix), 50
Labor and Desire (Rabinowitz), 101
Lacan, Jacques, 75
Lanier, Sidney, 101
Laqueur, Thomas, 10–11, 48
Larsen, Nella, 124
Le Conte, Joseph, 52–53, 59, 61
Leaves of Grass (Whitman), 5–7, 56, 112, 146n21
lesbianism. *See* homosexuality
Levander, Caroline Field, 31, 37
Leverenz, David, 7
Lewis, David Levering, 125
Lewis, H. H., 106
Lhamon, W. T., Jr., 29
"Life in the Iron Mills" (Davis), 81
local color, 101
Locke, Alain, 123–24
Locke, John, 3, 48
Log Cabin Settlement, 90
Looking Backward (Bellamy), 72
Loray textile mill, 80, 98
Lott, Eric, 120
Love's Coming of Age (Carpenter), 106
Lowell, Massachusetts, 48, 105
Lukács, Georg, 60

Lumpkin, Grace, 11, 15, 78–82 *passim*, 123, 156n57; and attacks on Agrarianism, 96, 142; childhood of, 98, 107; and conversion to socialism, 98–99; and rejection of radical past, 82, 99, 109, 142; and relationship with Michael Intrator, 99, 103; and return to Episcopal Church, 99; *To Make My Bread*, 15, 82, 97–105, 107–110, 142
lyric-epic, 5, 7, 56

M. B. H. (Union soldier), 10
Madonna/Whore Complex, 30
Male Fantasies (Theweleit), 135
"Man from Moscow, The" (Lewis), 106
Manhattan. *See* New York
Man-Made World, The. See Gilman, Charlotte Perkins
Männerbund, 142
"Manners of American Women, The." *See* James, Henry
Männerstaat, 142
Marbach, Dora, 118
Marx, Karl, 72–73, 81–82, 88, 93, 97, 101–3, 107, 141
Massachusetts, 35, 37–38, 105, 117
materialism. *See* Locke, John
Maxim Gorky Prize, 99
McClintock, Anne, 39
McKinley, William, 43
Memphis, Tennessee, 21–22
Methodism, 85
midwifery, 100
Millay, Edna St. Vincent, 93–95
Milledgeville, Georgia, 98
Miller, James E., Jr., 5
Miller, Monica L., 158n31
minstrelsy, 29–30, 120
miscegenation, 59, 117
"Miscegenation." *See* Du Bois, W. E. B.
Miss Ravenal's Conversion from Secession to Loyalty, (De Forest), 28
Modern Language Association, 12
modern sexuality, 8–9
modernism, 69, 79, 83, 85, 87, 102, 126–27, 138
Moi, Toril, 12–13, 147n44
Moral Re-Armament Movement, 99
Mosse, George L., 139, 142, 162n8
mugwumps, 8
Murie, James, 113
Mussel Slough shootout, 50–51
Musser, Judith, 160n65

Mussolini, Benito, 16, 96, 138–41, 162n8
My Lai, 143–44

"Narcissus" (Nugent), 126
Nashville, Tennessee, 82–83, 117
Nation, The, 21
National Association for the Advancement of Colored People, 114
National Consumers League, 90
National Emergency Council, 80
National Socialist German Workers' Party. *See* Nazi Party
National Urban League, 126
nationalism, 2–3, 5, 13, 15–16, 39, 61, 82, 86, 91, 107–9, 114, 117, 121–23, 130, 133, 136–38, 140, 142–43
Nationalism (Bellamy), 72, 153n53
naturalism, 53, 60–61
Nature (Emerson), 3
Nazi Party, 136, 140, 142, 162n8
New Criticism, The, 95–97, 108
New Criticism, The. *See* Ransom, John Crowe
New Hampshire, 40
New Masses, The, 98, 100, 102
New Negro, 123–24, 126, 160n65
"New Negro, The" (Locke), 124
New Negro Renaissance. *See* Harlem Renaissance
New South, 102, 118
New Soviet Woman, 94
New Woman, 21–22, 36–39, 45, 47, 83, 89, 140, 148n15
Nineteenth Amendment, 13, 19–20
Norris, Frank, 11, 14, 47, 49 *passim*, 141; education of, 52–53; "The Frontier Gone at Last," 57; "Novelists of the Future: The Training They Need," 50, 106; *The Octopus*, 14, 49–62, 73, 78, 88–89, 141, 152n32; populist politics of, 62; as student of Joseph le Conte, 52–53, 59, 61; and time in Paris, 62
"Nothing New." *See* Bonner, Marita
"Novelists of the Future: The Training They Need." *See* Norris, Frank
Novick, Sheldon M., 149n42
Nugent, Richard Bruce, 125–26, 160n56

Octopus, The. *See* Norris, Frank
Odum, Howard, 91

"On Being Young—a Woman—and Colored." *See* Bonner, Marita
"One's-Self I Sing" (Whitman), 6
Opportunity, 126, 132
Order of Railroad Telegraphers, 80
Ouida (Marie Louise de la Ramée), 21

Page, Myra, 96, 156n57
Painter, Nell Irvin, 75
Pater, Walter, 39–40, 56
People's Party, 153n53
Perkins, Mary Westcott, 62
Pettit, Katherine, 90
Petty, Leslie, 106
Philadelphia Negro, The. *See* Du Bois, W. E. B.
Pine Mountain Settlement School, 90
Plato, 3–4, 8, 49, 51, 59, 74–75, 138
Plato and Platonism (Pater), 39–40
"Poets Without Laurels." *See* Ransom, John Crowe
Popular Front, 105–6
Portrait of a Lady, The. *See* James, Henry
"Possible Triad on Black Notes, A." *See* Bonner, Marita
primitive accumulation, 101–2
producerism, 72–73
Progressive Era, 90, 97
proletarian literature, 15, 96–106, 156n48
Protestantism, 28, 85, 89
psychological realism. *See* realism
Psychopathia Sexualis (Krafft-Ebing), 18, 126
Pure Sociology (Ward), 70

"Question of Our Speech, The." *See* James, Henry

Rabinowitz, Paula, 101–2
racial uplift, 10, 15, 26–27, 91–92, 112, 119–121, 123, 128, 160n65
Radcliffe College, 126
Rado, Lisa, 69, 147n3
Ransom, John Crowe, 11, 15, 78–80 *passim*, 114, 123, 134, 141; and acceptance of New Deal programs, 92–93; and aesthetic theories, 81–82, 86–87, 93–98, 107–9; "Antique Harvesters," 86; "Art and the Human Economy," 93; *Chills and Fever*, 86; and editorship of *The Fugitive*, 83; and fear of socialism, 81, 88, 97; "Forms and Citizens," 94; *God With-*

out Thunder, 15, 84–89, 93, 96, 154n15, 155n34; Methodist heritage of, 85; and move to Kenyon College, 92, 96; *The New Criticism*, 95; and organic nationalism, 80, 82, 86–87, 106; and participation in *I'll Take My Stand*, 82–83; "Poets Without Laurels," 95; and reaction to the Scopes Trial, 84–85; "Reconstructed but Unregenerate," 84, 87–89, 91, 93; "Spectral Lovers," 86–87; *Two Gentlemen in Bonds*, 86; "What Does the South Want?", 92–93; "The Woman as Poet," 93–94, 108
realism, 25, 160n65
"Reconstructed but Unregenerate." *See* Ransom, John Crowe
Reconstruction, 17, 84
Reed, John Shelton, 91
Reign of Terror, 2
Report on Economic Conditions of the South, 80
Republic, The (Plato), 3
Republican Party, 8
Rhode Island School of Design, 62
Rice, Thomas Dartmouth, 29
Richmond, Virginia, 33, 46
Rollins, William, 156n57
romanticism, 1–2, 4, 10, 13–14, 17, 20, 24, 26, 35, 47, 54, 58–59, 70, 91, 109, 112, 116–17, 127, 130, 134
Room of One's Own, A (Woolf), 16, 138–40, 142
Roosevelt, Franklin Delano, 80, 93
Roosevelt, Theodore, 42–43, 45, 121–22
Rough Riders, 121
Rousseau, Jean-Jacques, 48, 75
Rowe, John Carlos, 44
Ryan, Father Abram, 107

Sainte-Beuve, Charles-Augustin, 41
Salisbury, Connecticut, 111
Sanger, Margaret, 74, 103
Schmoller, Gustav, 117
Scopes, John T., 84
Scopes "Monkey Trial," 84–85
Secor, Cynthia, 12
Sedgwick, Eve Kosofsky, 32
Seltzer, Mark, 53–54
Senate Sub-Committee on Government Operations, 99
Sex and Character (Weininger), 52, 64–65, 70
sexology, 7, 14, 17–20, 36, 58, 147n3
Shadow Before, The (Rollins), 156n57

Shaw, Robert Gould, 35
Silber, Nina, 27
Silvera, Edward, 160n56
slavery, 25–28, 67, 91, 112, 117
"Sleepers, The" (Whitman), 6–7
Smethurst, James, 125
Smith, Adam, 48
Smith, O. (Ola) Delight, 80
Smith-Rosenberg, Carroll, 21, 58, 148n15
"Smoke, Lilies and Jade" (Nugent), 126
social work, 90–91, 93–94, 97–98
socialism, 10–11, 59, 72, 81, 88, 90, 106, 109, 141
Somerville, Siobhan B., 19, 113
Souls of Black Folk, The. See Du Bois, W. E. B.
South Dakota, 43
Southard, R. P., 93
Southern Horrors (Wells), 22
Southern Pacific Railroad, 50–51
Southern Renaissance, 154n9
Southworth, Alvan S., 21
Spanish-American War, 12
"Spectral Lovers." *See* Ransom, John Crowe
"Speech of American Women, The." *See* James, Henry
Spencer, Herbert, 74
St. Augustine, Florida, 33
Stanton, Elizabeth Cady, 86, 154n16
"Statement of Principles" (Twelve Southerners), 88
Stepan, Nancy Leys, 116, 157n8
Stepto, Robert B., 160n69
Stetson, Charles Walter, 62, 68
Stevens, Wallace, 95
Stewart, Maria W., 25
stock market, 15, 80, 82, 98
Stowe, Harriet Beecher, 112
Strike! (Vorse), 156n57
suffrage. *See* women's suffrage
"Suggestion on the Negro Problem, A." *See* Gilman, Charlotte Perkins
Suydam, Levi, 111
Swedenborg, Emanuel, 3–5
Symonds, John Addington, 19
Symposium, The (Plato). *See* Plato

Talented Tenth, 114–16, 118, 120, 122, 125–27, 129, 132
Tate, Allen, 82, 88, 95, 156n50
Theory of the Leisure Class, The (Veblen), 49, 70
"There Were Three." *See* Bonner, Marita

Theweleit, Klaus, 135
Third Reich, 136
Thirteenth Amendment, 20
Thomson, J. Arthur, 113
Three Guineas (Woolf), 139
Thurman, Wallace, 160n56
To Make My Bread. *See* Lumpkin, Grace
Tocqueville, Alexis de, 1–2, 48, 137
transcendentalism, 3–7, 9, 14, 17–18, 23–24, 44, 47, 50, 112, 116–17, 134, 145–46n8
"Transcendentalist, The" (Emerson), 145–46n8
Treitschke, Heinrich von, 117, 122
Truth, Sojourner, 27
Twain, Mark (Samuel Clemens), 42
Two Gentlemen in Bonds. *See* Ransom, John Crowe

Ulrichs, Karl, 18, 23–24
Ulysses (Joyce), 83
Uncle Tom's Cabin (Stowe), 112
United Textile Workers of America, 80
Universal Negro Improvement Association, 121–22
Universalgeschichte, 2
University of Berlin, 117–18, 122
University of California at Berkeley, 52
University of North Carolina at Chapel Hill, 91
uplift. *See* racial uplift

Van Leer, David, 33
Van Vechten, Carl, 125
Van Wienen, Mark W., 153n53
Vanderbilt University, 82–84, 91–92
Veblen, Thorstein, 49, 70
Versailles Treaty, 135, 142
Virginia, 9, 33, 46, 92
Vision d'Hébal (Ballanche), 2
Volk, 2–3, 5, 15–16, 54, 57–58, 61, 91, 108, 114–17, 119–22, 127, 129, 132, 136, 141–42, 158–59n31
Vorse, Mary Heaton, 156n57
vox Americana, 14, 20, 35, 37, 41–42, 44–47, 61, 129, 140
Wagner, Adolf, 117
Wald, Lillian, 77, 90
Walkowitz, Daniel J., 90
Ward, Freda, 21–22
Ward, Lester, 70, 73
Warner, Charles Dudley, 42
Warren, Robert Penn, 82–83, 85, 91–92, 96, 155n34

Washington, Booker T., 120
Washington, D. C. *See* District of Columbia
Waste Land, The (Eliot), 83, 87, 152n44
Watson, Steven, 125
Weaver, Richard M., 141
Weber, Max, 117
Weil, Kari, 75
Weininger, Otto, 52, 64–65, 70
welfare state, 15, 78, 80–83, 89, 91–94, 97, 123
Wells, Ida B., 22
Welter, Barbara, 105
West, Lon, 151n12
Westphal, Karl, 18
"What Does the South Want?" *See* Ransom, John Crowe
Whitman, Walt, 5–7, 9, 14, 50, 56, 112, 116, 146n20
Who Owns America (Tate and Agar), 92–93
Wiggins, Ella May, 99, 105
Wilde, Oscar, 32, 120, 123, 125
Wilder, Thornton, 102
Wilhelm II, 118
Wilks, Jennifer Margaret, 127–28
Willard, Frances, 90
Wolff, Cynthia Griffin, 28, 112
"Woman as Poet, The." *See* Ransom, John Crowe
Woman in the Nineteenth Century (Fuller), 5, 112–13
Woman Today, 97
Woman's Bible, The (Stanton), 86, 154n16
Women and Economics. *See* Gilman, Charlotte Perkins
Women's Christian Temperance Union, 90
Women's Peace Parade, 77
women's suffrage, 11, 13, 20–21, 24–25, 32, 97, 106, 136, 139
Woolf, Virgina, 16, 138–40, 142, 147n44, 161n6
Working Woman, 97
World Tomorrow, The, 98
World War I, 12, 77, 137, 142
World War II, 12, 93, 136
World's Body, The, 93–95
Wyatt-Brown, Bertram, 30

"Yellow Wallpaper, The." *See* Gilman, Charlotte Perkins

Zip Coon, 120

www.ingramcontent.com/pod-product-compliance
Lightning Source LLC
Chambersburg PA
CBHW030521080526
44586CB00011B/280